MW00533181

BRAIDED SELVES

Braided Selves

Collected Essays on Multiplicity,
God, and Persons

PAMELA COOPER-WHITE

 CASCADE *Books* · Eugene, Oregon

BRAIDED SELVES
Collected Essays on Multiplicity, God, and Persons

Copyright © 2011 Pamela Cooper-White. All rights reserved. Except for brief quotations in critical publications or reviews, no part of this book may be reproduced in any manner without prior written permission from the publisher. Write: Permissions, Wipf and Stock Publishers, 199 W. 8th Ave., Suite 3, Eugene, OR 97401.

Cascade Books
An Imprint of Wipf and Stock Publishers
199 W. 8th Ave., Suite 3
Eugene, OR 97401

www.wipfandstock.com

ISBN 13: 978-1-60608-668-1

Cataloging-in-Publication data:

Cooper-White, Pamela, 1955–

Braided selves : collected essays on multiplicity, God, and persons / Pamela Cooper-White.

viii + 244 p. ; cm.—Includes bibliographical references.

ISBN 13: 978-1-60608-668-1

1. Pastoral Psychology. 2. Pastoral Counseling. 3. Psychotherapy—Religious Aspects—Christianity. 4. Women—Pastoral Counseling of. I. Title.

BV4012 .C66 2011

Manufactured in the USA.

Contents

Permissions and Credits

The author and publisher gratefully acknowledge the permission of the following journals and publishers for their permission to reprint articles and essays in adapted form in the present volume.

Chapter 1 was originally published as "Thick Theory: Psychology, Theoretical Models, and the Formation of Pastoral Counselors," in *The Formation of Pastoral Counselors: Challenges and Opportunities*, edited by Duane R. Bidwell and Joretta L. Marshall (Binghamton, NY: Haworth Press, 2006) 47–67; simultaneously co-published in the *American Journal of Pastoral Counseling* 8.3–4 (2006) 47–67. Copyright © Taylor & Francis/ Haworth Press, 2006. Adapted by permission of Taylor & Francis.

Chapter 2 was originally published in *Human Development and Faith: Life-Cycle Stages of Body, Mind, and Soul*, edited by Felicity Brock Kelcourse copyright © Chalice Press, 2004. Adapted by permission of Chalice Press.

Chapter 3 was originally published in *Pastoral Psychology* 50.5 (2002) 319–43. Copyright © 2002 Springer. Adapted by permission of Springer.

Figure 3.5 first appeared in Heinz Kohut, "The Two Analyses of Mr. Z," *International Journal of Psycho-analysis* 60 (1979) 11, used by permission of Dr. Thomas A. Kohut, Dec. 2, 2010.

Chapter 4 was originally published in *Pastoral Psychology* 57.1–2 (2008) 1–16. Copyright © Springer, 2008. Adapted by permission of Springer.

Chapter 5 was originally published in *Spiritual and Psychological Aspects of Illness: Dealing with Sickness, Loss, Dying, and Death*, edited by Beverly A. Musgrave and Neil J. McGettigan, copyright © Paulist Press, 2010. Adapted by permission of Paulist Press. Portions adapted from Cooper-White, *Shared Wisdom: Use of the Self in Pastoral Care and Counseling* copyright © Fortress Press, 2004; and *Many Voices: Pastoral Psychotherapy in Relational and Theological Perspective,* copyright © Fortress Press, 2007. Adapted by permission of Augsburg Fortress Publishers.

Chapter 6 was originally published in *Women Out of Order: Risking Change and Creating Care in a Multi-Cultural World,* ed. Teresa Snorton and Jeanne Stevenson-Moessner, copyright © Fortress Press, 2009. Adapted by permission of Augsburg Fortress Publishers.

Chapter 7 originally published in *Reflective Practice: Formation and Supervision in Ministry* 29 (2009) 23–37. Adapted by permission Herbert Anderson, editor, *Reflective Practice.*

Chapter 8 originally published as "I Do Not Do the Good I Want but the Evil I Do Not Want Is What I Do: The Concept of the Vertical Split in Self Psychology in Relation to Christian Concepts of Good and Evil," *Journal of Pastoral Theology* 13.1 (2003) 63–84.

Chapter 9 originally published in *In Search of the Self: Interdisciplinary Perspectives on Personhood,* edited by Wentzel Van Huyssteen and Erik P. Wiebe, copyright © Eerdmans, 2011, 141–62. Adapted by permission of Wm. B. Eerdmans Publishing Co.

Introduction

All writing is conversation. The intention is to get something going, to lob a thought or to return it with a new spin. Writing extends the reach of ideas beyond the immediate circle of students, friends, and colleagues to conversation partners the writer can hardly even imagine. The intention behind this book is to continue and expand a challenging conversation that has been going on for a while now, about what it means to be an "I," and how much more complex and fluid the understanding of "I" has become or is still becoming in postmodernity. This particular book is written from the perspective of a pastoral theology (an interdisciplinary field that works at the intersection of constructive theology and the theory and practice of spiritual care and clinical psychology), so the conversation further engages this question of the complexity of persons in light of who and what we believe and imagine God to be.

To the extent that all our beliefs about God begin in and amid human experience, the psychological and the theological must ring true to both realms—the realm of belief and the realm of experience. That experience itself is subjective, permeated with imagination, competing and contradictory beliefs, and even (as Sigmund Freud spent his career warning us) self-deception becomes less of a problem in postmodernity, because variability and even contradiction are now being valued in ways modernity could not conceive. As we begin to exchange static metaphors and models of the universe, the self, and even God for models that are less concrete and hard edged, more flexible and permeable; and as we mute our claims to possession of a universal truth in favor of a more modest, local, and culturally contingent approximation of truth(s), we may find new richness, openness, and expansiveness in both our theology and our anthropology (our under-standing of what it means to be a human person). Ultimately, I believe, the more complexity we can admit to in ourselves, other persons, and our conception of the transcendent or the divine, the more we will experience empathy and compassion toward ourselves, other human beings, and ultimately, the whole creation.

The premise of this book is that both persons and God are multiple, and that this multiplicity, although intuited in past generations, needs to be foregrounded in ways that were unthought and perhaps even unthinkable until the postmodern era. There has always been a dia-lectic of One and Many. In ancient times (e.g., with Plato's concept of the "tripartite soul/*psyche*"),[1] and in the biblical imagination, even as monotheism was becoming the dominant image that distinguished the Israelite cult from its neighbors, there is evidence of God/the gods, the *Elohim*, who created heaven and earth; and in Christian theology the doctrine of the Trinity. The thread of multiplicity has never gone com-pletely out of sight—for example, in the philosopher David Hume's comparison of "the soul" to "a republic or commonwealth, in which the several members are united by the reciprocal ties of government and subordination";[2] or Walt Whitman's famous saying, "Do I contradict myself? / Very well then I contradict myself, / (I am large, I contain multitudes.)"[3] However, a dominant theme in the West, particularly with the advent of the Enlightenment, has been unity/integration of the self (at least as an ideal) and an emphasis (through deism and theism) on God as singular prime mover and (only in Theism) shaker of the universe.

As we have been increasingly emerging in the twentieth and twenty-first centuries from the grip of modernity (in particular the legacy of Descartes and eighteenth-century rationalism), we are also beginning to question its foregrounding of unity, oneness, and inte-gration. The rhetoric and ideal of unity has served many admirable

1. Plato, *The Republic*, books 4, 8, and 9. See also Brown, "Plato's Ethics and Politics in *The Republic*." Heraclitus also conceived of the Logos in multiple dimensions (McLean, "Philosophical Notions of the Person," 58).

2. As cited in Bloom, "First Person Plural," 92. John Locke also admitted of the pos-sibility of multiple selves inhabiting one body, as the logical extension of conscious-ness as a separate entity, in *An Essay Concerning Human Understanding*, Book II, n20, as cited in McLean, "Philosophical Notions of the Person," 52. This disembodied view is quite different from the models of multiplicity for which I am advocating.

3. Whitman, *Song of Myself*, 194.

purposes—as a resident of Gettysburg, Pennsylvania, where one of the most pivotal battles of the Civil War was fought right here on seminary ground, I am especially mindful of the language of Union, and grateful that the horror of slavery was abolished in all the states and territories of the still fragile "United States of America." Yet I am also mindful of the ways in which the symbols of union, equality, and the "melting pot," fused with the Enlightenment image of the rational, free (white, male, and preferably Christian and landowning) citizen have actually served to exclude and disenfranchise women, persons of color, non-Christians, immigrants, non-English speakers, the landless, and the poor. By making the image of the ideal citizen, the normative image of the privileged One and holding out equal opportunity as a "fact" rendered invisible and unquestionable the realities of exclusion, inequality, and oppression.

Oneness has occupied the foreground of cultural discourse throughout most of Judeo-Christian history, and served both religious and political goals of uniting people within and across institutions and nations. In Christian history, rulers from Constantine to Charlemagne to the Catholic monarchs of the Renaissance to the Reformation princes recognized the power of religion to unite their realms. And in modern times even as religion per se became less hegemonic and as freedom of religion has been enshrined in many nations as the separation of church and state, religious values, ideals, and language continue to be invoked[4]—with an increasing return to explicitly religious rhetoric in American political life.[5]

Oneness, then, often as code for conformity, has been foregrounded in American life both public and domestic. While battles ensue about what the norm should be—often framed as liberal vs. conservative on a whole host of social issues—, privilege continues to accrue to those who fit a singular Enlightenment-imbued model of wealth, education, land (often in the form of corporate ownership), and power; and the entry gates are high and well guarded. The singular dream of

4. Zuckerman, *Society without God*, shows how many of the traditional religious values of care, honesty, goodwill, and community appear now to be best practiced in Scandinavian countries where personal faith in a supernatural God is waning, and religion is viewed as a vestige of cultural heritage.

5. Sixty-four percent of Americans surveyed believe that "politicians who don't believe in God are unfit for public office," compared to, for example, 8 percent of Danes and 15 percent of Swedes (ibid., 12).

such privilege continues to serve to erase other dreams and ideals from the popular imagination, and individuals envy and emulate wealth and celebrity, even if they claim to resent and hate those in power. Oneness, as long as it symbolizes the aspirational pinnacle of a hierarchical group, system, or society (whether religious or political), masquerades as an ideal of unity and well-being, while it perpetuates stratification and oppression.

Oneness has harmed us. Notions of being one-self and having One God have too often reified and reinforced the domination of one culture, one story, one gender, one race, one normative discourse. Awareness of the multiplicity of ourselves, one another, and the divine can interrupt such dominations and open new vistas for empathy and creative collaboration. It will not finally be our unity but our difference(s) in relation to the Other(s), both within ourselves, and in our relationships—across the boundaries of skin, subjectivity, clan, and culture—that can heal us: not "to make us one and the same" but to enlarge us and to make us whole.

All theology, but pastoral theology in particular, which has claimed healing, sustaining, guiding, reconciling, nurturing, empowering, and liberating as its central purposes,[6] needs such continual expansion,

6. Clebsch and Jaeckle, *Pastoral Care in Historical Perspective* and Ali, *Survival and Liberation*, 121. Note that in Thornton's *Broken Yet Beloved*, she disputes "healing" as a pastoral function analogous to the others, because "healing is something to be received, not something to be grasped or engineered. From this perspective healing comes not from inner strength and self-understanding alone, but through just relationships that are hospitable to the healing presence of the holy. The reign of God, the realm of the holy, is the locus of healing; it is a realm not conceived of or executed by technology, not even psychological or spiritual technology. Healing that is the basis for hope in history, a gift and a sign that the realm of justice is present in our midst, needs to be understood within this intricate web of human/divine relationships. Restoring wholeness refers to repairing the whole web. The aim of pastoral care as reconciliation means creating justice for this entire cosmos" (Thornton, *Broken yet Beloved*, 163–64.) I am nevertheless retaining the term "healing" here, and elsewhere in this volume, because it is still commonly understood as a central aim of pastoral care and counseling—at the very least in the form of creating a space for persons to be open to the healing power of the divine. I agree, however, that healing is ultimately the work of the Spirit, with our cooperation, and not solely by our own efforts. I also agree that the healing of individuals cannot be separated from the whole fabric of relationships and community. I agree with Thornton's emphasis on solidarity, political consciousness, and justice as a necessary part of healing and wholeness—moving in faith and hope toward the complete wholeness and reconciliation envisioned as the fulfillment of time-in-eternity (cf., Moltmann, *Theology of Hope*; and Moltmann, "Eschatology.")

needs continually to interrogate itself.[7] We need a "thick theory" and a corresponding "thick theology"[8]—multilayered, complex, and open to multifariousness and modes of symbolization in both our psychological and anthropological conceptualizations of persons, conflict, trauma, pathology, health, and wellness; as well as in our understanding of the transcendent, of God.[9]

As I will argue in chapter 1, our theory of the psyche needs to be "thick theory," one that (quoting anthropologist Clifford Geertz) "grows out of the delicacy of its distinctions, not the sweep of its abstractions."[10] It will be characterized as much by its capacity to generate helpful questions as by its capacity to assert answers. It will be open to further investigation of its own biases and assumptions about what it means to be a human person—both in terms of internal, subjective experiences and processes conscious and unconscious; and in terms of our relations to other persons, the immediate environment, and the larger physical and social world. Such a theory of the psyche requires imagination both generative and critical.

"Thick theology" similarly requires generative and critical imagination[11]—indeed, it invites a multiplicity of imaginations and imaginative moves. Assertions of concrete, universal-sounding truths about the nature of God, and for that matter, of persons, are too narrow. They fall too easily into human attempts to control, contain, or absolutize

7. Considering Derrida's critique of absolute knowledge of reality, e.g., Derrida, *Writing and Difference*; see also Lemke, "Postmodernism and Critical Theory." This theme will be elaborated in chapter 1.

8. Playing on Geertz, "Thick Description."

9. My method here is, like many pastoral and practical theologians, explicitly "correlational," beginning with Tillich's "method of correlation" (Tillich, *Systematic Theology* 1:3–68; see also Hammond, "An Examination of Tillich's Method of Correlation"; Loomer, "Tillich's Theology of Correlation"), but in this instance drawing more heavily on the mutual informing and critique of theology and the human sciences as developed in Tracy, *Blessed Rage for Order*. I further agree with Taylor (*Remembering Esperanza*) that the binary nature of such correlational thought tends to reify a false dichotomy between theology and anthropology, or between God and the world. For more on correlation and pastoral theology, see also and Browning, *A Fundamental Practical Theology*; Miller-McLemore, "Cognitive Neuroscience and the Question of Theological Method"; Doehring, "Minding the Gap: Response to Bonnie Miller-McLemore."

10. Geertz, "Thick Description," 25.

11. For a wonderful discussion of the role of imagination in theology, see Avis, *God and the Creative Imagination*.

the transcendent. Intuitions of God's omnipotence/sovereignty, omniscience, and eternal love reach toward the transcendent but finally collapse back into human categories, which are inadequate to name any experience, much less the divine. It is my contention that human experience is a part of the multicolored, intricately woven web of divine creativity and as such, can never be captured fully by words or images.

This is not to assert that God is "wholly Other,"[12] but to avow with awe that God is larger than all human conceptions, even while remaining immanent, even intricately woven into each person's internal experience. Our subjectivity always retains this intim|ation of the divine, in spite of our contradictory, complex, and even at times destructive aggression, unbalanced desires, brokenness, illness, or traumatic wounding. This enormity, this intimacy, is the paradox of divine multiplicity—God as *creative profusion, incarnational desire,* and *living inspiration.*[13] God-with-us (*Emmanu-El*) in all our multiplicity, arouses our creativity when we are tied up too much in one limited dimension of our selves, and braids us back together when we are too fragmented or torn apart. "Thick theology," like "thick theory," demands that we give up our certainties and shibboleths, interrogates what we have placed in the foreground and named as immutable truth. Because the foreground is merely an illusion. It is simply a ground, not primary or even solid. It is an island, made up of friable soil. We can choose to jump off, or navigate around to its backside to gain new vistas of landscapes previously unimagined, shining under the light of stars still uncharted.

Thick theology and thick theory together beckon us to step out onto a fragile, tender web of imagination, to pull back the curtain from the foreground, and allow multiple images and conceptions of God and our self/selves to emerge from behind the curtain. Such images may seem newborn to us, but they have their birth in the matrix of God's own fecundity. As daring as this may be—because to give up our own, personal certainties is always harder than asking others to give up theirs!—it seems to me that nothing less is required if we are

---

12. Contra Barth's famous formulation, e.g., *Epistle to the Romans,* 49 et passim; and "a God . . . overwhelmingly lofty and distant, strange, yes even wholly other," in Barth, *The Humanity of God,* 37. See also Barth, *Church Dogmatics.*

13. A reference to chapter 5, below, and to Cooper-White, *Many Voices,* 76–94.

genuinely to give ourselves in service to the pastoral dimensions of care and justice making to which we claim to aspire as pastoral and practical theologians. Our praxis may already be out ahead of us as we grope for theological images and claims that might truly empower change in the world, resist and confront oppression, and revivify faith wherever it may have grown stale or ritually devoid of meaning.

How, then, can we do "thick theology" that refuses concretizing, hegemonic assertions about God, and "thick theory" that refuses concretizing, hegemonic assertions about human persons? I am attracted to the word *metaphor* to explore the possibility of a theology and a theory of persons that do not take any assertions of truth so seriously that they lose the possibility of creativity and renewal. I am certainly not the first to do this, and much good theology is explicitly metaphorical.[14] But the idea of metaphor perhaps deserves revisiting specifically in the context of *pastoral* theology, because in our attention to drawing correlations between God and the suffering of the world, and between theology and praxis, we may at times have focused our energies on deepening the sophistication of our psychological and social-scientific knowledge about human persons while taking too literally and too much for granted the doctrinal assertions of our religious traditions about God, Christ, and even the church or institutional religion.

We are used to using the word *metaphor* to mean "a figure or speech in which a term or phrase is applied to something to which it is not literally applicable in order to suggest a resemblance, as in, 'A mighty fortress is our God.'"[15] Literally the Greek means "to carry across" (*phérein* + *meta*). A metaphor is something that gets us from one place to another. In modern Greek, the word is used not to refer to figures of speech, but quite concretely: a *metaphor* is the word for transportation. It's the bus you take to get across town or across the country. (It's also the word for the airport luggage trolley—in Greece you can find yourself carrying your baggage with a metaphor![16])

Multiplicity is a metaphor that gets us somewhere, potentially somewhere new, even previously unknown. Where does metaphor take us? It does not take us from the real to the unreal, but from the

14. E.g., McFague, *Metaphorical Theology*; and Avis, *God and the Creative Imagination*.

15. "Metaphor," in *Random House Dictionary*.

16. "Metaphor," in *WordIQ.com*.

literal to the imaginary or the creative. It does not take us from truth to untruth, but to a more complex truth that corresponds not only with tangible facts but with subjective experience and emotional feeling.[17] As such, it is a vehicle we need in pastoral theology to help us construct theologies that are adequate to the richness, complexity, and variability of the lives of those for whom we care, those with whom we share the work of justice. As pastoral theologians, we can little afford to continue to "get by" with totalizing images and doctrines that have upheld the status quo and have done little to join with Jesus in the reversal of exploitive powers in the world. There is a fundamental conflict between a mission of care and justice, and colluding with the status quo—which is essentially staying on a bus to nowhere.

Metaphors, moreover, are intrinsically relational, and as such are perhaps especially appropriate to pastoral speech, thought, and practice. As scholars of language have pointed out, metaphorical speech (and by extension, writing) requires participation by the hearer or reader to understand and respond to the vivid imagery metaphors entail: "There is a unique way in which the maker and appreciator of a metaphor are drawn closer to one another . . . the speaker issues a kind of concealed invitation; the hearer expends a special effort to accept the invitation; and this transaction constitutes the acknowledgement of a community."[18] Metaphor draws upon a set of shared cultural or communal images, or invokes new ones. Metaphor therefore is a "cultivation of intimacy."[19] Multiplicity, because it is itself an image of related parts, is therefore doubly relational, because it is both a metaphor that bridges realities, and a figure of the complexity and

17. Ricoeur, "The Metaphorical Process."

18. Cohen, "Metaphor and the Cultivation of Intimacy," 6. From a theological framework, see also McFague, *Metaphorical Theology*, 194; and McFague, *Models of God*, 7–8.

19. Ibid., 1, 6. Contemporary scholars of metaphor are now much more likely to give "attention to the ways that *context* shapes metaphor use and understanding" (Gibbs, "Metaphor and Thought," 3, emphasis added), rather than as semantic figures of speech. Indeed, the multiple domains touched by metaphorical language and thought have expanded metaphor studies beyond linguistics and rhetoric, into cognitive science, anthropology, the arts, and as a result, "the scope of metaphor studies has expanded enormously in recent years to cover the spectrums from brains to culture and from language and gesture to art and music" (Gibbs, "Metaphor and Thought," 4). Not only is metaphor inherently interactional and relational, but the study of it has also increasingly become so.

interrelatedness of life and persons that mirrors the divine dance of relationship: *perichōrēsis.*

The growing awareness that relationships are the heart of human experience, and of the interconnectedness of all life, further, invites us naturally into metaphorical thought as we ponder the truths of our experience of both persons and the divine. Metaphor is relational—and hence correlational/co-relational—by definition, bridging the realms of concrete, bodily experience and the realms of imagery, symbol, and mystery. Unlike abstract logical propositions that take us away from the livingness of our embodied subjectivity, or concrete fundamentalisms that refuse transcendental imagination altogether, metaphorical theory and theology allow us to bridge ordinary life and the numinous realm—in other words, to think metaphorically is also to think sacramentally and incarnationally—seeing the sacred in the ordinary.

As I have used the idea of "braided selves" as a metaphor for the multiplicity of persons, and the slightly more conceptual language of *"creative profusion, incarnational desire,* and *living inspiration"* as a pastoral formulation of the Trinity, it has been my intention to play in just such an ambiguous way with what is concretely in our embodied experience, and what we intuit ourselves, others, and God to be in an ultimately more ineffable, inexpressible sense. The image of multiplicity of persons I have developed, "braided selves," is explicitly metaphorical. People are not literally braids, of course, but the image of "braided selves" invites contemplation of the weaving together of multiple parts and subjectivities in the experience of self and other, and, further, implies an ongoingness—braiding is a continual process, and as such supports dynamic and relational views of multiplicity of persons.[20] My pastoral Trinitarian formulation of God as *"creative profusion, incarnational desire,* and *living inspiration,"* formally falls more in the category of a "model" rather than a "metaphor," strictly speaking, because the three proposed figures are somewhat more conceptual than images taken from everyday life. As McFague distinguishes, a *model* is "a dominant metaphor, a metaphor with staying power . . . models are a further step along the route from metaphorical to [abstract] conceptual language. They are similar to metaphors in that they are images which retain the

---

20. Cf., anthropologist Victor Turner's insistence that metaphors reflect the processional, not static or structural, nature of human social life and the world (in Turner, *Dramas, Fields, and Metaphors,* 24–25, also citing Richards, *The Philosophy of Rhetoric,* 93).

tension of 'is and is not' and, like religious and poetic metaphors, they have emotional appeal insofar as they suggest ways of understanding our being in the world."[21] At the same time, the conception of God as *"creative profusion, incarnational desire,* and *living inspiration"* retains the tension required of metaphor between the embodied experiences they evoke—fecundity, desire, and breath—and the ineffable intuitions of the transcendent that they seek to describe.[22]

Metaphors, finally, are also challenging and subversive. Turner calls metaphors "a species of liminal monster[!] . . . whose combination of familiar and unfamiliar features or unfamiliar combination of familiar features provokes us to thought."[23] Because a metaphor causes us to see an analogy we did not previously suspect, we are challenged to understand self, world, and even God in a new light. Metaphors do not so much confirm our embedded worldviews as they upset them by offering creative, even jarring juxtapositions or images. In the words of feminist theologian Sallie McFague, "metaphors redescribe reality, creating *tension* between oneness with existence and alternative ways of being in the world."[24] McFague draws on philosopher Paul Ricoeur for this insight,[25] and on his insistence that metaphors are not merely expressions of similarity, or simple naming of things. Metaphors, Ricoeur says, simultaneously "'make' and 'remake' reality."[26] The imagination is engaged,[27] as the concreteness of reality is suspended, at least in part, by linking it with something it is and is not—something that rings true

21. McFague, *Metaphorical Theology,* 23, also citing Black, *Models and Metaphors.* For more strictly metaphorical images of the Trinity, for example, see also McFague, *Models of God*—God as mother, lover, and friend—and Cunningham, *These Three Are One*—God as source, wellspring, and living water.

22. For detailed philosophical argument why metaphor is tensive in this way, rather nominative—simply drawing a similarity or analogy—see Ricoeur, *Interpretation Theory;* Ricoeur, "The Metaphorical Process"; and Ricoeur, *The Rule of Metaphor.*

23. Turner, *Dramas, Fields, and Metaphors,* 31. He goes on to write that this "liminal monster . . . provides us with new perspectives, one can be excited by them; the implications, suggestions, and supporting values entwined with their literal use enable us to see a new subject matter in a new way" (31).

24. McFague, *Metaphorical Theology,* 213n23.

25. Ricoeur, *Interpretation Theory,* 65.

26. Ricoeur, "The Metaphorical Process," 150.

27. Ibid., 155. Ricoeur uses the term "split reference" for the ability to entertain two different points of view simultaneously, and names this as one of the central attributes of metaphorical language (151).

(in the way a poem is felt to express deep truths) but is not concretely or empirically the case. So metaphors themselves draw us toward multiplicity, complexity, and ambiguity rather than uniformity, literalness, concreteness, and hierarchy disguised as conformity to the One.

For this reason, we cannot hang onto metaphors either, just as a passenger cannot indefinitely hang on the side of a bus without falling into mud or danger. Metaphors and the models drawn from them must be open to interrogation, revision, and testing against lived experience, lest they harden into dogmas that exclude or become idols.[28] So the very openness of metaphorical language itself requires of us flexibility and a continuing nimbleness of imagination. We must remain limber and open to new images, new areas of consciousness—both from within our own psyches, and from the creativity of others.

Our metaphors matter. The "metaphors we live by," to quote the well-known linguist George Lakoff,[29] create in large part the way we live—our values, our dreams, and our practices. To quote McFague again, "what we call something, how we name it, is to a great extent what it is to us . . . It follows, then, that naming can be hurtful, and that it can also be healing or helpful. The ways we name ourselves, one another, and the world cannot be taken for granted; we must look at them carefully to see if they heal or hurt."[30] She calls for images of God and persons that promote justice and care, and for language that "would support ways of understanding the God-world and human-world relationships as open, caring, inclusive, interdependent, changing, mutual, and creative."[31]

That has also been the goal of this project, represented by the various essays collected in this volume. A view of both God and persons as multiple is intended to promote a theology and an anthropology that is enlarging, empathic, and life enhancing. When we practice care and psychotherapy, when we write and teach theology, when we simply live as if both we and God are finally unitive beings, I believe we lop off much of our divinely inspired creativity, and we fall again and again into a binary vision of the world as the One and the Other. Our empathy suffers, and we fail in our capacity to recognize the

28. Cf., McFague, *Metaphorical Theology*, 27; Turner, *Dramas, Fields, and Metaphors*, 29.
29. Lakoff and Johnson, *Metaphors We Live By*.
30. McFague, *Models of God*, 3.
31. Ibid., 13.

value of those who are different from our one self—including those different selves who live within us (as will be discussed at length in the following chapters, especially in chapter 7). This book is an effort to challenge such narrow notions of self, other, and the divine, and to enter into an imaginative dialogue in which the complexity of life, lived sacramentally with an eye toward the sacred in the everyday, may become newly visible, and creatively practicable.

As we step, finally, into this imagined space of "thick theology" that refuses concretizing, universalizing assertions about One God, we may even find that we are stepping beyond any known categories of God, church, doctrine, or religion. In some sense, all metaphorical imaginings—whether in the form of psychological theory or theological reflection—finally participate in the holy—because metaphors operate at the boundary between what can and cannot be expressed in human language. In the words of Anglican theologian Paul Avis, "the creative human imagination is one of the closest analogies to the being of God. The mystery of imagination points to and reflects the mystery of God. As Coleridge (among others) suggested, human imaginative creativity is an echo, a spark, of the divine creativity that is poured out in the plenitude of creation."[32]

In the name of pastoral theology—which is, after all, itself simply *one* name for what we do, and how we conceive of both care and justice making—do we dare radically to question our inherited, unitive views of God and persons? But if our goal is to participate in the healing, liberating, and empowering movement of the Spirit in human lives, can we settle for less?

MORE ABOUT THIS BOOK

Volumes of collected essays, by their nature, do not flow seamlessly like a monograph. The essays in this book represent articles and chapters previously published in a variety of journals and anthologies, and, as such, do not provide a straight-line argument. They are more "multiple" and less "unified" than is a book laid out logically as a single argument. The chapters do, however, represent a long-standing conversation—or at least my side of it, interspersed with numerous references to others' voices and points of view. The chapters have also

32. Avis, *God and the Creative Imagination*, ix.

been arranged thematically to enhance the logical flow from one to another, and I have attempted to create linkages among the chapters—another form of braiding, perhaps!—in order to strengthen the coherence of the entire volume.

Another peril of an essay collection is that the chapters were not all written with the same readers in mind. If your interest lies primarily in pastoral psychology and the practices of care and counseling, chapters 1 and 2 provide foundational or background texts in the areas, respectively, of psychological theory (its necessity and complexity) and models of human growth and development in cultural context. If your interest is primarily, on the other hand, in the area of psychology and religion, and/or psychoanalytic theory, chapters 3, 4, and 8 will address more theoretical problems of concerns raised by multiplicity as a metaphor for understanding persons and the processes of care and psychotherapy.

Chapter 3 is the earliest essay in this volume (if the chapters were arranged strictly chronologically, it would have been the first) and represents the "opening sentences" of the twelve-year (or longer!) conversation represented here. If your interest is more purely in the area of constructive or systematic theology, chapter 5 is the most explicitly theological chapter in the book, in which the Trinitarian formula of God as "creative profusion, incarnational desire, and living inspiration" is explained (adapted from my earlier book, *Many Voices: Pastoral Psychotherapy in Relational and Theological Perspective*).

Chapters 6 and 7 delve into more specific areas of pastoral theology and psychology. Chapter 6 explores the implications of a theory and theology of multiplicity for gender, politics, and culture, especially focusing on women's experiences and intuitions of multiplicity. It is in this chapter that I introduce the metaphor of "braided selves," drawing from both philosophical images of folds and weavings, and on reflections with a friend whose grandmother's quilts provided a central image for the essay. In chapter 7, I explore in more detail the claims made earlier (especially in chapters 3 and 4) that a theory and theology of multiplicity has positive implications for social and political ethics and pastoral praxis. Chapter 8 extends this discussion into the realm of theodicy, and offers a correlational exercise in a pastoral theology and psychology of multiplicity, good, and evil.

The volume concludes with an in-depth examination of multiplicity from the framework of theological anthropology, and asks in particular the question whether there is a "core self." This chapter "picks up the thread" of the image of braided selves introduced in chapter 6, concluding with the image of a fourfold braid that weaves us together into a multiple yet coherent sense of self through the experiences of our bodies, our relationships, our spirituality, and our embodied ethical practices.

This imagery perhaps begs one last question, however: if we are braided selves, who does the braiding? The answer to that question is perhaps left best to prayer, but is implicit in my theology, as I have shared it throughout this volume: that as we are known and loved by God, and held, as St. Julian says,[33] by God's loving embrace, then the threads of the braid flow out from God as creative profusion. Some twists and turns will come into the braids of our lives from our environment, especially at the hands of others with whom we relate, through both gentleness and violence. There are knots and snarls of our own and others' making (as in a traditional soteriology) but we also participate actively in the warp and weft of creation, as it is woven by God day by day, and we are made and remade according to its ever-changing patterns. We find life-giving form and color through God's incarnational desire, working in us and others, sacramentally through this material world, across space and time. And in the fullness of time we are and will be made whole by God's living inspiration, fully fashioned in all our intricacy and complexity, and reconciled with one another and with the divine—the loving immanent/transcendent about which we can never speak with perfect knowledge, except by metaphors that bridge us, through God's love, to love for ourselves, God, and one another.

※ ※ ※

Just as all writing is conversation, real live conversations go into any piece of writing, and I am grateful for the embodied conversation partners who have helped this metaphorical bus to move in multiple directions over twelve-plus years! In particular, I am grateful to my colleagues in the Psychology, Culture, and Religion Group ("PCR") of the

33. Julian of Norwich, *Showings*, 300.

American Academy of Religion—especially with regard to the theme of multiplicity, Kathleen Bishop, Lisa Cataldo, Jim Jones, John McDargh, Lewis Rambo, Lallene Rector, and Hetty Zock—as well as Wentzel van Huyssteen of Princeton Theological Seminary, and my many wonderful colleagues in the Society for Pastoral Theology (SPT)—especially with regard to the theme of multiplicity, Herb Anderson, Felicity Kelcourse, Jeanne Stevenson-Moessner, Beverly Musgrave, and Teresa Snorton, among many others. I thank all these colleagues for their support and encouragement, challenging questions, and for keeping this conversation alive! I also thank my many mentors and colleagues at the Institute for Clinical Social Work, Chicago, especially Connie Goldberg, Harriet Meek, Joe Cronin, Joseph Palombo, and Sherwood Faigen, without whom I would never have read so much psychoanalytic literature or understood it so well "from the inside!"

I am also indebted to the faculty, staff, and students at Columbia Theological Seminary and the Atlanta Theological Association, the Lutheran Theological Seminary at Philadelphia, and the Lutheran Theological Seminary at Gettysburg, for personal and professional support over the years, for time, space, and resources to write, for wonderful, thoughtful feedback, and for creating such vibrant communities of diversity and collaboration. Thanks also go to the people of the Church of St. Martin's-in-the-Fields, Philadelphia, especially the Rev. Sharline Fulton, Christ Evangelical Lutheran Church, Gettysburg, PA, and the Sisters of St. Joseph of Chestnut Hill College, Philadelphia, for being my spiritual "holding environments" during most of the years I was writing these essays. Finally, I want to express heartfelt love and gratitude to my family, especially spouse Michael and daughter Macrina: for endless rounds of proofreading and thoughtful feedback—sometimes playing devil's advocate—and for always being the ones for whom I most gladly leave the task of writing behind!

ONE

Thick Theory

Psychology, Theoretical Models, and the
Formation of Pastoral Counselors

The head of music at my daughter's school e-mailed me with a request:
"As the chair of the performing arts committee, could you find me a
volunteer to accompany the middle school select chorus? And actually,
I was hoping it would be you." Daunted, I replied, "I'm a singer, not a
pianist. How hard is the repertoire?" She wrote back within the hour,
"You're on! Hey, it's middle school, how hard can it be?" My daughter
brought the music home to me a week later, and my worst fears were
realized. There was one piece in particular that snagged me every time
I attempted it. A wonderful "Gospel swing" piece with a heavy stride
base and large chords in the right hand, this song featured a sudden
key change midstream from G (one sharp) to A-flat (four flats). It was
like rafting down a calm river and suddenly hitting the rapids!

Feeling dutiful, and being somewhat obsessional in character, I
had no choice but to soldier on. Chord sequences in the second half
of the piece kept tripping me up every day. Finally, I took a mental
step back from my finger fumbling and growing panic, and put on my
musicology "hat" to think about the piece. What was its history: who
would have performed it originally? What was the theoretical analysis: what were the harmonic progressions, and why did certain chords
change as they did? The answers helped me immediately. The piece
was, of course, never meant originally to be learned or performed from

a written page. It would have been improvised at first, and then handed on from performer to performer by ear. A Gospel pianist would know instinctively how to move from chord to chord, because the harmonies followed certain formal patterns, and the creative departures from those patterns still belonged within the tonal universe of the style of music being presented. I needed to get my nose away from the sheet music in order to begin to feel my own way almost improvisationally, guided by the theory, into the movements of the melody, the chords, and the song's rolling rhythms.

WHY WE NEED THEORY IN PASTORAL CARE AND COUNSELING

Some students and some experienced therapists resist the need for theory, stating that they do not want to force individual patients with their unique issues into some kind of artificial or preconceived framework. Some pastoral colleagues believe that theory is too abstract, too removed from the flesh-and-blood realities of human thought, feeling, and behavior. While it may be true that some practitioners seem to treat their theoretical models like a procrustean bed, forcing every patient to fit their theory, and disregarding aspects of patients' lives that are not explained by their conceptual frame, this is not the fault of theory per se, but rather a faulty use of it. As Patrick Casement has warned from his psychoanalytic framework, "There is a temptation, rooted in the acquired knowledge of psychoanalytic theory, for analysts and therapists to try to mastermind the analytic process rather than to follow it."[1] This applies to all counselors' premature or overzealous applications of theory. But as Casement continues, "Patients will . . . often resist a therapist's premature application of theoretical knowledge, and preconceived ideas about them in order to reinstate the necessary 'period of hesitation' [citing Winnicott]. Without the space created by this hesitation there can be no room for analytic discovery or play. With it there is room, in every analysis and therapy treatment, for theory to be rediscovered and renewed."[2]

Rather than resisting theory as the culprit, then, it is perhaps more accurate to recognize that in fact *every practitioner has a theory*, whether it is articulated or not. The Greek word *theoría* literally means

---

1. Casement, *On Learning from the Patient*, 183.
2. Ibid., 53.

"a looking at, viewing, or contemplation," as well as "speculation" or *theory* in the sense we understand it. Our theory is, at its most basic meaning, our *viewpoint* as we enter into the work we do with patients.

Theory is classically defined as follows: "A scheme or system of ideas or statements held as an explanation or account of a group of facts or phenomena; a hypothesis that has been confirmed or established by observation or experience, and is propounded or accepted as accounting for the known facts; a statement of what are held to be the general laws, principles, or causes of something known or observed."[3] As it functions in the context of pastoral care, counseling, and psychotherapy, theory encompasses two domains. It represents a set of governing concepts about human behavior ("psychological theory")— encompassing explanations for human motivation, personality formation, emotional and cognitive development, and causes of pathology. And it also represents a framework for practice ("practice theory")—a rationale for using certain methods for both diagnosis and treatment. Various schools of thought within the vast range of contemporary counseling practice may place more emphasis on either the psychological or the practice domain. The most comprehensive theoretical frameworks encompass both, since a particular conceptualization of the human psyche would be expected to have implications for approaches to care.

Unarticulated theories, I would argue, can be as harmful to parishioners and patients as rigidly guarded conscious formulations. An unarticulated practice theory might be an unconscious conviction that "it is my job to be nice to everyone." Under the powerful sway of this unarticulated conviction, a therapist might end up avoiding exploring painful material with a patient, steering away from conflicts arising in the therapeutic relationship, fostering emotional dependency, and even crossing boundaries under the rubric of being a "special carer."[4] A corollary psychological theory might be that "all people are essentially good," and if given sufficient nurture, will naturally grow toward their highest potential. The pitfalls of this general theory include a failure to examine culturally and socially laden assumptions (including racial and gender constructions) about what constitutes "goodness,"

3. Weiner and Simpson, *Oxford English Dictionary*, 2:3284.

4. I have described the pitfalls of the need to be a "special carer" based on my empirical research in Cooper-White, *Shared Wisdom*, esp. 155–80; and in Cooper-White, "The Use of the Self in Psychotherapy," 5–35.

resulting in an empathic failure to recognize aspects of the patient's aggression, sexual desire, greed, hunger, fear, or hate.

Here, of course, I am already showing my own theoretical cards. Even one's approach to theory is already theory laden. My theoretical home is, broadly speaking, psychoanalytic, and within the ever-expanding range of psychoanalytic models, I have pitched my tent with the "relational" school[5]—a contemporary movement within psychoanalysis that follows postmodern, constructivist concepts of psychological reality as socially or interpersonally constructed, and regards "self" as a more multiply constituted subject than a unified or integrated core of identity or being. Its corresponding practice theory emphasizes the fluid interplay of self and other, and attention to countertransference as a primary tool for empathically identifying the thoughts, feelings, sensations, and enactments that continually bubble up in the "intersubjective"[6] or shared area of consciousness/unconsciousness between therapist and patient.[7] Because this school of thought has evolved out of earlier object-relations models, I also continue to find guidance and wisdom in its forebears, for example, the writings of D. W. Winnicott,[8] Harry Guntrip,[9] Melanie Klein,[10] and of Sigmund Freud himself[11]—whose multiply layered and ever-developing thought continues to be a rich resource.[12]

Given my own theoretical biases about theory, then, I am prone to believe that we are drawn to our favored psychological and practice theories (conscious and unconscious) by our own personal histories, experiences with people we are close to, and professional experiences

5. The foundational text for this school of thought is Mitchell, *Relational Concepts in Psychoanalysis*; see also Greenberg, *Oedipus and Beyond*; and Aron, *A Meeting of Minds*. The development of relational theory can be traced through the journal *Psychoanalytic Dialogues* beginning with volume 1 in 1991, and in Mitchell and Aron, *Relational Psychoanalysis*, ixff.; see also Greenberg and Mitchell, "Object Relations and Psychoanalytic Models," 9–20; and Mitchell, *Relationality*.

6. Term first coined by the phenomenologist philosopher Edmund Husserl, *Cartesian Meditations*.

7. Cooper-White, *Shared Wisdom*.

8. Winnicott, *The Maturational Processes*.

9. Guntrip, *Schizoid Phenomena*.

10. Klein, *Envy and Gratitude*; and Klein, *Love, Guilt, and Reparation*.

11. Freud, *The Standard Edition*.

12. For an argument for the continued relevance of Freud's work from a pastoral theological and psychological perspective, see Cooper-White, "A Critical Tradition"

—in other words, our countertransference. For example, I am gravita-tionally pulled toward Guntrip's and André Green's writings about the dead (depressive) mother;[13] Freud's explanations of neurotic symp-toms as an outbreaking of repressed sexual and aggressive desires;[14] Klein's unflinching descriptions of biting, guilt, and reparation;[15] and Jane Flax's and Jodie Messler Davies's theories about the emanci-patory qualities of multiplicity,[16] because they resonate symphoni-cally with my own personal and clinical experience. I am drawn to Winnicott's[17] descriptions of practice because they speak to the kind of "good-enough" care that touch my own yearnings to be cared for and understood, as well as my maternal longings and experiences as both a literal mother, and in the countertransference (the helper's uncon-scious reactions to the helpee)[18] as a professional caregiver.

The role of countertransference in the development, conscious and unconscious, of our psychological viewpoint, our theory, points to the need for self-knowledge, and to personal therapy as part of both the theoretical formation and the overall professional formation of pasto-ral counselors and caregivers. Formation involves not only training in skills—perhaps the most rudimentary part of formation—but acquir-ing a knowledge base from which to draw about the human psyche, the causes of dysfunction, effective modes of healing, and (as pasto-ral counselors) the spiritual dimensions of human growth and living. Moreover, formation suggests growth in the area of identity and even character—both in terms of one's role as a professional helper, and in terms of one's personal maturity, honesty, and sound judgment.

What constitutes mature character, of course, could be endlessly debated, and is conditioned by the particular era and culture in which one lives. A general view of the kind of maturity required of a pastoral caregiver or therapist might be summed up as follows (and always as a work in progress!): a capacity for honesty (with oneself and others),

13. Guntrip, *Schizoid Phenomena*; Green, "The Dead Mother."

14. Freud, *Three Essays*.

15. Klein, *Love, Guilt, and Reparation*.

16. Flax, *Disputed Subjects*; and Davies, "Multiple Perspectives on Multiplicity."

17. Winnicott, *The Maturational Processes*.

18. The literature on countertransference is vast and originates with Freud himself. For an overview of both classic and contemporary views of countertransference es-pecially in the context of pastoral care and counseling, refer to Cooper-White, *Shared Wisdom*.

self-reflection/introspection and self-awareness, empathy, compassion, graciousness, kindness, nonreactivity, self-restraint, respect, relatedness, and a willingness to be with and for another without losing one's own healthy boundaries (i.e., balancing one's own needs and another's).

The practices of professional care and counseling call especially for self-awareness as a person, because the knowledge of one's own wounds is a prerequisite both for avoiding the pitfalls of bias and projection, and for being open and available to the subjective experience of the other who comes to us for care. The hypothetical counselor mentioned above, whose unarticulated theory is to be nice at all times, has no less inward predilection toward his or her theory than I have toward mine. We cannot escape the force of our own internal landscape. But to the extent that we can come to recognize some of the elements within it, we can make choices about what makes the most mature sense to us, how to conduct ourselves as professionals, and what is most likely to be genuinely therapeutic in our work with patients— putting their emotional and developmental needs above our own during the time we spend with them. Learning from the highly developed and carefully articulated theories of those who have gone before us gives us a richer repertoire from which to form our own models of psychology and pastoral practice.

WHAT MAKES A "GOOD" THEORY?

Not all theories are created equal. I like mine, and you like yours, but we need better reasons for these inclinations than that they somehow "ring true," or even that we can identify how they resonate with our personal experience, as I described above. What is good theory, and how can we tell?

Good theory, first of all, should be useful to actual processes of healing. A theory should be internally consistent, and may even be brilliant or fascinating in its speculations about the motives and meanings of human behavior, but if it does not connect to the struggles of real human persons, it is not enough. Especially for the practice of psychotherapy a theory should have sufficient explanatory power to help illuminate both *what* is happening to the patient internally, and in his or her relationship to others in the world in terms of some larger patterns common to human behavior, and *why*.

Second, as pastoral counseling belongs under the larger umbrella of ministry disciplines and practical theology, good pastoral care and counseling theory must also be in dialogue with pastoral theology, in which theory, theology, and practice are seamlessly interwoven. As postmodern philosophers such as Michel Foucault and Jacques Derrida have pointed out, the separation of theory and practice is itself an artificial dichotomy. Don Browning[19] and Edward Farley[20] have both argued that all authentic theology is at heart "practical in its import."[21] Browning advocates for an inductive "practice-theory-practice" orientation in which practice is recognized both as implicitly theory laden, and offering a rich source, via "thick description,"[22] for building theory.

Further, the claims human beings make *ethically* upon one another —each encounter with difference, each encounter with the unique face of the other (to borrow from the philosopher Emanuel Levinas[23])—call us continually to draw from, and at the same time to reappraise and revise, our theological premises in light of whatever new form of love and justice this new "I-Thou"[24] encounter demands. As theologian David Tracy has argued,[25] there must be, indeed, a mutual dialogue or "critical correlation" back and forth between theology and the human situation. Pastoral theology always takes suffering as its starting place[26]—in Jürgen Moltmann's words, "the open wound of life in this world."[27] The classic pastoral functions, as articulated in the mid-twentieth century (and amplified in recent decades), immerse the pastoral theologian directly in this open wound, through a commitment

19. Browning, *A Fundamental Practical Theology*.

20. Farley, "Practical Theology."

21. See also Ramsay, *Pastoral Care and Counseling*.

22. Geertz, "Thick Description." See also chapter 1, above.

23. E.g., Levinas, *Totality and Infinity*.

24. Buber, *I and Thou*, as both elaborated and contested in ibid.

25. Tracy, *Blessed Rage for Order*, drawing also from Tillich, *Systematic Theology* 1:40–47.

26. This method is characterized by Anton Boisen's foundational concept of the "living human document" as a corrective for approaching pastoral care and therapy with human subjects through the lens of theory first rather than examining the patient's experience as the primary "text" to guide assessment and care, in Boisen, *The Exploration of the Inner World*. This expression was further developed by Charles Gerkin, in *The Living Human Document*. See also Bonnie Miller-McLemore's further creative and feminist elaboration as "The Living Human Web."

27. Moltmann, *The Trinity and the Kingdom*, 49.

to ministries of healing, sustaining, guiding, reconciling, nurturing, empowering, and liberating.[28]

In order to serve this purpose well, theory needs to be *thick theory*, borrowing from anthropologist Clifford Geertz's term for good ethnographic observation, "thick description."[29] The goal of good theory is, to quote Geertz, "not an experimental science in search of law but an interpretative one in search of meaning. It is explication I am after, construing social expression on their surface enigmatical."[30] As Geertz continues, "What generality it [theory] contrives to achieve grows out of the delicacy of its distinctions, not the sweep of its abstractions . . . [T]he essential task of theory building here is not to codify abstract regularities but to make thick description possible, not to generalize across cases but to generalize within them."[31]

A thin theory, like thin description, imagines far fewer questions. A theory is a paradigm,[32] which can only explore the questions its adherents can imagine. Thus thick theory is marked not by its factual *accuracy*, but by its power to generate more and better *questions*.[33] Pastoral psychological theory must be "thick": layered and detailed enough to take into consideration the complexity and multifariousness of human living and its many modes of symbolization, together with the vicissitudes of psychological unfolding over time.

Finally, following Derrida, I would argue that good theory is theory that also has the capacity to interrogate not only its subject of investigation but *itself*. Thick theory raises questions about its own presuppositions and biases, thus generating queries that are both more rigorous and more creative. Therefore, a good theory is one that continually breaks itself open. In the words of one scholar of post-

28. The first four functions were classically articulated by Clebsch and Jaeckle in *Pastoral Care in Historical Perspective*; Ali expanded these to include the last three functions in *Survival and Liberation*, 121. See also Thornton's critique of "healing" as a "function," described in more detail above in the introduction, n6.

29. Geertz, "Thick Description."

30. Ibid., 5.

31. Ibid., 25–26.

32. Kuhn, *The Structure of Scientific Revolutions*; cf., Geertz, "Thick Description," 27, on the process by which unproductive theories are retained beyond their usefulness.

33. Geertz, "Thick Description," similarly evaluates his "interpretive anthropology" as "a science whose progress is marked less by a perfection of consensus than by a refinement of date. What gets better is the precision with which we vex each other." (ibid., 29).

modernism: "Derrida in particular mounted a radical philosophical critique in which he pointed out that the very act of meaning making always presupposes an unanalyzable ground of the possibility of meaning and of sign systems, and that the dialectic of sign and ground produces an inherent instability or indefiniteness in any meaning."[34]

To the extent that theory is itself a practice of naming, Derrida's reflections about the slipperiness of words caution us that there is an irreducible gap between the act of naming and whatever may exist as actual reality: "It is . . . simultaneously true that things come into existence and lose existence by being named."[35] The reality of our parishioners' and patients' subjective experience can never be fully known, even as its contours may be traced and given meanings in the ongoing dialectic between the caregiver's and care recipient's respective theoretical knowledge (or speculations), and the narrative(s) they construct together. So meaning grows and changes more and more with each successive encounter. What I am calling "thick theory," then, grows out of an ongoing dialectical relationship between each moment of engagement (including its symbolic representation in words), and our contemplation of the relationship especially before and after each meeting (also interpretation, also symbolic, but at another level of remove[36]).

This approach has emancipatory implications. Rather than a tool by which to measure or evaluate patients, used in a unilateral act of power on the part of the professional caregiver as expert, theory is fluid and malleable as it passes through the ongoing floes (both conscious and unconscious) of the therapeutic relationship. Foucault wrote in detail about the intrinsic link between knowledge and power, and in particular the use of theoretical knowledge to set the medical, psychiatric, or other professional in a position of superior political power by virtue of the expertise accorded. We hold legitimate power that we cannot shed, in the form of responsibility and trust based on a nonreciprocal ethical duty to care for our parishioners, patients, and clients.[37] Our use of theory involves serving this trust faithfully—using

34. Lemke, "Postmodernism and Critical Theory."

35. Derrida, *Writing and Difference*, 70.

36. For a further discussion of hermeneutics and theory, see Geertz, "Thick Description," 24–30.

37. For more on a relational reframing of the reason for good boundaries, see Cooper-White, *Shared Wisdom*, 58–60.

our analytical abilities and therapeutic skills to *em*power rather than *dis*empower those in our care, as we engage in mutual rather than unilateral practices of exploration, interpretation, and meaning making. We bring a fund of theoretical knowledge with us as part of our training, and then our theory, in turn, is shaped and challenged by each new encounter. Thick theory, to borrow words from Foucault, "does not express, translate, or serve to apply practice: it is practice. But it is local and regional . . . and not totalizing. This is a struggle against power, a struggle aimed at revealing and undermining power when it is most invisible and insidious."[38]

THE CASE OF "BRITT"

To bring this abstract theorizing about theory down to earth, let me offer an example. I once had a pastoral psychotherapy patient in California, Britt,[39] a competitively ranked figure skater, who was involved in self-injury. Britt was pushed early and hard by her parents to perform. By the time she had become an adult, her perfectionism and related self-punishment for imperfection were unrelenting. Initially my theoretical understanding was a fairly standard conceptualization of self-injury available at that time:[40] that her cutting was an externalization of inner pain, an effort to restore a sense of personal control, an expression of a rescue fantasy or a cry for help, and also a physiological addiction to the endorphins released by cutting. This was a supportive understanding that corresponded well to Britt's own conscious understanding of her motives for cutting, her inability to stop it, and the relief it provided her.

That year during the winter Olympics, I saw a magazine advertisement for a brand of kitchen knives. The ad consisted of a full-page photograph of just the legs and feet of a female figure skater, clad in sheer tights and boots with chef's knives for skate blades. The ad jolted me, both because of the violent and sexual fetishization implicit in

---

38. Foucault, "Intellectuals and Power," 208; see also Foucault, "Power and Strategies," 145. For a good discussion of Foucault's writings on social theory, see also Lemert and Gillan, *Michel Foucault*.

39. Name and identifying information have been altered for confidentiality.

40. My main resource was Karen Conterio and Wendy Lado, *Bodily Harm*. For a more recent in-depth discussion of self-injury, drawing on psychodynamic attachment theory, see Farber, *When the Body Is the Target*.

the image, and because of my immediate association to Britt. I realized that my theory had been too thin. It had not allowed my reverie about the patient to entertain the possibilities of either the erotic or the more violent, aggressive aspects of her self-harm. I went back to my theoretical resources and began to consider more widely some of the possible unconscious meanings that had eluded me before—partly in unconscious collusion with the patient's own need to be seen only as victimized, innocent, and pure in motive. I thought from a self psychological perspective about skates and knives as selfobjects. I thought from a Kleinian perspective about themes of eroticism fused with aggression, guilt, and reparation. I thought about gender theory and the female figure-skating world, its sexual performativity,[41] and its enforcement of a certain paradoxical image of child-woman femininity (think of star performers being pelted by fans with both flowers and teddy bears). More associations came to me, but suffice it to say that suddenly my theory was now thick with multiple associations having to do with both the erotic and the aggressive dimensions of Britt's cutting. Issues that had previously seemed unrelated came into focus in a new way—body image, erotic desire and inhibition, bravado, rage, issues of power, and revenge.

Note that my "aha!" moment of viewing the knife ad did not suddenly lead me to make ham-handed interpretations, catalyzing a clichéd cathartic, cure-all moment for Britt. Rather, my inner shift from thin to thick theory *sensitized* me to the many more possible meanings of Britt's cutting that had previously been opaque to me, so that over time I could hear more, explore more, and empathically understand more. My new openness helped make a space for Britt to verbalize more—thoughts, feelings, and fantasies she previously had kept both unconsciously repressed and consciously suppressed out of shame and fear of judgment. Thick theory thus facilitated a form of "hearing into speech."[42] Britt experienced this as empowering and freeing for her, and as less consciously acceptable aspects of her motives and behavior became more tolerable to her, her crises of self-injury ceased through-

41. Judith Butler's *Gender Trouble* is relevant to this discussion. For a fascinating discussion of Butler's theories and cultural meanings of female figure skating, see also Kestnbaum, *Culture on Ice.*

42. Morton, *The Journey Is Home.* Teresa Snorton points out an additional caution: that "hearing into speech" can be romanticized when other variables, such as culture, race and class are not taken into consideration. (Personal communication.)

out the latter part of our therapy work together. She found more constructive modes of expression for a myriad of unconscious feelings and needs that had previously been relieved through cutting.

THREE IMPORTANT USES OF THEORY FOR PASTORAL PRAXIS

There are many ways in which theory can be helpful, and many theories about theory itself. I will highlight three that I believe to be particularly important for pastoral praxis: 1) diagnostic sensitivity, 2) empathic anticipation, and 3) play and imagination.

Diagnostic Sensitivity

Diagnosis, like theory itself, has fallen on hard times in some therapeutic quarters. *Pastoral* diagnosis in particular has seldom been addressed as a topic per se. The three major exceptions to this are Paul Pruyser's now classic text, *The Minister as Diagnostician*,[43] Chris Schlauch's article, "Re-Visioning Pastoral Diagnosis" (in which he includes both a biblical-exegetical and self psychological approach),[44] and Nancy Ramsay's *Pastoral Diagnosis: A Resource for Ministries of Care and Counseling*.[45] Because of reductionistic and sometimes sexist misuses of diagnosis to label, (mis)define and pathologize patients, some therapists and chaplains, and probably many more parish pastors, are wary of assessment and diagnosis.[46] Resistance to intrusive

---

43. Pruyser, *The Minister as Diagnostician*.

44. Schlauch, "Re-Visioning Pastoral Diagnosis."

45. Ramsay, *Pastoral Diagnosis*.

46. Largely driven by managed care, a trend has arisen in the last decade or so, variously called Outcome-Based Practice or Empirically Validated Treatment (EVT) —see, for example, Seligman, *Selecting Effective Treatments*. It is a pragmatically oriented practice theory of sorts, a teleological theory in which the ends—as defined by the interests of insurers as much as by patients—not only justify but dictate the means. This is the approach adopted by the National Board for Certified Counselors, and by extension, most state licensure requirements. It appeals to the desire of legislators and the medical establishment to validate counseling practices from a positivist scientific model, and to regulate practice from a risk-management perspective, i.e., to minimize malpractice liability. In large part, however, it is a practice theory without a psychology, so in its worst manifestations, an EVT approach would suggest that the same therapist, based on quantitative outcome research, should be a cognitive-behaviorist with depressed patients, a behaviorist with anxious ones, a family-systems therapist with couples in conflict, a psychopharmacologist with psychotic patients, and perhaps—only after cognitive methods have been tried first—a psychodynamic therapist

oversight by managed-care and third-party payers can also play into this distrust. Some therapists and pastoral professionals therefore prefer to take a more intuitive approach to assessment, allowing the therapeutic process to unfold without formal evaluations or case formulations. Implicit in this resistance sometimes is a parallel resistance to the notion of pathology itself, with some therapists feeling that to identify problems with living as pathology is automatically to assume a superior position to the patient and to patholog*ize.*

I agree that concepts of pathology and diagnosis, and a medical or "disease" model of psychology and psychotherapy have rightly become suspect in recent decades, to the extent that they set up an expert therapist / passive patient dynamic, in which patients come to be identified globally and impersonally with their suffering and impairments, or labeled as "problems" in order to impose political and social conformity. However, I believe that to do away with all forms of assessment or diagnosis would be to pretend that various recognizable forms of illness and pain did not exist.[47]

I would argue on the contrary that *pathology* does not have to be construed as a pejorative term by which individuals may be labeled and thereby dismissed, but rather that *pathology* be understood as a means of naming a quality of suffering. The root of the word *pathology*, like the origin of the word *patient*, is not sickness but *pathéma/páthos*—"suffering"or"passion." *Pathology* is the study of suffering and passion: "*pathos-logos.*" To quote Schlauch, pastoral diagnosis can be practiced as "holy regard" and one form of "faithful companioning."[48] Understanding pathology in all its nuances requires care-full diagnosis or assessment, in order to have some means of categorizing the shapes that mental and emotional suffering tend to take, at least in any given cultural location. Consensus about these categories and specific terminology evolves and changes over time as different theories hold sway, but there is a shared language and at least a broadly consensual conceptualization in the field of psychology, without which professional communication and consultation regarding practice, research,

---

working with traumatized patients. The inherent bias of this research is toward short-term interventions that restore a baseline of functioning but rarely focus on helping a patient to reach any deeper understanding of the root causes of his or her problems.

47. For further discussion, see Cooper-White, *Many Voices*, 96–117.

48. Schlauch, "Re-Visioning Pastoral Diagnosis," 65.

and training would be very limited. *Diagnosis*, from the Greek word *diagnoskō*, means "to distinguish or inquire," "to make a decision," or "to make something known." If the word is broken down, it simply means "to know (*gnōskō*) through" (*día*). In this regard, pathology and diagnosis belong to pastoral practice and are especially crucial in the work of pastoral psychotherapy. Diagnosis remains an important area of disciplined focus, in order to shape the care given and receiving with a thoughtful assessment of "what ails."[49]

The reigning understanding of diagnosis taught in pastoral clinical training programs is codified in the United States in the *Diagnostic and Statistical Manual of Mental Disorders* (DSM),[50] currently in its fourth edition since 1952, with a fifth edition scheduled to be published in 2013.[51] The DSM offers a taxonomy of symptom descriptions, based on observations of clinicians over several decades, and not primarily on theoretical formulations or etiology (causation).[52] While the "reliability" of its classifications continues to be a subject of some controversy and even diatribes against the DSM,[53] the utility of having some common clinical vocabulary is valued by most professional therapists. But it should be noted that the DSM is not in and of itself a *theory*, although its categories were originally developed with underlying theoretical biases (often functioning invisibly, like all effective ideologies). Sophisticated readings of the DSM and other diagnostic manuals require the clinician to pay attention to their ever-changing and evolving definitions and underlying theoretical constructs. The *Introduction* to the DSM itself includes cautions on the limitations of a categorical approach, and the still-fledgling efforts of the DSM task force to incorporate "ethnic and cultural considerations."[54] Very

49. Quoting a favored phrase to open a therapy session from Yalom, *Love's Executioner*, 89, 232.

50. American Psychiatric Association, *Diagnostic and Statistical Manual* (hereafter: "*DSM-IV-TR*").

51. American Psychiatric Association, "DSM-V Development."

52. The one obvious exception to this is Post-Traumatic Stress Disorder and its related brief form Acute Stress Disorder, which by definition require a trauma to have occurred as the origin of the disorder (American Psychiatric Association, *DSM-IV-TR*, 463–71.)

53. Kirk and Kutchins, *Making Us Crazy*.

54. American Psychiatric Association, *DSM-IV-TR*, xxii, xxiv; see also Lukoff et al., "Toward a More Culturally Sensitive DSM-IV."

different constructions of mental health and spiritual well-being are authoritative in non-Western cultures.

As Ramsay has written, "Diagnosis is not a neutral process; it has both interpretive and constructive functions. Diagnosis reiterates the anthropological and philosophical assumptions of the practitioner and validates the usefulness of those assumptions for naming reality."[55]

Optimally, therefore, diagnosis should be self-reflective and self-critical, watchful for biases and gaps in one's own understanding, and above all, engaged in collaboration with the patient, in an ongoing process of shared reflection, dialogue, and continual revision as the patient's sufferings come to evolve, change, and carry different meanings over time.

The value of theory for diagnosis lies beyond—often far beyond—the descriptive shells of DSM categories. Fluency in psychological theory helps the clinician to move beyond such quantitative measures toward a more subtle and nuanced, empathic interpretation of the causes of an individual's distress. Such an interpretation (which must always be acknowledged as such, and not as a factual account) may be summarized as a *case formulation*. Such a formulation is a working sketch of a patient's inner world and external relations, drawn for the purpose of offering the best, most sensitive therapeutic response. Therefore it is always provisional and subject to ongoing revision. As psychoanalyst and training supervisor Nancy McWilliams has written, "it is a more inferential, subjective, and artistic process than diagnosis by matching observable behaviors to lists of symptoms . . . A good tentative formulation . . . attends to the following areas: temperament and fixed attributes, maturational themes, defensive patterns, central affects, identifications, relational schemas, self-esteem regulation, and pathogenic beliefs."[56]

Case formulation, while often associated with psychoanalytic psychotherapy, is a valuable tool for counselors practicing from a variety of theoretical orientations, ranging from family-systems to cognitive-behavioral therapies. A good formulation, regardless of the practitioner's theoretical orientation, is one that begins with a nuanced and detailed understanding of the patient's concerns in the patient's own language and connected to the patient's own sensibilities.

55. Ramsay, *Pastoral Care and Counseling*, 9.
56. McWilliams, *Psychoanalytic Case Formulation*, 11, see also ibid., 208–9.

Only a thick theory aids the pastoral counselor, as well as the chaplain or pastor, in forming a thick description (encompassing what is observed in fine detail both about the other, and about one's own affective experience within the flow of the therapeutic relationship). Only such a thick description, in turn, can sensitize the counselor to the minute, specific, and detailed vicissitudes of the patient's or parishioner's speech, behavior, affect, and communication—expressing the delicate turns of his or her life, both inner and outer. And as observations are shared and explored with the patient, the formulation of "what ails," and why, is mutually constructed. Diagnosis becomes a relational process rather than a product created by an expert solely for communication with other experts. This leads naturally from diagnosis to care as deepening relationship—and theory becomes helpful once again as an empathic tool.

Empathic Anticipation

While theory may be most obviously associated with initial diagnosis and case formulation, it is also invaluable in the continuing pastoral assessment that flows inseparably throughout the pastoral relationship. Patrick Casement describes this contemplative turn within the therapeutic work in terms of an "internal supervisor."[57] The "internal supervisor" is a composite metaphor for a therapist's internalization of his or her own supervision, personal therapy, and clinical experience. This internal supervisor functions, at least in part, as a metaphor for the way theory continues to function for a therapist or counselor, sometimes subliminally, as an internal compass when in the midst of working with a patient.

Especially in psychotherapy, part of the way in which this internal supervisor functions is to facilitate a variety of different imagined empathic connections with the patient's material, beyond what occurs in session. In my experience, allowing for an associative process of making such "trial identifications," including a free-floating consideration of transference-countertransference dynamics and enactments as they have begun to bubble up in the therapeutic relationship, helps the therapist to be more nimble and sensitive when actually in session with the patient. Drawing on a musical analogy, Casement writes:

57. Casement, *On Learning from the Patient*, esp. 29ff.

In order that we can develop a more subliminal use of the internal supervisor when we are with a patient, it is valuable to use (or in a Winnicott sense, to 'play' with) clinical material outside of the session. A musician plays scales, or technical studies, in order that these can become a natural part of his [or her] technique. So too in psychotherapy: when a therapist is 'making music' with a patient [s/]he should not be preoccupied with issues of technique. That technique can be developed by taking time, away from the consulting room, for practicing with clinical material. Then, when in the presence of a patient, the process of internal supervision is more readily available when it is most needed.[58]

Theory thus enhances our ability to be truly, empathically present with a patient from moment to moment. The work we do in actual therapy sessions has a performative dimension—it is an enacted narrative, constructed by both therapist and patient, that operates simultaneously at a verbal and an embodied level. Therefore the work and the *play*[59] of therapy is akin to improvisation, rather than to the production of a scripted drama. Thick theory requires a multidimensional capacity to enter vicariously into the worldview and affective life of the patient, and to be open, as well, to the subtleties of feeling and fantasy arising spontaneously within one's own frame of reference, one's own countertransference. While we are focusing here on psychotherapy, there are certainly aspects of this empathic imagination that are relevant to pastoral care and parish practice—indeed, all practical theology draws upon the pastor's capacity for creativity and imagination.[60]

Heinz Kohut defined *empathy* as "vicarious introspection,"[61] and contended that sustained empathy, or "empathic-introspective inquiry" is the primary tool of therapeutic observation and insight.[62] Empathy works primarily through the medium of the therapist's own subjectivity or countertransference, as the therapist experiences af-

58. Ibid., 38, also citing Winnicott, *Playing and Reality*.

59. Winnicott, *Playing and Reality*.

60. Dykstra, "Pastoral and Ecclesial Imagination"; and Dykstra, "Imagination and the Pastoral Life."

61. Kohut, "Introspection, Empathy, and Psychoanalysis," 459.

62. Stolorow et al., *Psychoanalytic Treatment*; Stolorow et al., *The Intersubjective Perspective*; Orange et al., *Working Intersubjectively*.

fects, resonances, fantasies, and images that are drawn from the pool of unconscious material and "shared wisdom" in the intersubjective dynamic of the therapy.[63] We ourselves are the most sensitive instruments to "catch" the vibrations of the music that is occurring between the patient or parishioner and ourselves, especially at the level of unconscious relationship. At first we may not even be able to sing the melody back, i.e., to verbalize in our own minds what is happening. But as the relationship continues, and we consider the interactions between our parishioners and patients and ourselves—particularly moments that seem deeply affect laden or powered by nonverbal enactment—, both our personal self-awareness and theoretical knowledge can aid us in our understanding of the other person (and especially in psychotherapy) of the therapeutic relationship. As the British analyst Christopher Bollas has written:

> In order to find the patient, we must look for him[/her] within ourselves . . . By establishing a countertransference readiness I am creating an internal space which allows for a more complete and articulate expression of the patient's transference speech than if I were to close down this internal space and replace it with some ideal notion of absolute mental neutrality or scientific detachment . . . What the [therapist] feels, imagines, and thinks to himself while with the patient may at any one moment be a specific element of the patient's projectively-identified psychic life . . . that creation of a total environment in which both patient and [therapist] pursue a 'life' together.[64]

Such readiness, I would suggest, is enabled and facilitated by a combination of a discipline of introspection and an ongoing engagement with the best theoretical thinking available, both historically and in the present. Finally, this readiness requires a willingness on our part to *play*.

Play and Imagination

Scripture scholar Frances Young uses the metaphor of a concerto performer's virtuosic cadenza for preaching and teaching, but this analogy could just as easily be extended to the improvisational virtuosity of the pastoral counselor in session with a patient: "The performer of a

---

63. For a detailed discussion of this dynamic, see Cooper-White, *Shared Wisdom*.

64. Bollas, *The Shadow of the Object*, 201–2.

cadenza keeps to the style and themes of the concerto" [here, we might substitute *psychological and practice theory* for "the style and themes of the concerto"], "but also shows virtuosity and inspiration in adapting and continuing in keeping with the setting and form."[65] All the technical training, all the theory and analysis, all the historical study that a musician or a therapist has internalized becomes crystallized in a moment of creative imagination in the irreducible present moment of performance or therapeutic encounter. This creativity is not constrained but rather is carried by the boundaries of setting, and it is resourced by the received theoretical structure and its theoretical underpinnings. In this way, especially in an ongoing in-depth psychotherapy, but even in briefer series of conversations in a parish or other pastoral setting, each subsequent encounter becomes a duet, in which the harmonic resolution desired is healing, growth, or revitalization for the patient or parishioner.

Paradoxically, given the reams of psychotherapeutic publications over the last one hundred years, and the tooth-and-claw fights among therapists of differing theoretical persuasions, perhaps the most important capacity of a therapist is "the moral courage not to understand."[66] A favorite quotation among relational analysts is Wilfred Bion's statement that therapists should approach the work of therapy "without memory or desire."[67] The therapist, like the poet, should be "capable of being in uncertainties, mysteries, doubts, without any irritable reaching after fact and reason."[68] It is ironic that Bion, of all possible theorists, wrote so much toward the end of his life about therapy as an "act of faith,"[69] when one of his greatest concerns was laboriously categorizing modes of cognition, including the creation of an elaborate grid of algebraic symbols. Yet, Bion's own symbol for the ineffable, "O,"[70] literally went "off the charts"—it does not appear on Bion's complicated grid.[71] "O" referred to a reality beyond what can

65. Wells, *Improvisation*, 60; also citing Young, *The Art of Performance*.

66. Reik, *Listening with the Third Ear*, as cited in McWilliams, *Psychoanalytic Psychotherapy*, 21.

67. Bion, *Attention and Interpretation*, 32, 41–54.

68. Ibid.

69. Ibid., 32, 41.

70. First described in Bion, *Transformations*.

71. Ibid., frontispiece.

be grasped, like Derrida's ineffable "ground" that lies as a trace in the gaps between sense and representation.

This is perhaps the paradoxical value of deeply critical, theoretical thinking—that it finally leads to the recognition of its own limits, and a lifting of one's gaze past books and papers and theories toward the horizon of that which, inevitably, appears in the distance as a shimmering Unknown. Bion's own slipping into theological language shows how thin the membrane finally is between the "faith" of secular therapy and a religious sensibility: "O . . . can 'become,' but it cannot be 'known'. It is darkness and formlessness, but it enters the domain K [knowledge] when it has evolved to a point where it can be known, through knowledge gained by experience, and formulated in terms derived from sensuous experience; its existence is conjured phenomenologically."[72]

CONCLUSION: MAKING MUSIC

Finally, the knowledge of theory and practical skills must dissolve into the immediacy of the pastoral encounter. One should not be theorizing as a primary activity in the presence of a parishioner or patient! But one must first *have* a theoretical foundation in order to suspend it. It is perhaps only once one is secure in one's capacity to play theoretically, based on a thoroughgoing acquaintance with respected theoretical models, that one is freed to hold such "knowledge" lightly. We suspend it within the practice of "evenly hovering attention"[73] to all the registers of the therapeutic encounter—affective, cognitive, sensory, and in the realms of nonverbal enactment and unconscious/semiconscious fantasy. Theoretical speculations are precisely that—they are *speculi*, mirrors, or, more aptly, prisms, by which one facet of theory after another can be held up to our experience with a patient, to see what lights and patterns may be reflected—, always with the benefit of the patient and not merely the brilliance of the therapist as the aim. Theory ultimately does not provide us with "information" about the patient but rather a sensitivity to multiple meanings that arise in the intersubjective matrix of the therapeutic relationship. It does not

---

72. Bion, *Attention and Interpretation*, 26.

73. Freud, "Recommendations to Physicians Practicing Psycho-analysis."

provide us with answers, but over time it may provide us with more complex and sophisticated questions.

Some Recommendations

In conclusion, to return to concrete training and practice, how can we as pastors, chaplains, pastoral counselors, psychotherapists, supervisors, consultants, and teachers, foster "thick theory?"

1. First, we can make it a lifelong habit to read widely in pastoral, clinical, theoretical—and of course, theological[74]—literature, both contemporary and historical. Just as a musician can learn new pieces more readily when s/he has already learned an extensive repertoire, we gain in theoretical sensitivity and a capacity for vicarious introspection by assimilating a broad range of theoretical ideas.
2. We can foster a capacity for critical reflection on our theoretical (and also theological) resources. Questions to ask include the following: What is the underlying paradigm being presented? Who is served, and who is left out in this paradigm? What are the cultural, social, and political biases behind this theoretical formulation, and how is power being mediated?
3. It is essential that we reflect often, and deeply on our countertransference reactions to theoretical formulations themselves. What in a given theory excites, disturbs, attracts, or repels us? What might be the inner sources of such reactions, and how might such self-awareness enhance the use of this theory for the benefit of those we serve?
4. Finally—and perhaps this is especially warranted for pastoral counselors, therapists, and supervisors—, we should foster an awareness of desires on our own part either to resist theoretical *play and reverie* about a given patient, or to fall too rigidly into a single fixed formulation. What might such resistances to imaginative speculation and improvisation mean in the ongoing dynamic of a particular patient or helpee? And what does the particular interplay of our desire to know, our desire not to know, and our

74. While theology is not the focus of this chapter, it is assumed that a pastoral identity is formed not only in psychological theory, but in theological reflection, and that theological reflection itself has much to do with both self-knowledge and pastoral assessment. For an elaborated pastoral theological method, see Cooper-White, *Shared Wisdom*, esp. 74–81. For a pastoral theological framework and its rationale, see Cooper-White, *Many Voices*, 1–132; and, more briefly, chapter 5 in this volume.

"negative capacity" for suspending knowledge suggest empathically about the patient's or parishioner's own subjective life and experience?

The Theory behind the Improv

I eventually had five rehearsals with the middle-school chorus, and a final, nail-biting performance. I am never going to be an exceptional pianist, but I have come a long way since the first day of practicing that challenging music. Practicing strengthened my skill, and I became basically fluent with all the pieces that at first I stumbled my way through. But especially by taking a step back and thinking about the theory and the history of the notes on the printed page, I was able to let go and recapture just a bit of the improvisational genius behind the written composition. Paradoxically, it was connecting to the theory behind the notes that allowed me to really *play* the music, fearlessly, with pleasure, and "well enough."[75]

75. A play on Winnicott's term, "the good enough mother" in "Ego Distortion in Terms of True and False Self," 145.

TWO

Human Development in Relational and Cultural Context

"In the beginning is the relation."—Martin Buber[1]

Human development does not occur in a vacuum. To be human is to be in relation from the moment of conception. The development of human consciousness is a process of meeting, an increasingly rich and complex knowing and experiencing oneself in context. There is never a moment of human existence without a surrounding environment of sensations and relations, beginning with the experience of the mother herself as total environment and living, breathing home. While researchers and theory makers differ somewhat on the perception of differentiation between self and others that is possible at birth, life begins in the matrix of "I and Thou."[2] Martin Buber wrote, "It is not as if a child first saw an object and then entered into some relationship with that. Rather, the longing for relation is primary, the cupped hand into which the being that confronts us nestles."[3]

1. Buber, *I and Thou*, 69.
2. Ibid.
3. Ibid., 78.

TOWARD A NEW METAPHOR FOR HUMAN DEVELOPMENT

This basic relationality of human existence may seem obvious, but traditional models of human development have tended to paint a different picture. Human development is still frequently taught as an extension of Descartes's famous seventeenth-century dictum:"I think, therefore I am,"[4] or in a perhaps more accurate translation,"I am thinking, therefore I exist."[5] Traditional models of development, while recognizing the challenges of interpersonal relating, particularly from early childhood onward, have tended to focus on the (mostly cognitive) growth of individuals, as solitary "I's" rather than as persons-in-relation. With the individual as foreground, the environment and the people in it mostly form a backdrop against which the individual's development proceeds. Frequently, the environment is depicted as posing obstacles or impediments to forward movement of the individual. An overarching pattern or archetype presented in these traditional models of development is the hero's journey.[6] The individual yearns, or is "hardwired" from birth, to move forward toward ever increasing capacities, particularly in the realm of cognitive, rational, and principled moral thought. Obstacles are seen as problems to be overcome, and each developmental stage or level is an achievement over the previous one. The use of the term *mastery* in many developmental theories is not accidental. The hero's journey has a goal, that of increasing mastery of the environment through ever more efficient thought and skilled action.

The hero's journey is also depicted as linear. Traditional models have tended to present human psychological growth as progressing forward along a developmental path. Furthermore, the path has milestones. Development is understood in virtually all traditional models as occurring in *stages*, that is, as a predictable sequence of psychological achievements that could be charted as a series of rises and plateaus. The most famous of these perhaps is Erik Erikson's "Eight Stages of Man,"[7] but the basic idea of stage theories originates as early as 1905 with Freud's psychosexual stages (oral, anal, and phallic/genital).[8] Jean Piaget also presented his highly detailed theories of cognitive develop-

4. Descartes, *Discourse on Method and Meditations on First Philosophy,* 18.

5. Author's translation.

6. Jung, *Symbols of Transformation.*

7. Erikson, *Childhood and Society.*

8. Freud, *Three Essays.*

ment in terms of minute changes that he observed over time in infants' and children's perceptual and cognitive capacities.[9] The stages are understood as normative—when all goes well, the psychological stages should occur more or less in synchrony with advances in physiological maturation. From Anna Freud's point of view, pathology could also be understood as occurring along a series of parallel developmental lines, which needed to proceed more or less synchronously toward healthy maturity.[10] Pathology is thereby understood as a failure to achieve stages more or less on time, whether this delay is caused by constitutional deficits, or disruptions from the environment. Another way of thinking about what goes wrong would be a "boxcar" model, in which each stage is a boxcar being added to a train; if something goes wrong at a particular stage, the individual's growth is "derailed."

Stage theories have a place in the understanding of how the individual human person acquires capacities for increasingly complex cognitive and physical tasks. The stages described in traditional developmental theories do have descriptive power. They represent physiological and cognitive "milestones" that serve a heuristic and diagnostic purpose, allowing for the measurement of a child's growth against a norm of average, expectable development. All stage theories are based either on close observation of infants and children directly, or, in psychoanalytic theories, also on reconstructions from adult patients' memories and experiences. Beginning with Erikson, the study of developmental stages expanded beyond early childhood to encompass the lifespan. Longitudinal studies, such as Vaillant's *Adaptation to Life*,[11] have contributed important observations about normative phases of human life. Stage theories have also served as the framework for more specific research into the development of morality,[12] of lifelong meaning making,[13] and of faith.[14]

The whole notion of stage theories has, however, increasingly been challenged in the last two decades, with regard to most if not all

9. Piaget, *The Construction of Reality in the Child*; see also Ginsburg and Opper, *Piaget's Theory of Intellectual Development*.

10. Freud, "The Concept of Developmental Lines"; Freud, "The Concept of Developmental Lines: Their Diagnostic."

11. Vaillant, *Adaptation to Life*.

12. Kohlberg, *Collected Papers on Moral Development*; Gilligan, *In a Different Voice*.

13. Kegan, *The Evolving Self*; and Kegan, *In Over Our Heads*.

14. Fowler, *Stages of Faith*; Meissner, *Life and Faith*; Loder, *The Logic of the Spirit*.

of its fundamental presuppositions: linearity, progress, the prescriptive quality of stages, individualism, and the privileging of rational thought. Advances in both philosophical and scientific realms have brought a collective critique of the notion that truth itself is singular, universal, or even wholly knowable. The broad philosophical movement called postmodernism and the scientific field of quantum physics both have questioned, from very different perspectives, the Enlightenment-age assumptions that the world is always orderly, that all knowledge is rational, and that objective knowledge of a phenomenon (whether of a person, other living being, thing, or event) can be possible apart from entering into a relationship with that phenomenon, which relationship in turn influences it. Some of the limitations of research in the 1960s and 70s have also been challenged, particularly the establishment of norms based on white, middle-class boys and college-educated men.[15]

A sense of directionality may be unavoidable in the way we experience development phenomenologically, as growth occurring in a forward movement over time. But development is not only linear. It is an organic unfolding, similar to the process shown in slow-motion films of the growth of flowers. Growth occurs not in a single direction, but outward, like the concentric rings of a tree trunk. Plants and trees do not only grow up but toward all their sources of energy. They reach up toward the light, outward into the air, and downward into their source of nourishment. Trees also build structure as they grow—over the years, layers are added to the trunk, building a structure of support, storage of nutrients, and an outer layer of bark that protects the tree against the buffeting realities of wind, fire, and the axe. *Unfolding* is a more adequate and organic metaphor for human psychological development than a linear model.

In theological terms, these two developmental models also correlate with two Greek conceptions of time. The organic model is more closely related to *kairos* (time-in-eternity) than to *chronos* (the category of hourly time marked progressively by the ticking of a clock). Time is not only linear, but participates in eternal cycles of birth, change, death, and renewal. Such a concept of time might be represented not by a straight line but by a Moebius strip, a symbol of eternity. This is an image that can represent the diversity and complexity of hu-

---

15. Gilligan, *In a Different Voice*; Belenky et al., *Women's Ways of Knowing*; Brown and Gilligan, *Meeting at the Crossroads*; Taylor et al., *Between Voice and Silence*.

man developmental phenomena such as love, dependency, grief, fear, pleasure, power, and attainment (as well as their opposites), and the narratives about them, which appear, change, multiply, and loop back to reappear in new configurations with many different meanings over the lifespan.

In the model presented in this chapter, development is not conceived with the individual in sharply focused foreground, as it is in the more linear stage theories of development. Rather, growth is conceived in this chapter as *a multidimensional interrelation*. The individual self participates in and co-constructs the realities of intimate relationships, culture, class, and society, and shares mutually in endowing these with meaning and the power to impact ongoing being. As Erikson himself recognized,[16] social context has an important influence on the formation of identity, including cultural, historical, sexual, racial, ethnic, and religious influences.

It is therefore the thesis of this chapter that development is not only a linear, heroic, individualistic process, but also a complex, organic, and intrinsically relational human phenomenon that operates simultaneously and dynamically in at least four multiply constituted dimensions: 1) the internal or intrapsychic world of fantasy and experience (conditioned by the earliest relationships with primary caretakers); 2) the interpersonal, gendered world of intimate relationships and families; 3) the wider context of the cultures and subcultures into which the person is born, and the other cultures with which s/he comes to interact; and 4) the overarching dimension of time, both linear and eternal.

THE INTERNAL WORLD OF EXPERIENCE AND FANTASY

> *"There is no such thing as a baby . . . If you set out to describe a baby, you will find you are describing a baby and someone. A baby cannot exist alone, but is essentially part of a relationship."*[17]

Although no one can say for certain what goes on in the interior life of an infant, it is quite clear that environment and context play an ongoing role in development. A baby is not born as a psychological *tabula rasa* or "blank slate." The human person comes into the world already

16. Erikson, *Childhood and Society*; Erikson, *Identity and the Life Cycle*.

17. Winnicott, "Further Thoughts on Babies as Persons," 88. See also Winnicott, *The Maturational Processes*, 39n1.

equipped with the capacity to receive and process information on a number of levels, including bodily sensations, cognitive abilities, affects, feelings, and emotions, all of which have a relational dimension:

1) *Bodily Sensations.* These may include internal and external perceptions of pressure and touch, smells, taste, sounds, and sight. On the inside, the baby experiences his or her own vital functions and digestive system as central, organizing events. Breath, heartbeat, the bubbling of stomach juices and gas, the sensations of hunger and satiety, sleepiness and urges to perform vigorous movement constitute the core inner rhythms of daily life. But even in this most interior realm, the inside is in constant relation with the outside world, the "cupped hand" to which Buber refers. The baby is utterly dependent on the environment for the alleviation of all internal discomfort—especially hunger. External sensations also bring comfort or discomfort. Sounds can be intriguing and pleasurable, or painfully loud or startling. Light can bring objects into better focus, or hurt the eyes. There are wonderful smells and horrible smells. The milk from breast or bottle can taste sweet, rich, sour, or watery thin. The surfaces of things—clothes, diapers, beds, blankets and stuffed toys—can be cozy and comfortable, or they can be scratchy, cold, squishy, or wet. The baby's own skin can betray, with rashes that itch and burn. At the most primal level of the skin the baby first experiences the boundary between self and other.[18] While the primary caretaker(s) cannot soothe every sensory pain and irritation (no cure for colic has yet been discovered!), a "good enough"[19] response by a caretaker who is reliably present establishes from the earliest days of life a sense of trust in the potential goodness of the outside world, the core of faith.

2) *Cognitive abilities.* Infants come "hardwired" neurologically to receive and process a huge variety of stimuli. Recent neurological research suggests that particularly in the years between birth and age three there is an explosion of growth in neurological pathways that become the basis for learning even in adulthood.[20] When a child's brain is given optimal stimulation, neurological pathways develop and patterns of recognition are laid down. In the absence of stimulation,

18. Bick, "The Experience of the Skin in Early Object Relations"; Ogden, *The Primitive Edge of Experience.*

19. A term coined by Winnicott, e.g., in "Ego Distortion in Terms of True Self and False Self."

20. Greenspan, *The Growth of the Mind*; Siegel, *The Developing Mind.*

certain pathways do not develop, and there is a process of "pruning" that takes place. Over time, every baby's brain becomes more specialized, as certain pathways are developed and others diminish with lack of stimulation.

While a great deal that is still not known about the neurobiological bases of development, researchers have identified a close relationship between infant brain development and such developmental areas as emotions, behavior, learning, the acquisition of language, and social development. Evidence supports the idea that the environment strongly impacts development. Positive or negative stimulation from primary caretakers and others early in life can nurture or interfere with healthy brain growth and can have ramifications for all areas of a child's psychological and social development.[21]

3) *Affects, feelings, and emotions.* Researchers have now recognized that not only are infants "hardwired" for cognitive learning; they also come equipped with a set of eight basic affects, which can be observed by facial expressions: surprise-startle, interest-excitement, enjoyment-joy, distress-anguish, contempt-disgust, anger-rage, fear-terror, and shame-humiliation.[22] These early affects are not quite the same as emotions.[23] They are biological reflexes originating in the autonomic nervous system, not yet attached to voluntary action or symbolic or verbal meaning. But they do represent primal reactive states that are excited by environmental stimuli in a range from mild to intense. Environmental stimuli may be personal, such as a parent's smell or touch, or impersonal, such as a bright light or loud sound. Basch defines *feeling*, which arrives developmentally around eighteen to twenty-four months, as an affective reaction connected to a sense of self, with a basic verbal capacity not only to experience, for example, the state of anger, but to articulate it: "I am angry."[24] Emotion is a yet more mature affective phenomenon, in which feelings, experiences, and the meanings given to them are joined to produce complex concepts such as love, hate, and happiness.[25] Basch proposes that "the final maturational step in affective development is the capacity

21. Schore, *Affect Regulation and the Origin of the Self;* Perry et al., "Childhood Trauma"; Siegel, *The Developing Mind.*

22. Tomkins, *The Positive Affects;* Tomkins, *The Negative Affects.*

23. Basch, *Understanding Psychotherapy.*

24. Ibid.,78.

25. Ibid.

for empathic understanding,"[26] similar to the concept of "emotional intelligence,"[27] in which the individual is capable of entering into the affective, feeling-toned experience of another outside the self.

These powerful relational tools of affect, feeling, emotion, and empathy further confirm the intrinsic relationality of human nature, and of the close relationship between affective communication and the development of identity.[28] Researchers have, for example, studied the importance of the affect of *shame* on development of the self, concluding that an overwhelming amount of shame-laden experiences in early childhood can create serious deficits in all areas of development.[29] The quality of early *attachment* between infants and their primary caretakers also may have a profound effect on later learning, social relationships, and even mental and emotional health.[30] Warm, sensitive nurturing by primary caregivers tends to result in healthy, secure attachment, while inconsistent, unresponsive, or rejecting parental interactions tend to result in patterns of attachment that are "anxious," either in the form of ambivalent clinging or avoidant distancing behaviors.[31] Significant negative effects on development have been observed in cases where the infant's experience of attachment is traumatically interrupted.[32] Trauma, although seldom discussed in the literature of developmental psychology, has a profound impact on multiple aspects of development.[33]

The emotional surround of early childhood, in fact, impacts brain development itself. One of the leading researchers on the neurobiology of emotional development, Allan Schore, asserts, "the early social environment, mediated by the primary caregiver, directly influences the evolution of structures in the brain responsible for the future socioemotional development of the child."[34] Thus, cognitive and emotional development and neurological maturation are not separate pro-

26. Ibid.

27. Salovey and Sluyter, *Emotional Development and Emotional Intelligence*; Goleman, *Emotional Intelligence*.

28. Beebe and Lachmann, "The Contribution of Mother-Infant Mutual Influence."

29. Lewis, "Shame and Guilt in Human Nature."

30. Bowlby, *Attachment*.

31. Ainsworth et al., *Patterns of Attachment*.

32. Spitz, "Hospitalism."

33. Cooper-White, "Opening the Eyes."

34. Schore, *Affect Regulation and the Origin of the Self*, 62.

cesses but are intertwined. Growth in all areas is intrinsically dependent upon relationships. It is not too much to say that the brain itself
is shaped by social and emotional relations from birth.

Recent studies based on infant observation confirm the inherently relational nature of human development at the earliest phase
of life.[35] In particular, the level of *attunement* of a primary caretaker
with the infant's and small child's shifting affect states will have an
impact on the child's own capacity for affective maturation. As the
child acquires verbal ability, the parent's ability to observe and accurately name feelings for the child lay the foundation for the child's
own ability to recognize and name his or her own feelings, and in
time, complex emotions. Empathy, the foundation of all capacity for
"I-Thou" relationship, is thus a learned capacity. It is first acquired at
a rudimentary level through the experience of empathic attunement
from primary caretakers, and later (sometimes remedially) through
both experiencing and practicing the affective recognition, respect,
and mirroring from and with others. This process is never finished but
continues to increase in depth and complexity over the lifespan.

Such infant observation studies have added credence to many
of the more relationally centered concepts of psychoanalytic theory,
particularly from the school of psychoanalysis known as "object relations." Melanie Klein, an analyst from Freud's own circle who im-
migrated to London, was one of the first theorists to investigate the
earliest relationship between mother and infant.

Object-Relations Theory

Klein proposed a theory of the infant's inner experience that did not
entirely replace Freud's view of the centrality of sex and aggression,
but placed far more emphasis on the formative nature of the infant's
earliest inner experience of caretakers.[36] Based on reconstructions
from her adult patients' memories, fantasies, and projective processes
at work in the analytic relationship, Klein proposed that the infant's
experiences of hunger, thirst, pain, satisfaction, soothing, or fright
were stored by the infant in a rudimentary system of classification
into "good" and "bad." Relational experiences of the primary caretaker
(for Klein, this was always the mother) could be good if perceived as

35. E.g., Stern, *The Interpersonal World of the Infant.*
36. E.g., Klein, *Envy and Gratitude*; and Freud, *The Psycho-Analysis of Children.*

adequately responsive, or could be bad in either of two ways: overwhelming and intrusive, or depriving and inadequately responsive. These good and bad experiences coalesced in the realm of fantasy into symbolic mental representations, or "objects." Initially, good and bad were split domains, with an all-or-nothing quality. A primary caretaker, or in the earliest months even a part of a caretaker, particularly a breast, could exist multiply in the interior fantasy world as both a good object and a bad object or objects. Klein called this early period of development the "paranoid-schizoid position," in which the infant's early mental life was organized around an absolute split between good and bad, and efforts to avoid experiencing the bad.

After the first six months of life, Klein proposed, the infant began to gain a rudimentary experience of the destructive potential of his or her own hunger and need. There could be a dawning sense that the wish to devour the breast could destroy it. With this sense could come a feeling akin to sadness, and a desire for reparation. She called this the "depressive position" and considered it the lifelong foundation for emotional and psychological health. It is significant that Klein did not use the term "stage" but rather "position."[37] Because her theorizing was based on adult clinical cases, she saw the relevance of both positions throughout life, and saw the paranoid-schizoid position as one in which adults might still be predominantly functioning, or to which they might regress during times of great stress or trauma.

Other object relations theorists extended Klein's theories further, in particular, British psychoanalysts W. R. D. Fairbairn,[38] D. W. Winnicott,[39] and Harry Guntrip,[40] and, more recently, a loosely related "relational" group of psychoanalytic theorists who have posited a two-person, relational or "intersubjective" dimension to every individual's construction of meaning and even reality.[41] For these theorists, the inner world, from infancy throughout the lifespan, is made up of varying

37. Ogden, *The Primitive Edge of Experience*.

38. Fairbairn, *Psychoanalytic Studies of the Personality*.

39. E.g., Winnicott, *The Maturational Processes*; Winnicott, *Playing and Reality*.

40. Guntrip, *Schizoid Phenomena*.

41. For an overview of this school of thought, see Aron and Mitchell, *The Emergence of a Tradition*. These theorists are also represented in the journal *Psychoanalytic Dialogues*, and the International Association of Relational Psychoanalysts and Psychotherapists (IARPP). Emerging out of self psychology, see also Stolorow et al., *Psychoanalytic Treatment*; Stolorow et al., *The Intersubjective Perspective*; and Orange et al., *Working Intersubjectively*.

numbers of internalized others, or "objects," as well as multiple representations of the self or aspects of oneself at different times and under different circumstances. These inner mental representations function somewhat like templates against which new experiences, particularly relational experiences, are tested. As a child grows up, he or she comes to expect certain kinds of behaviors from other people, based on the internalization of earlier experiences. The earliest internalized objects or representations, because they occur in infancy and toddlerhood, are preverbal and therefore not necessarily attached to any sort of narrative memory.

Narrative meaning, when attached to these early representations, is always necessarily retrospective, from the vantage point of an older, verbalizing self. Not all early representations are ever explored or processed verbally, but nevertheless these exist as powerful forces governing behavior and experience. Some of a person's earliest childhood experiences may not even reach the cognitive level of symbolization but rather may be retained at the level of behavior patterns or bodily sensations.[42] Particularly in the case of trauma, researchers have observed that overwhelmingly terrifying or painful events are not processed cognitively, as are other narrative memories, but are stored in fragments that separate cognition, affective or emotion-toned experience, behavioral patterns, and/or visual, auditory, olfactory, taste, and tactile sensation. Some traumatic memories may only exist as unsymbolized body memories.[43]

Inner objects or representations are also not merely inert pictures or sensations in the mind. As object-relations theorists have proposed, inner objects also have their own dynamic life. They function as internal motivating forces or parts of the self, with varying degrees of autonomy, acting and reacting in relationship with external and internal others. A person may feel "fragmented" or "divided" internally as different forces come into play based on differing childhood experiences and internalized significant others. The child may have little or no conscious awareness of these inner forces or parts of the self. The less aware s/he is, in fact, of these inner forces, the more likely they are to be projected, in a manner similar to the way a movie is projected,

42. Segal, "Notes on Symbol Formation."

43. Van der Kolk, "The Body Keeps the Score"; Davies and Frawley, *Treating the Adult Survivor*.

onto the "screen" of other people. This process has the power to distort the person's perception of others, and to cause the person to misperceive a new reality as an old (usually painful or self-destructive) one. When early experiences have been consistently painful or depriving enough, projections tend to be negative and bring even more pain. Expectations that in childhood might have been helpful or even life saving often outlive their usefulness, and in adult life may serve to create more problems than they solve.

Especially in cases where childhood experience has been consistently depriving or traumatic, a more intensely projective process called "projective identification"[44] may occur. In projective identification, projections may be experienced by the other as entering *inside* them and actually changing their behavior in relation to the person doing the projecting. Considered mysterious or quasi-telepathic by some, this process is really conveyed by a series of subtle or not-so-subtle behavioral cues, which invoke reciprocal behaviors in the other person. A form of self-fulfilling prophecy results, in which the inner expectations of the person doing the projecting become incarnated in the other. A vicious cycle may ensue, in which the expectation based on a negative experience of a primary caretaker in early childhood becomes confirmed again and again in ongoing living.

This cycle is hard to break because projective processes are not only powerful but frequently mutual: individuals become locked into mutually reinforcing negative patterns of projection. The cycle can be broken, however, by the inbreaking of an unexpected new relational experience that is powerful enough and feels real enough to overcome the veil of projections and allow for the internalization of a more positive reality, a new object that neither abandons nor retaliates.[45] Sometimes this can happen in everyday living, but more often, if the inner representations are too painful or persecutory, a therapeutic relationship is needed to allow for and contain the projective processes at the level of intensity necessary for healing. Much clinical work in object relations–oriented psychotherapy is founded on this principle, and the projective processes that begin to develop in the therapeutic relationship become the focus for mutual exploration between therapist and patient.

44. Klein, "Notes on Some Schizoid Mechanisms."
45. Winnicott, *Playing and Reality*, 86–94.

The object-relations model also has implications for faith, particularly as individuals conceive of God and the quality of their relationship to God or the sacred. Internalized representations of primary caretakers early in life are not only projected onto other people. These representations, particularly internal parental figures, also constitute the core of a person's internal representation of God, or God-*imago*. Ana Maria Rizzuto demonstrated in her studies of children's and adults' drawings of their concepts of God that God images are powerfully influenced by the positive or negative internalized experiences of primary caretakers in early childhood.[46] Valerie DeMarinis and M. Kathryn Armistead have also found that the processes of pastoral care and counseling can facilitate the emergence of more complex, healing, and life-sustaining images of God.[47]

Thus the inner life is the place of primary experience, mediated through ever increasingly complex symbols and verbal narratives, which are continually co-created in the intersubjective matrices of intimate relationships. Inchoate experiences, symbolizations, and narratives (both positive and negative) combine to form the deep structures underlying each individual's motivation, moral choices, and construction of ultimate or spiritual meanings—the unconscious foundation of an individual's faith (religious or secular).

THE INTERPERSONAL WORLD OF INTIMATE RELATIONSHIPS AND FAMILIES

Individuals most often are raised in the context of families—not narrowly defined as the white, middle-class, nuclear family of *Leave It to Beaver*—but in many more varied, culturally normed configurations of dual- or single-parent, cross-generational, and extended families. The relational life of every family includes both conscious and unconscious dimensions, with an interlocking network of mutual projective processes at work among the individual "I's" and "Thous" within it. These processes result over time in the formation of certain characteristic patterns, boundaries, and styles of relating within the family (whether harmonious or conflictual). Conflicts may harden

---

46. Rizzuto, *The Birth of the Living God.*

47. DeMarinis, "The Body's Sacred Containing." See also DeMarinis, *Critical Caring*; Armistead, *God-images.*

into predictable polarities between certain dyads or rigid triangular configurations.[48] The functioning of families as whole organic entities or systems has been elaborated by family-system theorists,[49] who emphasize the transmission of these family patterns across generations. These multigenerational patterns can be observed using a family-tree-like diagram called a genogram.[50]

Families, like individuals, also have a developmental "life cycle," with certain somewhat predictable "stages" that occur as the family moves through time.[51] Intergenerationally, this cycle has no definite beginning or end. Betty Carter and Monica McGoldrick chose leaving home as the entry point to describe the family life cycle, a time at which single young adults "leave the nest" and accept responsibility for themselves. A new generation of adults is thus launched. The cycle continues with a number of steps, not all of which apply to all families or generations: the joining of families through marriage of adult children; the expansion of families with the birth of young children (with the family's new task being to incorporate and nurture new dependent members); the further development of families with adolescents (with the family's new task shifting toward greater tolerance for children's growing independence, as well as to caring for elder family members); the launching of children from the family home (making the transition to the "empty nest"); and finally, the stage of families in later life (whose task is to accept a shifting in their generational roles from parents to grandparents or nurturing elders). Individual development is closely entwined with larger family realities. Individuals' identities are profoundly shaped by the roles, conflicts, and particular phases of the life cycle that characterize the experience of collective family life. Certain other groups, particularly close work groups[52] and religious groups such as churches and synagogues,[53] also function unconsciously and systemically, and may have a reciprocal formative impact on the development of the individuals within them.

Contemporary American media frequently depict family life, at its best, as representing a place of safety and nurture for children, and

48. Bowen, *Family Therapy in Clinical Practice*; Friedman, *Generation to Generation*.

49. E.g., Bowen, *Family Therapy in Clinical Practice*.

50. For an excellent, detailed explanation see McGoldrick et al., *Genograms*.

51. Carter et al., *The Expanded Family Life Cycle*, 2.

52. Bion, *Experiences in Groups*; Obholzer and Roberts, *The Unconscious at Work*.

53. Friedman, *Generation to Generation*.

as a haven for adults from the pressures of the outside world. This ideal of domestic life as separate and fortressed from reality is limited, however, and at worst may become insular and self-absorbed. Sociologists such as Robert Bellah[54] have increasingly begun to challenge the privatization of family life as a symptom of unhealthy individualism in American society. Just as individual development usually proceeds within the interpersonal context of family life, so do families grow and develop within and contribute to the wider context of culture and society, and contribute to it.

THE WIDER CONTEXT OF CULTURES AND SUBCULTURES

Psychoanalytic theorists have become increasingly sensitive to the formative impact of the interpersonal context of relationships. Group-relations and family-systems theories have extended this sensitivity to the context of groups and families. However, most theorists stop short of considering the significance of the wider circles of cultures and subcultures in which individuals and families are embedded. This shortsightedness is in part due to the once unquestioned practice, particularly in developmental psychology, of establishing norms based on the study of white, middle-class, male subjects. But it is also due to the tendency inherent in psychoanalysis to focus on the interior life of individuals and to pay less attention to the real impact of the environment.[55]

Cultures and Subcultures

Just as individuals do not exist and grow in a vacuum, neither do couples, families, or groups. All children are born and develop within a culture—or, more typically, within multiple cultural systems that may overlap. Culture is often thought of as the particular imprint of an individual's national or ethnic heritage; a world into which a child is born and develops that includes distinctive languages or dialects and patterns of speech; styles of dress, particular aesthetic forms of music, art, drama and literature; particular foods; and particular forms of religious expression and identity. Culture may also include social mores, proper manners for social and business interactions, and moral taboos. Accepted norms for forming intimate social friendships and sexual

54. Bellah, *Habits of the Heart*.
55. Cf., Altman, *The Analyst in the Inner City*.

partnerships, and for child rearing, also fall within the umbrella of culture. They are the cultural maps through which "I-Thou" relationships are expressed. These are most often the rich qualities that come to mind when considering the value of cultural identity. They are the cultural treasures that individuals and groups love, identify with, and seek to protect.

Culture is not only a national or ethnic phenomenon. Cultures and subcultures may form around particular occupations, lifestyles, or sexual practices. Movements for social change frequently begin as "countercultural" groups that question the authority of prevailing cultural paradigms. Religious groups may become cultures or subcultures organized around religious identity and practice as a primary definer of self and group. Religious, artistic, social, and political subcultures frequently exist as havens of protection for individuals who do not conform to the mainstream of social norms and privilege. While an individual child may not grow physically, intellectually, or socially according to traditional developmental criteria, which are normed to middle-class, able-bodied male Anglo-American subjects, there may be a subculture in which that child can flourish. Schools for the deaf, schools for the arts, religious schools, and all-girls' schools are all quite different examples of places in which the growth of children who do not necessarily do well according to established competitive norms may be positively encouraged so that they may reach their own unique potential. Such subcultures also allow for individual growth without sacrificing each child's unique constitutional or cultural endowment to a goal of assimilation.

Particular ideologies can also serve as organizing cores of cultures or subcultures, some more positive and growth fostering than others. Ideological cultures, which do not necessarily identify with a national or ethnic heritage, may attract or even recruit new members. The more strongly ideological the subculture, whether a political group or a religious group or cult, the more likely it is to interact at an unconscious, projective level with the psychodynamics of the individual member to create a strong bond of mutual need, loyalty, or loss of autonomy in favor of a group identity. While ideological groups and cults are not rare, they do not constitute the center of most individuals' lives. No one escapes the force of culture, however. Ultimately, culture is the medium for all development, and for reality itself.

The Social Construction of Reality

Reality does not exist apart from the meaning that humans make of it. Therefore, the perception of reality is the chief product of all cognitive and emotional development. Because development does not occur in a vacuum but in the context of culture and society, *reality is socially constructed*.[56] This social construction, further, is a construction not only of what is, but of how things happen. At the scientific level, this is the construction of "paradigms," in which theories about the way the world works generate certain questions for investigation and preclude others.[57] At the social level, it is the construction of familial, group, social and institutional arrangements, and structures of political power. It is the usually unconscious and unnamed "way things are" that keep decision making in the hands of some groups and individuals, and not others. How does this work?

All development takes place in a social matrix in which reality is defined in and through relationships. People, places and things, and particular aspects of them, are given existence through the social act of naming. This act of naming is inescapably an exercise of power, which can take the form of either stewardship or domination. As in the biblical creation story in Genesis 2:19–20a, God entrusts Adam with the stewardship of all the animals by giving Adam the power to name them. But not all practices of naming are so benign. Power and privilege are distributed according to the meanings given to certain realities, and the naming or lack of naming of certain individuals' experiences. Groups hold social dominance by naming and conferring meaning on certain realities, but also by refusing to see and to name realities that are experienced by other social groups. Many realities are not named, especially realities experienced by groups who do not share social dominance and privilege. These are most often realities that if named, would reveal the pernicious aspects of the prevailing social power structure, such as gender and race discrimination, or assumptions about able-bodied-ness.[58] They are therefore left unnamed and not given the status of reality. Individuals and groups who do attempt to give voice to their experience often find themselves in the position of having to choose between their own reality and the authorized, named reality of the dominant

---

56. Berger and Luckmann, *The Social Construction of Reality*.

57. Kuhn, *The Structure of Scientific Revolutions*.

58. Eiesland, *The Disabled God*.

group. The act of choosing their own reality is an act of courage, because it carries the risk of being labeled delusional.

Language, Power, and Violence

Language is central to the maintenance of structures of power in another way as well. As the philosopher Michel Foucault[59] showed in his monumental studies of early twentieth-century mental institutions and medical clinics, professional training often is not only an education about the subject matter of concern to the profession, but also an initiation into an exclusive world of coded language, to which only professionals are given the key. Foucault showed how much of the role of the professional or expert revolved around the maintenance of social power, again, conferred by the power of naming.[60]

All human persons are thus born into a world of language, in which the acquisition of language itself serves as a primary initiation into a social and systemic construction of reality. In the theory of the French psychoanalyst Jacques Lacan,[61] this primary acquisition of language is both a vehicle for and itself a constitutive element of the child's inevitable acquiescence during the oedipal phase to what Lacan terms the "Symbolic Order," and the "Law of the Father." Feminist theorists, particularly Julia Kristeva,[62] Helene Cixous,[63] and Luce Irigaray,[64] have further clarified that language itself is both the medium and the message of patriarchy.[65]

Development, particularly cognitive development, is inextricably related to the capacity first for symbolization and then verbalization of experience. But all verbalization is learned in a social context, and the acquisition of language is a culturally mediated process that also is inextricably related to social structures of power and privilege. At the most obvious social level, children who grow up in environments of

---

59. E.g., Foucault, *Power/Knowledge*; Foucault, *Madness and Civilization*; and Foucault, *The Birth of the Clinic*.

60. Foucault, *Power/Knowledge*.

61. Lacan, *Écrits: The First Complete Edition in English*.

62. For a useful selection, see Kristeva, *The Kristeva Reader*.

63. E.g., Cixous, *The Hélène Cixous Reader*; Cixous and Clément, *The Newly Born Woman*.

64. E.g., Irigaray, *Speculum of the Other Woman*.

65. Moi, *Sexual/Textual Politics*; for a view through a theological lens, see especially Kim et al., *Transfigurations*.

relative lack of power and privilege not only are frequently deprived of the material resources that would support their growth (such as adequate housing, nutrition, clothing, and education) but also grow up within a different "language game."[66] Children of privilege tend to learn only the dominant language of the culture and are initiated into increasingly complex usages of that one language. Children who because of racial or economic oppression grow up excluded from circles of privilege often learn to become "bilingual," or in the words of W. E. B. Du Bois, develop a "double consciousness."[67] Like all children, they are acculturated into the language and meaning-making patterns of their own immediate cultural environment but also, as a matter of survival, may become increasingly adept at decoding the language of privileged groups as well. This brings the benefit of survival, but with it also comes the absorption of meanings from the dominant culture's language that devalue and denigrate oppressed groups, and name them as inferior. As this "language game" is internalized, so hatred can be internalized as self-hatred. The saying "Black is beautiful," coined by the Black Power movement in the 1960s, is a good example of a conscious attempt to counter this process of internalizing oppression. It was a reclaiming of sacred, creative power of naming, to restore pride in African American identity and to declare it good. It takes many such acts of power to overcome the dominant social structures of power and to reclaim the power of naming for oneself and one's own group.

Gender and sexual orientation are social constructions that exist in complex relationship to other realities of power, privilege, and oppression. While the biological realities of male and female bodies may be understood as givens, the meanings given them are again socially constructed. What it means to grow up in a male or female body may be taught as an unquestioned reality but is, in fact, an interpretation. Similarly, to grow up gay, lesbian, or bisexual may have very different meanings in different cultures and subcultures. In most contexts, feminine gender and gay, lesbian, or bisexual sexual orientation are categories of oppression. For women, and for lesbians and gay men of color, these socially constructed realities add a "double whammy" to the experience of racial and economic oppression. For white women, and for white lesbians and gay men, there is a fragmentation experience in

66. Wittgenstein, *Philosophical Investigations*; Lyotard, *The Postmodern Condition*.
67. Du Bois, *The Souls of Black Folk*, 272–78.

which social and institutional power is conferred due to race privilege, but at the same time, gender or sexual-orientation oppression is a constant, though often unnamed, reality. Children who grow up female, or homosexual, may be initiated into the language game of privilege, only to find that, for them, it does not open the doors that it opens for white, heterosexual males. Economic class oppression further heightens this disparity of power, so that working-class and poor women and girls, gay men and lesbians, are excluded even more from decision-making positions in institutions of power, including education, industry, and government.

All forms of ongoing, structural, institutional oppression are maintained by economic, physical and sexual violence, which are the largest, but often least clearly named signs of injustice. In the United States, certain forms of oppression, especially racial violence, economic oppression, and violence against women and homosexuals, establish the particular map of reality into which each person is born. Every human person without exception around the world is also born, and must develop, embedded in his or her own culture. And every culture is formed by a combination of language and, to varying degrees, violence, which may be racial, economic, or gender-based, or a combination of these and other forms of oppression. Language and violence combine to create a "reality" that defines each individual's identity, and names his or her place within the hierarchical structures of power.

Developing a Critical Stance

Persons are not only born into cultures and receive their imprint. Individuals are also constitutive members of their cultures and from birth help to shape and construct the cultures in which they are embedded. Culture itself, then, is a "Thou" with whom a person, an "I," may enter into a mutually formative relatedness. What gives individuals the resilience to take one step back psychologically from the culture(s) in which one is embedded, to see and name realities that commonly have been left unseen or unnamed, and to develop a critique of one's own cultural inheritance, including its most oppressive aspects?

At least two factors seem to be essential in allowing an individual to develop a critical stance toward his or her own cultural surround: exposure to other cultures and worldviews, and a capacity for empathy and mutual perspective taking. First is the exposure to alternative cultures, which present alternative "language games" and ways of understanding one's own embedded world view. One cannot take the perspective of another person, another worldview, without coming into meaningful contact with the other. The more insulated an individual is from other national, ethnic, and linguistic communities, the less opportunity there is to place one's own assumptions into a critical or even self-reflective light.

But the capacity for taking the perspective of another is also, as traditionally understood by most developmental theories, a cognitive and emotional achievement. It requires, at minimum, the cognitive capacity for reciprocal operations.[68] Making the imaginative leap of seeing from another's point of view also means taking the risk of being exposed to criticism or harm, as well as the risk of being changed by what one learns from the new perspective. This requires a capacity for empathy, the ability to stand in another's shoes. This capacity, as discussed above, requires a sufficient foundation of having been treated empathically, and responded to in such a way that the world seems safe enough to risk setting aside one's own aims, at least temporarily, in the service of greater understanding.[69] Empathy can be seriously impaired by childhood trauma, which has the power to wound one's primal sense of security, basic goodness, trust in the reliability of the world, and also one's confidence in the basic sufficiency and goodness of one's own self.

One of the benefits of greater knowledge and insight about one's own individual developmental process and the contours of one's own inner landscape is that the tendency to project one's own fantasies, experiences, and inner objects onto (or into) other persons and institutions tends to recede. Sometimes, especially where there has been significant trauma or deprivation, psychotherapy can foster a healing process of self-reflection that can in turn nurture one's capacity for empathy. Sometimes constructive new relationships and learning experiences can serve a similar function in strengthening one's ability to enter into meaningful encounters with other points of view.

Cultures are not monolithic.[70] Whenever the issue of cultural context is invoked, individual cultures tend to be described in terms of

68. Piaget, *The Construction of Reality in the Child.*

69. Kohut, *The Restoration of the Self.*

70. Geertz, "Thick Description."

general characteristics, which frequently do not adequately depict the richness of variations within their communities. Individuals within cultures are not only embedded in them but act upon them and create new variations within them. As an individual grows and develops, he or she makes meaning of the cultural surround. Some of these meanings will subtly or even radically shape the culture itself.

Further, cultures themselves do not simply exist; they also grow and develop, like the individual self. And, like the individual self, they do not grow in a vacuum. Multiple national, ethnic, and linguistic groups coexist and comingle, and international migration brings increasing numbers of groups into contact with one another. Each contact has the potential for genuine encounters in which new meanings may be made and thus new realities. Idealized or "pure" cultures that are invoked to represent the identity of individuals, families, and groups actually function as "imagined communities."[71] Artifacts of nineteenth-century historicism, these exist more in the imagination than in everyday life. As Seyla Benhabib has pointed out, recent debates about culture have tended to operate upon four faulty assumptions: regarding cultures and value systems as "self-consistent, pre-reflexive wholes; as sealed off from one another; as internally unified"; and as "systems of meaning, value, and interpretation which must also be reproduced over time by individuals under the constraints of a material way of life."[72]

Just as interpersonal relationships are increasingly being recognized as co-constructing the reality that is shared between two individual "I's" and "Thou's," and thereby in some sense continually recreating and reconstituting the sense of self, meaning and purpose of each partner, so too do cultures interact in a "potential space"[73] in which new meanings are given and new realities can be created. This interaction of cultures does not usually happen en masse, however. It is carried out most often in intimate dyads and in genuine interactions among small groups of people. Individuals who are committed to justice can work for social change most effectively not through maneuvers to replace one dominant force with another but rather through engagement with others and participation in a process of mutual creation.

71. Anderson, *Imagined Communities*, cited in Benhabib, "Complexity, Interdependence, Community," 243.

72. Benhabib, "Complexity, Interdependence, Community," 244.

73. Winnicott, *Playing and Reality*, 41.

Lives of Commitment

Within most developmental schemata, there is usually a stage assigned to the years beyond midlife, in which individuals are said to achieve a more altruistic, generative, or universal perspective.[74] Beyond the capacity for one-to-one perspective taking comes a capacity for commitment to constructive change in the world. In order to inquire about what constitutes such commitment, social researchers Daloz, Keen, Keen, and Parks interviewed 145 individuals whom they identified as having a commitment to the common good, evidenced in their ability to articulate how their lifework served the well-being of society as a whole, as well as qualities of perseverance, resilience, and ethical congruence between life and work.[75] Through these interviews, the authors identified several key factors that appeared to be significant in the development of these "lives of commitment." These factors include a loving home environment in childhood, the example of at least one parent who worked actively for the public good, opportunities and challenges to be of service to others during adolescence, exposure to cross-cultural experiences, and a good mentoring experience in young adulthood.[76] The more such experiences were present, the authors found, the more likely the individual would be to grow into a mature adult life of commitment to the common good.

Families collectively may also participate in this ongoing process of mutual influence and social change. It is not only true that "it takes a village to raise a child," but it might equally be said that it takes individual children and adults, families, and groups to "raise a village." Anderson and Johnson, grounded in a Christian theological framework, have proposed a model of family as a "just community,"[77] and a "crucible" of social responsibility, in which "the needs of the individual and the needs of the community are negotiated and balanced."[78]

All such social and cultural developments finally occur, not as single events, but as ongoing processes within the overarching framework of time. In the context of faith, this may also be understood as

74. E.g., Erikson, *Childhood and Society*; Fowler, *Stages of Faith*; Maslow, *Toward a Psychology of Being*.

75. Daloz et al., *Common Fire*.

76. Ibid., 17.

77. Anderson and Johnson, *Regarding Children*, 81.

78. Ibid., 107.

occurring, not only within the generally linear human perception of time, but within the eschatological future-present of God's time.

TIME AND ETERNITY

Theologians are familiar with the notion that there are at least two kinds of time, represented by two words in biblical Greek: *chronos* and *kairos*. As mentioned at the beginning of this chapter, development is usually discussed only in terms of the first: a concept of time as linear, forward moving, and measurable. But development occurs in the context of both linear time and eternity.

Chronos and the Cohort Group

In linear time individuals are born, grow, and die within identifiable historical epochs. Every individual is born into a "cohort group" of persons born roughly during the same political and historical era.[79] Significant events, particularly traumatic ones, such as natural disasters, wars, or assassinations, can serve as symbolic markers for the experience of entire generations of people. Generations are sometimes even identified by the dramatic events, social trends, or political movements that occurred during their formative years. A child born at the turn of the twentieth century and a child born at the turn of the new millennium might go through nearly identical physiological stages of maturation, and somewhat similar psychological changes, but theories of individual development would not adequately explain the differences in the lives of those two individuals and their respective beliefs and behaviors. Technological changes alone could account for a very different experience of the world and a different set of expectations about how to live and even about longevity itself. Large-scale historical events can also shape the worldview of entire groups of individuals. For example, the generation who served in World War II has tended to have a very different view of the morality of war and the trustworthiness of political institutions than those who were drafted during the Vietnam War. Children of individuals who experienced historical periods of enduring hardship or crisis also tend to be formed in their worldview by the experiences of their parents—for example,

79. Ryder, "The Cohort as a Concept"; Elder, *Children of the Great Depression*; Elder et al., *Children in Time and Place*.

the children of parents who lived through the Depression. Children whose parents survived extreme trauma, as in the Holocaust, also may be heirs to the previous generation's worldview, as shaped by those traumatic historical events. Meanings, philosophies, and commitment or lack of commitment may be shared by large groups of people who have endured shared losses, victories, or disillusionments.

Kairos: Time in Relation

Time is not only linear. The human life journey is not only a forward-moving line but a circle or spiral in which meanings are made, changed, remade, and regathered in dynamic relation with persons, groups, and cultures past, present, and in potential. The meaning of a life cannot adequately be charted only as a story of progress. Life is also a pro-cess of continual formation and re-formation, as other lives enter the story. Finally, our stories are given residence within the hearts and experiences of other people and their stories.[80] Religiously committed individuals further understand their personal stories and the stories of others with whom their own lives are intertwined as resonating with God's eternal story as revealed in their holy scriptures. The stories of individuals, families, and groups also participate in ancient sacred pat-terns, such as biblical narratives of liberation from bondage, of exile and return, of brokenness and healing, and of death and resurrection.

All human life from before birth is created within and for relation-ship. Genuine encounter with the other, however, past the inner realm of fantasy and projection, past reified boundaries and mores of family and group, past cultural barriers, often is fragile and fleeting. Moments of joining nevertheless do take place at both conscious and unconscious levels, and in the space between individuals: in the words of Winnicott, in the "potential space" where imagination, fantasy, and mutual experi-ence come together to create new understandings. Furthermore, true meetings, however fleeting, are not simply isolated moments. When individuals become intentional about seeking genuine I-Thou encoun-ters with the other, this has the potential for building greater ongoing possibilities for connection and cooperation. In the words of Buber, "the moments of supreme encounter are no mere flashes of lightning

---

80. E.g., Wimberly, *African American Pastoral Care*, esp. 71–90; Anderson and Foley, *Mighty Stories, Dangerous Rituals*.

in the dark but like a rising moon in a clear starry night."[81] When this openness to encounter becomes a *habitus*, a committed practice, it promotes dialogue not only between individuals but also among groups, communities, and cultures. We study development in relational and cultural context, finally, so that our awareness may expand and enable us to participate more fully in the sacred, storied conversation that embraces all people across all time. To close, I invoke Buber once more: "The anchoring of time in a relation-oriented life of salvation and the anchoring of space in a community unified by a common center: only when both of these come to be and only as long as both continue to be, a human cosmos comes to be and continues to be around the invisible altar, grasped in the spirit out of the world stuff of the eon."[82]

81. Buber, *I and Thou*, 163.
82. Ibid.

THREE

"Higher Powers and Infernal Regions"[1]

Models of Mind in Freud's *Interpretation of Dreams* and Contemporary Psychoanalysis, and Their Implications for Pastoral Theology[2]

While Freud's *The Interpretation of Dreams* is popularly best known for his detailed illumination of the symbolic meaning of dreams, it actually represents one of Freud's most significant achievements as the first explication of Freud's "discovery" of the unconscious (the "system Ucs.") and in particular the concepts of repression and unconscious conflict. It also represents his first major work after his revision of the "seduction theory" (that is, his initial impression that all neuroses were caused by sexual trauma).[3] Over the next decade and a half,

1. Freud, *The Interpretation of Dreams*, 608, quoting Virgil's *Aeneid*, to picture "the effects of the repressed instinctual impulses."

2. A briefer version of this essay was presented to the Person, Culture and Religion Group Session on the one hundredth anniversary of Freud's *Interpretation of Dreams* at the American Academy of Religion meeting in Boston in November 1999.

3. This shift from an emphasis on actual external trauma toward attention to the inner, unconscious dynamics of the psyche has sometimes been critiqued as an "abandonment of the seduction theory" (Masson, *The Assault on Truth*) and a betrayal of sexual abuse survivors in Freud's practice. While there is certainly some truth to this, e.g., the disastrous case of "Dora" (Freud, "Fragment of an Analysis"), a review of Freud's entire opus demonstrates that he never completely abandoned his concern for the impact of

65

Freud worked out the details of what has come to be known as his "topographical" model of the mind, in which conscious/preconscious and unconscious are conceptualized as separate spatial areas of mind, divided by the repression barrier but each having its own strong influence on behavior, cognition, affect, and sensation—and potential pathogenesis. It was this model that was first transmitted to pastoral caregivers in America, through the "Emmanuel movement" in Boston, clergy and seminary faculty who attended lectures by Abraham A. Brill in Boston and New York, and the Clark University lectures of Freud and Jung in 1909.[4] Freud's further contributions of the stages of infantile psychosexual development—the oedipal situation and the structural model with its tripartite institutions of the mind, the ego, id, and superego—were not to come for another two decades. These further strengthened the notion of repression as the central mechanism by which certain contents of mind, conceived of as unacceptable or even intolerable, could be swept from consciousness into the "infernal regions" by the "higher powers" of a well-civilized, well-socialized ego. This model of conscious/preconscious and unconscious divided by a repression barrier thus has had a powerful and formative influence on pastoral psychology and pastoral theology from its earliest days.

Freud first conceived of conscious, preconscious, and unconscious as dynamic regions laid out spatially along a horizontal line or plane, with a system of barriers similar to locks in a dam, as shown in this so-called picket fence diagram in *The Interpretation of Dreams*[5]

---

actual trauma. However, his recognition of the inner forces of desire in the form of the drives of sex and aggression led to a significant shift from a more materialist view of the human personality to one that recognizes the complexity and motivational impact of intrapsychic as well as interpersonal dynamics. Contrary to popular critiques, Freud never actually denied the reality of child abuse or the disastrous impact of trauma (e.g., Freud, *Introductory Lectures* 16:370 and Freud, "An Outline of Psychoanalysis," 187; also cited in Lear, *Freud*, 234n27; as well as the case of "Wolf Man" (Freud, "From the History of an Infantile Neurosis"). It is a fair assessment, however, that when Freud turned his focus away from the impact of the environment and onto the internal dynamics of the psyche, he left the field of trauma largely uninvestigated. This shift in attention no doubt blinded Freud to some reality-based suffering of his own patients, notably "Dora" (whose analysis could well be understood as an autocratic retraumatization of a sexually abused teenager), and set psychoanalysis on a trajectory of privileging internal reality over the external for almost a century (Mitchell and Black, *Freud and Beyond*, 207–14; Cooper-White, "Opening the Eyes."

4. Holifield, *A History of Pastoral Care in America,* 195.

5. Ibid.; Freud, *The Interpretation of Dreams,* 541.

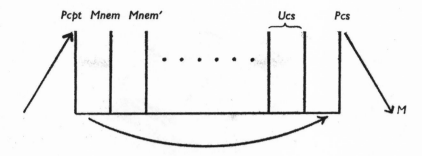

Figure 3-1. Freud's Topographical Model (*The Interpretation of Dreams*)

Soon within Freud's own thinking this was rotated ninety degrees, to become a vertical conception of mind. In an explanatory footnote added to the *Interpretation* in 1914, he likened the mechanism of repression and the unconscious to the hydraulic system in a pyramid: "a thought becomes repressed as a result of the combined influence upon it of two factors. It is pushed from the one side (by the censorship of the Cs.) and pulled from the other (by the Ucs.), in the same kind of way in which people are conveyed to the top of the Great Pyramid."[6] In the same time period, Freud was further likening this vertical pull of the unconscious to the downward or inward pull of gravity: "the concept of the mind is a wider one than that of consciousness, in the same kind of way in which the gravitational force of a heavenly body extends beyond its range of luminosity."[7] The unconscious thus came to be understood not only as removed from conscious awareness, but privileged as the *deepest* layer. Freud went so far as to name this as the "*true* psychical reality."[8]

This dynamic, vertical conception was retained and incorporated into Freud's later structural model in *The Ego and the Id*, with the repression barrier shown as a partial "lid" over the unconscious, and the ego resting atop the id "as the germinal disk rests upon the ovum."[9]

6. Freud, *The Interpretation of Dreams*, 547.
7. Ibid. 612n1.
8. Ibid., 525, emphasis added.
9. Freud, *The Ego and the Id*, 24.

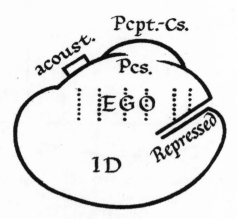

Figure 3-2. Freud's Structural Model (*The Ego and the Id*)

While there are important differences between the topographical model per se and the later tripartite structural model,[10] it is the vertical ordering of conscious and unconscious mental contents and the economic principle of bound mental energy, shared by both models, that is of concern in this chapter. This vertical model of conscious and unconscious is still commonly taught and used in clinical practice theory and has enjoyed a long tenure as the most commonly accepted theory of mind (with the exception of the most strictly behavioral counter-models) during the past one-hundred-plus years in North America, including in the fields of pastoral care and counseling.

The language of conscious, preconscious, and unconscious (in German *das Unbewusste*)[11], resonates with late nineteenth-century fascination with mystery, the occult realms of the unseen and the un-

10. For example, "in the topographic model, defense was considered synonymous with repression, and repression produced anxiety. In the structural model (after Freud, *Inhibitions, Symptoms and Anxiety*, 1926) this view was exactly reversed, and anxiety evoked defense. Furthermore, anxiety was linked to object relations from earliest infancy; anxiety evoked defenses of which repression was only one; and the central significance of early developmental factors became far more important than they had been in the topographical model" (Boesky, "Structural Theory," 497), citing Arlow and Brenner, *Psychoanalytic Concepts and the Structural Theory*.

11. The term *das Unbewusste* (as well as *das Bewusstsein*, the word for "consciousness") has its roots in the verb *wissen*, "to know," as in an idea, a fact, or a skill. *Wissen* does not encompass, as does the word *know* in English, the sense of knowing a person or thing, which in German is carried by the verb *kennen*. It may be of interest, given the relational paradigm of this paper, that *wissen* does not carry the meaning of "recognition."

known. As Peter Gay and others have pointed out, the idea of unknown "depths beyond depths" in the mind was already a feature of nineteenth-century romantic literature,[12] the poetry of Goethe and Schiller, whom Freud could "quote by the hour."[13] Parallel ideas were also afloat in the philosophical works of Schopenhauer and Nietzsche. The mysteriousness of the dream itself was a favored subject of late eighteenth- and nineteenth-century romanticism, producing such art works as *The Nightmare* (1782), by Henry Fuseli [FIGURE 3-3], and a widespread fascination in literature, theater, and the opera with nocturnal themes blending the erotic, horror, and the supernatural—as seen, for example, in the proliferation of stories, plays, and operas about vampires.[14] (I'm sure we are all quick to recognize the thinly veiled sexual and aggressive drive derivatives in such art, but let's reserve that interpretation for future discussion, bearing in mind that vampires have much in common with Kleinian digestive themes as well!)

Freud's collection of archaeological artifacts, and his own likening of the psychoanalytic process with an archaeological dig, betray the broader influence of the European fin-de-siècle romance with "dark continents,"[15] also manifested in movements such as orientalism, spiritualism, the rise of historicism and a new historical consciousness across many disciplines, and colonial exploration and expansion. In this sense, the "dream's navel" is the ultimate unknown continent: "the spot where [the dream] reaches down into the unknown," the "tangle of dream-thoughts which cannot be [further] unravelled," and "which has to be left obscure."[16] In some sense, Freud's wish was not only to be a great scientist (his own most conscious aim[17]) or even a great artist-philosopher and hermeneut (as he is now sometimes being recast), but also a heroic explorer, penetrating further and further to bring back artifacts from the uncharted regions of the mind.

12. Gay, *Freud,* 128, 366.

13. Ibid., 128.

14. Cooper-White, "Two Vampires of 1828," 22–57.

15. Freud used this term as a metaphor for "the sexual life of adult women" in "The Question of Lay Analysis," 212. Shengold has written about Freud's fascination with nineteenth-century geographical exploration in "The Body and the Place," in *"Father, Don't You See I'm Burning?"* 29–41. For a feminist, postcolonial analysis and critique, see also Khanna, *Dark Continents.*

16. Freud, *The Interpretation of Dreams,* 525.

17. Freud, *Project for a Scientific Psychology.*

Figure 3-3. *The Nightmare* (1782) by Henri Fuseli

As with all exploration of his time, the attendant agenda of conquest and colonization was never far behind. In several papers, perhaps most notably his 1912 paper "The Dynamics of the Transference,"[18]
Freud employed the language of a heroic military struggle to describe
the psychoanalytic process. The conflict was staged between three
pairs of opposites: doctor vs. patient, intellect vs. instinct, and recognition (insight) vs. striving for discharge (we might say "acting out.")

18. Freud, "The Dynamics of the Transference."

Psychoanalysis became the battleground on which, in Freud's own words, "the victory must be won." The heroic, military tone of this paper may reflect a consciousness of the gathering political tensions in Austria, which would culminate in the Great War two years later. But the heroic tone also reflects, perhaps, the power of forces of opposition with which Freud felt himself personally to be contending in the years 1911–1912. The defensive, combative tone also reflects tensions with Jung, and in particular Freud's upset about Jung's tempestuous sexual involvement with a patient Sabina Spielrein, and the dangers inherent in such mishandling of the transference, both for individuals and for the advancement of psychoanalysis as a movement.[19]

Thus, the topographical model came riding in to America at the turn of the twentieth century on the twin horses of romanticism and expansionism, both congenial animals in the stables of America's heroic, imperial self-concept and doctrine of Manifest Destiny.[20]

The topographical model incorporated a similarly hierarchical ordering of consciousness itself. The conscious portion of the ego was privileged as the executive function in daily life, but the unconscious was admired as the "true psychic reality," and therefore accorded an aura of mysterious power.

In this model the psychoanalyst (and by extension, the psychoanalytically devoted psychiatrist, social worker, and pastor) was the shaman of rationality, the experienced voyager to these deep recesses of the mind, who could initiate new acolytes on their own voyages of discovery and colonization. Freud reputedly told his biographer

19. For more on the history of this period, see Gay, *Freud*; Carotenuto, *A Secret Symmetry*; Kerr, *A Most Dangerous Method*.

20. For a fascinating discussion of Manifest Destiny from a feminist, postcolonial perspective, see Greenberg, *Manifest Manhood*. John Gast's painting *American Progress* (1872) was a popular and frequently reproduced symbol for the American doctrine of western expansion, romanticizing and spiritualizing the conquest of native lands and indigenous peoples. George Crofutt, who made a widely distributed print of the painting described it as follows: "a diaphanously and precariously clad America floats westward through the air with the 'Star of Empire' on her forehead. She has left the cities of the East behind, and the wide Mississippi, and still her course is westward. In her right hand she carries a schoolbook—testimonial of the National Enlightenment, while with her left she trails the slender wires of the telegraph that will bind the nation. Fleeing her approach are Indians, buffalo, wild horses, bears, *and other game*, disappearing into the storm and waves of the Pacific Coast. They flee the wondrous vision—the star "is too much for them"(emphasis added). Online: http://www.webpages.uidaho.edu/~rfrey/422gast.htm.

Figure 3-4. *Manifest Destiny* (1872) by John Gast

Ernest Jones that he considered himself not "really a man of science . . .
nothing but by temperament a conquistador."[21] Freud compared *The
Interpretation of Dreams* itself to a heroic journey, with explicit parallels
to Dante's *Inferno*. He was, in fact, reading the *Inferno* during the period of drafting *The Interpretation of Dreams*. The quotation from Virgil
that served as the motto for the book reflects the tone of the conquer-
ing explorer.[22] Mastery of these infernal regions was seen as capable
of freeing initiates from self-generated neurotic limitations, and conferring upon them the ability to harness these mysterious powers for
productivity and conquests of all kinds. This model of the unconscious,
to varying degrees, has held sway for a large portion of this century in
a variety of psychotherapeutic disciplines and has had great influence
in other fields as well, including philosophy and the arts.

21. Ernest Jones, *The Life and Work of Sigmund Freud*, 1:348.

22. For a deeper discussion of *The Interpretation of Dreams* as a heroic journey and
its parallels to the *Inferno*, see Shengold, *"Father, Don't You See I'm Burning?"* 44–50.
Shengold also points out how the journey narrated in *The Interpretation of Dreams* itself was conceived as "descent from the heights and the penetration of depths where
'every path will end in darkness'" (54–55, quoting Freud, *The Interpretation of Dreams*,
511). The sexual symbolism is perhaps self-evident.

CONTEMPORARY CHALLENGES

The hegemony of this vertically conceived model of mind, with repression as the central mechanism of removing mental contents from consciousness, is now increasingly being challenged *within* psychoanalytic schools of thought. These challenges are arising from a number of separate theoretical and clinical spheres, generating ideas that are just now in the process of being crystallized. These ideas may be seen to have converged in the postmodern era toward a model of mind conceived of as more multiple, more dispersed, and depicted spatially (horizontally or even three dimensionally) rather than vertically or hierarchically.

The sources of these challenges are numerous. Common to these contemporary movements is a challenge to the centrality of the function of *psychic conflict* in Freud's concept of the formation of the unconscious. Freud's concept of *repression* increasingly relied on drive theory (i.e., the theory of sex and aggression as the central motivators of human behavior) to explain why mental contents had to be removed from conscious awareness. Repression was a by-product of psychic conflict. Object-relations theory (originating with Melanie Klein [23]) has for many decades now challenged this notion in favor of a model of splitting, in which human behavior is no longer viewed primarily as motivated by forbidden drives and terror of castration, but by irresolvable fractures between and among fantasied and real experiences of parental/environmental provision and lack, and one's own hunger and aggression.[24] Regardless of the specific school of object relations (and here I include self psychology as well), every object- relations theory has stated in its own way that it is these irreconcilable relational contradictions that create splits in mental life. Over time an entire inner landscape comes to be populated with "objects" (or, in self psychological terms, "selfobjects"), i.e. inner representations of strongly cathected people, part-people, and other figures that dwell in both conscious and unconscious regions. These inner objects are further understood both to inhabit and to provoke different states of consciousness with different accompanying affective atmospheres and cognitive capacities. Internal objects may be invoked and prompted into behavioral enactment by various shifts in the external environment that may have

---

23. E.g., Klein, *Envy and Gratitude*; and Freud, *The Psycho-Analysis of Children*.
24. Described in more detail in chapter 2, above.

resonance with them. It is not surprising, then, that the various contemporary heirs of object-relations theory, from both self psychology and the new "relational" school of American object relations, have rejected the centrality of the concept of repression in favor of models that might be understood more horizontally, and even multidimensionally.

THE CHALLENGE FROM SELF PSYCHOLOGY

In self psychology this stems from Kohut's idea of the vertical split—a split born not from oedipal conflict but from a more primitive, narcissistic splitting of reality based on preoedipal experience. This idea was first introduced and diagrammed by Heinz Kohut in his paper "The Two Analyses of Mr. Z."[25]

In this paper, regarded by some as autobiographical, Kohut describes two separate analyses of the same patient, a socially isolated young man who presented with narcissistic traits and an unusually close peer-like relationship with his widowed mother, with whom he was living. The first analysis, conducted along classical structural lines, framed Mr. Z's pathology in terms of unconscious conflict and defense:

> The centre of the analytic stage was occupied by transference phenomena and memories concerning his, as I then saw it, pathogenic conflicts in the area of infantile sexuality and aggression—his Oedipus complex, his castration anxiety, his childhood masturbation, his fantasy of the phallic woman, and, especially his preoccupation with the primal scene—and, on the other hand, by his revelation that, beginning at the age of 11, he had been involved in a homosexual relationship lasting about two years, with a 30-year-old high school teacher, a senior counsellor and assistant director of the summer camp to which he had been sent by his parents.[26]

25. Kohut, "The Two Analyses of Mr. Z."

26. Ibid., 5. Contemporary readers are usually quick to note the disturbing fact that in neither of Mr. Z's two analyses is the behavior of the thirty-year-old camp counselor framed as sexual abuse. In the first analysis it was interpreted as a reactivation of the fantasied bliss of preoedipal merger with the idealized mother. In the second analysis it was reframed as again a largely positive enactment of the yearning for a strong idealizable father figure—although Kohut did "only once, briefly," voice his opinion hat "Mr. Z would have obtained more lasting benefits from the friendship with this man, who, as far as I can judge was indeed a remarkable person, if their closeness had remained free of sexual contacts" (19). In the best construction,

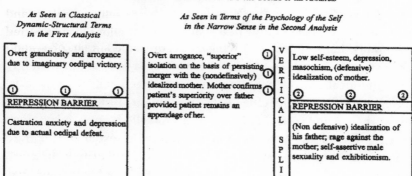

THE CASE OF MR. Z - HIS PSYCHOPATHOLOGY AND THE COURSE OF HIS ANALYSIS

As Seen in Classical Dynamic-Structural Terms in the First Analysis

As Seen in Terms of the Psychology of the Self in the Narrow Sense in the Second Analysis

Overt grandiosity and arrogance due to imaginary oedipal victory.

REPRESSION BARRIER

Castration anxiety and depression due to actual oedipal defeat.

Overt arrogance, "superior" isolation on the basis of persisting merger with the (nondefinsively) idealized mother. Mother confirms patient's superiority over father provided patient remains an appendage of her.

VERTICAL SPLIT

Low self-esteem, depression, masochism, (defensive) idealization of mother.

REPRESSION BARRIER

(Non defensive) idealization of his father; rage against the mother; self-assertive male sexuality and exhibitionism.

The analytic work done on the basis of the classical dynamic-structural concept takes place throughout the analysis at the line indicated by ① ① ①.

The analytic work done on the basis of the self-psychological concept is carried out in two stages. The first stage is done at the line indicated by ① ① ①; Mr. Z confronts fears of losing the merger with the mother and thus losing his self as he knew it. The second stage is done at the line indicated by ② ② ②; Mr. Z confronts traumatic overstimulation and disintegration fear as he becomes conscious of the rage, assertiveness, sexuality, and exhibitionism of his independent self.

Figure 3-5. Heinz Kohut's Vertical Split ("The Two Analyses of Mr. Z")

The split in consciousness, as diagrammed, was understood as a conscious sense of entitlement born of an often enacted narcissistic wish to regress to a preoedipal, pregenital state of merger with the mother, vs. an unconscious oedipal rivalry and accompanying fear of castration resulting in depressive anxiety and social inhibition.

The second analysis, separated from the first by a space of about five years, was conducted along the lines of Kohut's then newly developing "psychology of the self." In this second analysis, Mr. Z's difficulties were understood as resulting not from repression of conflictual aims but from the splitting off from awareness of intensely negative aspects of his mother's emotional domination, which had been known and experienced but not allowed expression. The breaking of this taboo was accompanied by intense anxiety, as the loss of the idealized archaic selfobject of the mother threatened the dissolution of his sense of his own self—notably, in Kohut's words, "the loss of *a* self that at

this probably must be understood as Kohut's wish not to impose judgments on the patient's own positive perception of the relationship and, particularly in the second analysis, Mr. Z's use of the camp counselor as an idealized paternal selfobject. The suggestion that this article was semi-autobiographical further complicates our reading of this apparently rather mild acceptance of the sexual exploitation of a child.

these moments—and they were more than moments—he considered to *be his only one*"[27] (emphasis added). In this sentence, Kohut quite matter-of-factly ushers into psychoanalysis the idea that one could have more than one self. And in the model presented in Mr. Z's second analysis what we see are at least three selves: a self based on merger with the idealized mother; a split-off, depressed self that behaviorally manifests the difficulties with the mother through compulsive masturbation and social inhibition; and a so-called repressed vital self that represents Mr. Z's self- assertion and male sexuality. This third self, which Kohut also calls the "nuclear self" (similar to Winnicott's formulation of the "true self"),[28] is associated with a (male-identified, even patriarchal) longing for an idealized and idealizable father, and is enraged at the mother's domination. It is not clear, nor does Kohut elaborate in this article, whether the use of the term *repression* for the horizontal split depicted in this second model is really accurate, or whether some other mechanism of removing mental contents from awareness is being conceptualized here. Rather than the pushing back of conflictual aims, the "downward" push in the second model resembles more a schizoid withdrawal from consciousness, as in the works of Klein, and later Guntrip,[29] which also might be understood as a form of dissociation.

The mechanism of the vertical split, in any case, is clearly not repression in any formulation. Kohut uses the term *disavowal*, in which certain aspects of oneself are accessible to consciousness, in the sense that they are not repressed but so uncomfortable to one's own sense of oneself that they are normally kept out of awareness. In a new book devoted entirely to the concept of the vertical split in self psychology, Arnold Goldberg explains: "Rather than being inaccessible, as the repressed is, one can attend to them, [the contents of the vertically split-off segment] are similar in form in the sense of being characterized as a secondary rather than primary process, and they manifest an organization reflecting a total personality. It is often only in respect

27. Ibid., 13.

28. Winnicott, "Ego Distortion in Terms of True Self and False Self."

29. Klein, "Notes on Some Schizoid Mechanisms"; and Guntrip, "Deeper Perception of the Schizoid Problem."

to their relationship to the world that something different and even strange may be seen."[30]

While repression is usually implicated in neurotic processes, the vertical split is considered by self psychologists to be ascribed to narcissistic pathology and behavioral disorders. The split-off aspects of the self are considered to be manifested primarily in behaviors rather than thoughts, usually taking the form of compulsive acts that the person would ordinarily find completely alien. Goldberg cites Montaigne (1588):"We are, I know not how, double in ourselves, so that we believe what we disbelieve, and cannot rid ourselves of what we condemn."[31] Pastoral theologians might hear echoes of St. Paul's own protestations, "For I do not do the good I want, but the evil I do not want is what I do. Now if I do what I do not want, it is no longer I that do it, but sin that dwells within me" (Rom 7:19–20, NRSV). What a perfect description of the vertical split! The origins of such a split are attributed to attempts in the earliest year of life to"turn a blind eye"or to rid oneself of unwanted experience, which in some personalities may become habitual. Goldberg cites Bowlby's attachment theory, drawing a parallel with Bowlby's own term, *cognitive disconnection*, observed as a reaction to loss or lack in very early childhood, especially of a parent's or both parents' attention.[32]

The principal contribution of the theoretical construct of the vertical split in self psychology is, I believe, in clarifying that repression of conflictual aims is not the only means by which mental contents may be removed from awareness. It is, perhaps, the first and certainly the clearest depiction of a process in which consciousness *itself* is divided into two separately functioning areas of awareness and self-knowledge. It serves particularly well to explain certain forms of inconsistent behavior in which different behavior patterns are governed by the two separate arenas of consciousness: for example, in cases of sexual misconduct by revered clergy and other moral leaders. Still, the construct of the vertical split in self psychology is a mainly binary model. Some other contemporary psychoanalytic theories are now going even further in exploring an even greater variety or multiplicity

30. Goldberg, *Being of Two Minds*, 10.
31. Ibid., 12, citing Montaigne, *Essays*.
32. Ibid., 22, citing Bowlby,"An Information Processing Approach."

of mental states that may coexist at varying levels of consciousness within the same self or mind.[33]

THE CHALLENGE FROM RELATIONAL THEORY

In relational theory, a new movement centered largely in New York, with origins in the Interpersonal (or Sullivanian) school of psychoanalysis, increasing attention has been given to dissociation as a nonpathological phenomenon, being placed alongside or even replacing repression altogether as the primary model of mental geography. In Adrienne Harris's words, explicitly countering Freud's archaeological analogy, "This model of consciousness is less archaeologically organized and more a set of surfaces or representations with boundaries of varying permeability."[34] Jody Messler Davies has elaborated on this dimension of relational theory "that has begun to conceive of self, indeed of mind itself, as a multiply organized, associationally linked network of parallel, coexistent, at times conflictual, systems of meaning attribution and understanding."[35] Elaborating in another article, she wrote:

> Not one unconscious, not the unconscious, but multiple levels
> of consciousness and unconsciousness, in an ongoing state of
> interactive articulation as past experience infuses the present
> and present experience evokes state-dependent memories of
> formative interactive representations. Not an onion, which
> must be carefully peeled, or an archeological site to be me-
> ticulously unearthed and reconstructed in its original form,
> but a child's kaleidoscope in which each glance through the
> pinhole of a moment in time provides a unique view; a com-

33. In an offshoot of self psychology, intersubjectivity theorists Stolorow and Atwood have proposed three interrelated forms of unconsciousness: the "prereflective unconscious—the organizing principles that unconsciously shape and thematize a person's experiences; 2) the dynamic unconscious—experiences that were denied articulation because they were perceived to threaten needed ties; and 3) the unvalidated unconscious—experiences that could not be articulated because they never evoked the requisite validating responsiveness from the surround. All three forms of unconscious, we have emphasized, derived from specific, formative intersubjective contexts" (Stolorow and Atwood, *Contexts of Being*, 33). For the sake of brevity, I have omitted a detailed examination of this contemporary movement in psychoanalysis here, since most of its contributions are similar to those of the relational school, whose appropriation of object relations and constructivist paradigms in my view carry more explanatory power.

34. Harris, "False Memory?" 159n2

35. Davies, "Multiple Perspectives on Multiplicity," 195.

plex organization in which a fixed set of colored, shaped, and textured components rearrange themselves in unique crystalline structures determined by way of infinite pathways of interconnectedness.[36]

In this view, dissociation is not necessarily regarded as pathological per se, although it may become problematic, as in severe posttraumatic states in which continual experiences of fragmentation interrupt the normal sense of a seamless continuity of consciousness. However, dissociation, or multiplicity, is increasingly being recognized as inherent in mental functioning, and not only as a sequela of trauma. The idea that the mind begins as a unitary phenomenon and is gradually fragmented by traumatic experience is itself increasingly being challenged. Philip Bromberg, a relational psychoanalyst who has written considerably about dissociation, the unconscious, and clinical process, has observed,

> The process of dissociation is basic to human mental functioning and is central to the stability and growth of personality. It is intrinsically an adaptational talent that represents the very nature of what we call 'consciousness.' Dissociation is not fragmentation . . . There is now abundant evidence that the psyche does not start as an integrated whole, but is nonunitary in origin—a mental structure that begins and continues as a multiplicity of self-states that maturationally attain a feeling of coherence which overrides the awareness of discontinuity. This leads to the experience of a cohesive sense of personal identity and the *necessary illusion of being "one self."*[37]

Bromberg and others point to a body of psychoanalytically informed research based on infant observation. Researchers such as Robert Emde,[38] Daniel Stern,[39] and Beatrice Beebe and Frank Lachmann[40] have observed that the earliest experiences of the self appear to be organized around a variety of shifting self states that encompass cognitive, affective and physiological dimensions, and appear to include

36. Davies, "Dissociation, Repression, and Reality Testing," 197.

37. Bromberg, "'Speak! That I May See You.," 521 (emphasis added). See also Bromberg, "Standing in the Spaces," and Bromberg, *Standing in the Spaces*.

38. Emde, "The Affective Self"; and Emde, "The Prerepresentational Self and its Affective Core.

39. Stern, *The Interpersonal World of the Infant*.

40. Beebe and Lachmann, "The Contribution of Mother-Infant Mutual Influence."

internalized representations of relational or interactive experiences.[41] Therefore, a central aspect of the developmental process consists of being increasingly able to move smoothly and seamlessly from one self state to another with an increasing sense of self-continuity and an increasing capacity for self-regulation. This process is facilitated (or not facilitated) by primary caretakers' responsiveness (or lack thereof). The quality of the boundaries between self and other also gradually comes to be established through mutual recognition and regulation, or, in less desirable scenarios, comes to be impaired by parental non-recognition and/or intrusion.

THE CHALLENGE FROM TRAUMATOLOGY

The interest in multiplicity in relational theory has been highly influenced by clinical work with trauma survivors, particularly survivors of sexual abuse.[42] In fact, one of the central recent sources of disruption of Freud's topographical and structural models has been the reemergence of serious attention to the sequelae of severe trauma in mental life. Relational authors are, in part, reclaiming models of dissociation advanced by Freud's predecessors, Charcot[43] and Janet,[44] whose studies of hysteria took seriously the link between trauma and dissociation; as well as the writings of Ferenczi,[45] whose continuing emphasis on the actual impact of environmental trauma contributed to his ejection from Freud's inner circle.

The mutability or robustness of memory, particularly traumatic memory, is one particular arena in which questions of consciousness and unconsciousness have been hotly debated in recent years. Both *repression* and *dissociation* as terms have been appropriated—sometimes incorrectly—by combatants in recent wars about the reliability of memories of adult survivors of childhood sexual abuse. The politicization of issues surrounding trauma, sexual abuse, and so-called recovered-memory therapy has unfortunately obscured or skewed a

41. Stern's "representations of interactive experience as generalized," or "RIGs," in *The Interpersonal World of the Infant*.

42. E.g., Davies and Frawley, *Treating the Adult Survivor*; Bromberg, *Standing in the Spaces*.

43. Charcot, *Clinical Lectures*.

44. Janet, *The Major Symptoms of Hysteria*.

45. Ferenczi, "The Confusion of Tongues."

growing body of serious research on both traumatic and nontraumatic memory. We have already seen that "forgetting" is not conceived of within psychoanalytic models as a single process, but may involve repression in Freud's original sense of banishing once-known but intolerable thoughts, particularly wishes; disavowal, in which something fully known but dystonic with one's sense of oneself is split off from everyday awareness; and dissociation, in which multiple arenas of cognition, affect, sensation, and behavior[46] may be split off from consciousness, for varying lengths of times and with boundaries of varying permeability. Exegeting beyond political rhetoric for valid evidence about the nature of memory, a somewhat less politically clouded but no less complex consensus may now be beginning to emerge:

Some basic principles seem to include:

a) Memory is not a single phenomenon or process. Neuropsychological studies by Bessel Van der Kolk and others have determined that memory is "state dependent," i.e., determined by whether the external circumstance is relatively calm or threatening. Trauma specialists working in the medical and neurobiological fields are now validating the importance of dissociative processes on a spectrum from normal and universally experienced shifts in states of affect and cognition to highly fragmented states of consciousness resulting from efforts to adapt to extreme trauma.[47] Psychobiologists have also begun to offer evidence for the impact of a normative, nontraumatic early social environment on the brain, pinpointing neurochemical changes resulting from affect-regulating functions of the primary caretaker. They suggest a model of mind with greater developmental plasticity throughout the lifespan, and in some ways more in keeping with lateral moves among multiple mental states than a vertical model of repression as the sole mechanism of removing mental contents from awareness.[48]

---

46. These four domains were first specified in Braun, *The Treatment of Multiple Personality Disorder*.

47. Van der Kolk and Fisler, "Dissociation and the Fragmentary Nature"; see also van der Kolk et al., *Traumatic Stress*.

48. Moskowitz, et al., *The Neurobiological and Developmental Basis for Psychotherapeutic Intervention*; Schore, *Affect Regulation and the Origin of Self*; Schore, *Affect Dysregulation and Disorders of the Self*; and Schore, *Affect Regulation and the Repair of the Self*.

b) Not all memory is cognitively processed into a narrative or even a symbolic framework. Different types of memory are stored differently in the brain. Ordinary narrative or "declarative" memory is generally associated in neurobiology with the frontal lobe and the hippocampus, while nondeclarative memory (including emotional responses, reflexive actions, classically conditioned responses, and memories of skills and habits) appears to be associated with the central nervous system.[49] There is growing evidence that certain experiences, including severe trauma, may only be encoded in portions of the brain that do not primarily involve cognition and therefore are accessible to consciousness only through visual fragments; intense waves of affect; or olfactory, auditory, or bodily sensations.[50] Hormonal hyperarousal resulting in chronic anxiety states, and dissociative responses may themselves be memory traces.[51]

c) In severe trauma, there is rising evidence that "memory" itself is not a unitary phenomenon, but that an event may be encoded in several separate domains at once, including affect, sensation, and cognition, but never connected up to make what we would ordinarily understand as a full narrative memory of an event by subsequent cognitive processing.[52] The capacity to process an experience is strongly influenced by the safety of the environment at the time of the event and immediately thereafter, and whether the environment is hospitable or inhospitable to the act of processing into memory. Distortion may be introduced during the time period immediately surrounding the trauma; for example, in a situation of familial incest when a painful sexual violation is framed by

49. Van der Kolk and Fisler, "Dissociation and the Fragmentary Nature," 4.

50. Ibid. 8; Perry et al., "Childhood Trauma."

51. Van der Kolk, "The Body Keeps the Score." Gender differences have also been seen. Adult males and older male children may be more likely to respond to threat with a "fight-or-flight" response associated with hormonal hyperarousal and sensitization of brain-stem and mid-brain-mediated catecholamine systems. Female children and adult females are more likely to respond with a "freeze-and-surrender" reaction, involving CNS activation but also increased vagal tone, increased dopaminergic system activity, and in some cases the appearance of endogenous opioids which reduce pain sensation and induce dissociative responses. (Perry et al., "Childhood Trauma.")

52. Van der Kolk and Fisler, "Dissociation and the Fragmentary Nature of Traumatic Memories."

the abuser as something good and wanted, and treated by other family members as unreal and unseen.

d) Some memories *may* be fabricated, or, more likely, elaborated from a kernel of actual experience. However, the heavily touted evidence that false memories can be implanted by an outside person has frequently been overstated for political purposes.[53] In most cases, a core of memory persists, although it may not have narrative form. Surrounding details may be shaped in consciousness by the relational surround at any given time, including both personal and wider societal canons affecting what is believable.[54]

e) Finally (and this has perhaps the most important implications for clinical and pastoral work) memory cannot be divorced from *meaning*. Details of a remembered event may in fact shift and change, particularly in what is background vs. foreground, depending on the meaning or multiple meanings assigned to the experience. This process of meaning making is not a solitary one but is co-constructed (for good or for ill) in the intersubjective "shared wisdom," conscious and especially unconscious, of both therapeutic and nontherapeutic relationships.[55] A constructivist framework for therapeutic and pastoral care does not imply that original events are being "made up" by therapist and patient. Donnel Stern likens the constructivist view of memory to figures emerging from a dense fog:

> They do have shapes, rough or 'fuzzy' shapes, and those shapes, while allowing a number of interpretations, forbid many others . . . We are not free to assign any interpretation we please to our experience, not without violating the semiotic regularities of our culture . . . Such violations are so meaningful that we notice them immediately, and the conclusions we draw from them are either dire or terribly interesting: that is, when the wrong use of signs does not indicate psychosis, it

53. In Elizabeth Loftus's oft-cited study of implanting memories of being lost in a shopping mall (described in Loftus and Ketcham, *The Myth of Repressed Memory*), only 10 percent of research subjects actually came to accept the story as their own, and 90 percent resisted (noted in "Miscoding Is Seen as the Root of False Memory," *New York Times*, May 31, 1994, pp. C1, C8, cited in Davies, "Dissociation, Repression and Reality Testing," 193).

54. Cf., Harris, "False Memory? False Memory Syndrome?" 171.

55. Cooper-White, *Shared Wisdom*.

either indicates willful disregard (a lie) or playful disrespect (as in art) of the codes of communication in which we live.[56]

What is co-constructed is not the core of experience, but what the experience comes to mean. The process of meaning making is not and should not be viewed as moving toward some single, incontrovertible truth or concrete certainty.

The "truth" of an experience, when given an open, nonleading and nonintrusive exploration in a context of mutual, empathic curiosity, will usually become increasingly rich, complex, and multiple over time. The question thus shifts from the narrow forensic one of "Did 'it' happen?" to "What does 'its' presence—in my feelings, senses, thoughts, fantasies, memories, and behavior—mean?" Different meanings will then lead to different choices and actions at different times. There is no one right action (i.e., prescriptions for confrontation, litigation, or forgiveness), and "right" actions will also change over time as meanings continue to grow in subtlety and complexity. Increasing recognition of the complexity of memory, traumatic and otherwise, leads to more complex understandings of consciousness itself as influenced by the vicissitudes of loss, grief, and desire, and by the co-construction of reality in the context of relationships.

CHALLENGES FROM COGNITIVE SCIENCE

A somewhat parallel paradigm shift in cognitive science is a movement variously called "connectionism" or "parallel distributed processing," which draws analogies between "human information processing" and digital computers.[57] Researchers in academic psychology are also joining the multiplicity bandwagon. Yale psychologist Paul Bloom writes:

> Like any organ, the brain consists of large parts (such as the hippocampus and the cortex) that are made up of small parts (such as "maps" in the visual cortex), which themselves are made up of smaller parts, until you get to neurons, billions of them, whose orchestrated firing is the stuff of thought. The neurons are made up of parts like terminal buttons and receptor sites, which are made up of molecules, and so on.
>
> This hierarchical structure makes possible the research programs of psychology and neuroscience. The idea is that

56. Stern, "Commentary on Papers by Davies and Harris," 262–63.

57. Bechtel and Abrahamsen, *Connectionism and the Mind.*

interesting properties of the whole (intelligence, decision-making, emotions, moral sensibility) can be understood in terms of the interaction of components that themselves lack these properties. This is how computers work; there is every reason to believe that this is how we work, too.[58]

Bloom draws also from researchers in the fields of artificial intelligence and cognitive science. Marvin Minsky, with his "Society of Mind" theory, asserts that intelligence is built "from many little parts, each mindless by itself."[59] Steven Pinker makes the analogy to computers even more explicit in his "computational theory of mind."[60] For example, Pinker writes:

[The computational theory of mind] is one of the great ideas in intellectual history, for it solves one of the puzzles that make up the "mind-body problem": how to connect the ethereal world of meaning and intention, the stuff of our mental lives, with a physical hunk of matter like the brain . . .

The computational theory of mind resolves the paradox. It says that beliefs and desires are information, incarnated as configurations of symbols. The symbols are physical states of bits of matter, like chips in a computer or neurons in the brain. They symbolize things in the world because they are triggered by those things via our sense organs, and because of what they do once they are triggered. If the bits of matter that constitute a symbol are arranged to bump into the bits of matter constituting another symbol in just the right way, the symbols corresponding to one belief can give rise to new symbols corresponding to another belief logically related to it, which can give rise to symbols corresponding to other beliefs, and so on. Eventually the bits of matter constituting a symbol bump into bits of matter connected to the muscles, and behavior happens. The computational theory of mind thus allows us to keep beliefs and desires in our explanations of behavior while planting them squarely in the physical universe. It allows meaning to cause and be caused.

Such comparisons between the human mind and computers, or even the Internet, are problematic if taken to extremes. The metaphor of cyberspace and computers is a mechanistic one, and may tend back

58. Bloom, "First Person Plural," 92. See also Bloom, *How Pleasure Works*.

59. Minsky, *The Society of Mind*, 17.

60. Pinker, *How the Mind Works*, 24–25.

toward a more abstract Cartesian conception of mind, in which time and the body again are disregarded.

Sherry Turkle, a sociologist who has studied psychoanalysis, artificial intelligence, and the seductive appeal of cyberspace and virtual alternate identities, recognizes a tension between the view that the mind is multiply constituted of microprocessors that learn through trial and error, causing a group intelligence to emerge, and the subjective feeling of being an "I." Theories that propose a decentered model of mind—whether we are considering Freud's theories of conscious and unconscious or Minsky's computer-like society of mind—are "hard to live with," she states, because "the cornerstone of ordinary life is that there is an 'I' that causes things to happen."[61] "[T]hese images of decentered minds do not sit easily with the sense of being a person and acting in the world."[62] This motivates us to seek out a role for a "reconstituted center."[63] For some, this is the role of a traditional view of the soul. Turkle finds the way out of this dilemma through a paradox of strength and weakness. The inevitability of slips—whether Freudian or computational—means that true strength (whether mechanical or cultural) always requires vulnerability, and this, in turn, bridges the gap from pure computational logic to the subjectivity of the human mind.[64]

Paul Bloom's formulation, which he links with his inquiries into happiness, both short-term and long-term, is perhaps the most compatible with some of the other conceptions of multiplicity described

61. Turkle, *The Second Self*, 267.

62. Ibid., 269.

63. Ibid., 266.

64. Turkle draws on Douglas Hofstadter's *Gödel, Escher, Bach*, quoting mathematician Kurt Gödel's theorem: "A crystal glass can be shattered by a singer who hits exactly the right note. By extension, for any piece of matter, including a phonograph, there is a pitch that will shatter it. If a record whose 'song' contains this pitch is played on the phonograph, the machine will 'self-destruct.' Thus any phonograph must be imperfect in one of two ways. It can be imperfect because it is unable to play notes with enough fidelity to reproduce the destructive tone, in which case it does not destroy itself, but is obviously imperfect, imperfect through weakness. Or it can be imperfect through strength, in which case it is able to reproduce notes in full fidelity, and the record with that 'certain note' will shatter it to pieces. The paradox at the heart of Gödel's theorem is this: if the formal system is really powerful there will be a question that can be posed within it which it cannot answer." Her student poses, and then answers the question "'If we are machines, are we perfect?' No, he comes back saying, 'if we are the most powerful kind of machines, the kind that God would create,' we are limited, vulnerable, weak . . . "[I]f we are machines, we are human" (275–78).

in this chapter. Adopting a view of a "community of selves" characterized by competing long-term and short-term aims, Bloom values the expensiveness of our plural "imaginary worlds" and argues for a middle way that makes room for a multiplicity of voices rather than a hegemony of one or a few: "We benefit, intellectually and personally, from the interplay between different selves, from the balance between long-term contemplation and short-term impulse. We should be wary about tipping the scales too far. The community of selves shouldn't be a democracy, but it shouldn't be a dictatorship either."[65]

CHALLENGES FROM POSTMODERNISM

This view coincides with a final source of challenge to Freud's topographical model, which is being advanced on the philosophical front by postmodernism. Postmodernist thinkers have, from a slightly different vantage point, also called into question the whole notion of a unitary self. Some have drawn analogies between the mind and cyberspace, which has been described by Graham Ward as "an undefined spatiality, like the contours of a perfume."[66]

In a different, more embodied postmodern vision, drawing more from the feminist writers Luce Irigaray and Hélène Cixous and from contemporary psychoanalysis, Jane Flax presents a critique of modernist conceptions of a unitary self as potentially repressive of subjugated inner voices. Flax has written:

> I believe a unitary self is unnecessary, impossible, and a dangerous illusion. Only multiple subjects can invent ways to struggle against domination that will not merely recreate it. In the process of therapy, in relations with others, and in political life we encounter many difficulties when subjectivity becomes subject to one normative standard, solidifies into rigid structures, or lacks the capacity to flow readily between different aspects of itself . . . No singular form can be sufficient as a regulative ideal or as a prescription for human maturity or the essential human capacity . . . [I]t is possible to imagine subjectivities whose desires for multiplicity can impel them toward emancipatory action. These subjectivities would be fluid rather than solid, contextual rather than universal, and

65. Bloom, "First Person Plural," 98. On the relationship of daydreaming, imaginary worlds, and multiple selves, see also Bloom, *How Pleasure Works*, esp. 197–202.

66. Ward, *The Postmodern God*, xv.

process oriented rather than topographical. Emancipatory theories and practices require mechanics of fluids [a quote from Luce Irigaray] in which subjectivity is conceived as processes rather than as a fixed atemporal entity locatable in a homogeneous, abstract time and space [Flax's reading of the Cartesian idea of the self]. In discourses about subjectivity the term 'the self' will be superseded by discussions of 'subjects.' The term 'subject(s)' more adequately expresses the simultaneously determined, multiple, and agentic qualities of subjectivity.[67]

While Flax is not addressing states of consciousness per se, her work as a psychoanalyst includes a deep respect for mental contents that exist both in and out of awareness. What I find in Flax's conception of a multiple, fluid, contextual conception of self and subjectivity is the possibility for greater passage between conscious and unconscious domains, and a sense of mental contents shifting in and out of awareness as contexts and subjective states shift and change. The "return of the repressed"[68] gives way to a more variable process in which we move in and out of multiple areas of our own knowing and unknowing. "Knowing" itself may be understood as more than cognitive appreciation alone, or even cognitive and affective experience together, which is usually possible to verbalize, but also as nonverbal mental contents that are only symbolic, or even presymbolic, the knowledge of the body and physical sensation—in Christopher Bollas's words as "the unthought known."[69]

As unsettling as we may find a more multiple, fluid, and spatially conceived model of mind, advances both in psychoanalytic clinical theory grounded in listening to patients' inner experiences, and in neurobiology, especially research into the sequelae of traumatic experience, suggest that the postmodern view may be a more generous and apt description of the true complexity and multiplicity of mental life. In fact, given the complex, pluralistic nature of our postmodern world and society, mental health may depend as much on the capacity for "identity complexity"[70] and the ability to entertain multiple meanings as it

67. Flax, "Multiples," 93.

68. A term used by Freud throughout his life from 1896 "Further Remarks on the Neuro-Psychoses of Defense," 169, to the his last publication in 1939, *Moses and Monotheism*, 124.

69. Bollas, *The Shadow of the Object*.

70. Cf., Saari, "Identity Complexity as an Indicator of Mental Health."

does on unity, integration, and a capacity to synthesize. Postmodernist writers further highlight the emancipatory implications of such theories of mind, especially as they influence the social construction of self and others, and the resulting social construction of categories such as gender, race and class, and the distribution of power.[71]

IMPLICATIONS FOR PASTORAL THEOLOGY

What are the implications for my discipline of pastoral theology of this very new shift away from a depth-oriented repression model toward these newer, more spatially dispersed models emphasizing dissociation and multiplicity?

As we have seen, the topographical model privileged the unconscious, and the early generations of psychoanalysts and their enthusiasts, including the Emmanuel movement and early pastoral psychologists,[72] understood themselves as heroes, often misunderstood and even persecuted by the uncomprehending masses, but pioneers into uncharted territories where deeper truths would be unearthed to cathartic effect. This romantic ideal lives on, even at the turn of a new millennium. Who among us has not at one time or another thrilled to the notion that deep somewhere resident in our own psyche are regions of which we know little, even nothing, and that we contain within ourselves deep wells of unknowability that a knowledgeable guide could help us to plumb?

I am not disputing the phenomenological evidence that people, especially when engaged in an experience of introspection, and perhaps especially in the ritualized context of psychoanalysis, realize that there are domains of knowledge and desire that have been inaccessible to everyday states of consciousness. I am not even disputing that the mechanism Freud identified as repression, in an increasingly rich and complex theoretical formulation, has a place in our understanding— as *one* possible way in which mental contents come to be removed from awareness. What the accumulation of new research and theory suggests, however, is that everyday consciousness itself is more complex and multiple than our nineteenth-century-informed models of mind have suggested to us, and that domains hitherto referred to as

71. For further elaboration of the relationship between postmodernism and justice, including an appropriation of Winnicott's *Playing and Reality*, see Flax, "The Play of Justice."

72. Holifield, *A History of Pastoral Care in America*.

preconscious and unconscious may not be *deeper* in the psyche, but simply *other*—states that become accessible under different conditions than everyday activity.

I am further suggesting that this is less comfortable to us than the notion of plumbing a single, vertically drilled well deeper and deeper into the territory labeled "the unconscious." As disquieting as that notion is, do we not find it more manageable in some sense than the idea that the mind is more disparate than we had even thought, and that our late Victorian maps do not begin to show all the "infernal regions" that might exist? In Kuhnian terms,[73] the psychoanalytic model worked because it was a paradigm: it produced evidence and answers based on what was phenomenologically observable when asking the questions that could be conceived within its own worldview. The topographical model gave us at least the illusion of a certain element of control over the unknown: the "infernal regions" could be scary, but they constituted an increasingly recognizable region with categorizeable contents based on the cartography of Freud and his followers. This may feel preferable to us as compared with the idea of our minds as an "undefined spatiality, like the contours of a perfume." And yet, contemporary researchers and clinicians are challenging us to entertain the possibility that our minds, and indeed our selves, are more like highly complex, networked systems, not discrete entities, more like the "clouds" of chaos theory than the "clocks" of Newtonian physics.[74] What might this do to our theology, our theological anthropology, and our work as pastoral theologians and caregivers?

It seems to me that as we embrace a model of greater complexity and multiplicity of the human mind, this will lead us to a more complex and nuanced appreciation for the diversity and mutability of human persons, and a similarly more variegated, nonlimited, and nonlimiting *imago Dei*. In contemporary Trinitarian theology, process theology, and feminist theology, we find resources that support a theology of complexity, diversity, and mutability. Elizabeth Johnson has described how the very image of the Trinity is one that challenges unitary, totalizing images of God.[75] Johnson presents us with a

73. Kuhn, *The Structure of Scientific Revolutions*.

74. Polkinghorne, Trinity Institute Lectures 1997: *Quarks, Chaos and Christianity*.

75. As Johnson herself exhaustively catalogs (*She Who Is*, 210), there are numerous twentieth-century articulations of Trinitarian theology, many of which could be considered relational. E.g., Moltmann's influential idea of the Trinity as "divine society" (*The*

Trinitarian image of God as fluid, multiple, and profoundly relational: "At its most basic the symbol of the Trinity evokes a livingness in God, a dynamic coming and going with the world that points to an inner divine circling around in unimaginable relation. God's relatedness to the world in creating, redeeming, and renewing activity suggests to the Christian mind that God's own being is somehow similarly differentiated. Not an isolated, static, ruling monarch but a relational, dynamic, tripersonal mystery of love—who would not opt for the latter?"[76] In her vast mining of the Catholic theological tradition, Johnson finds support for this idea in numerous sources, including Aquinas: "relation really existing in God is really the same as His essence, and only differs in intelligibility. In God relation and essence do not differ from each other but are one in the same."[77] She quotes feminist theologian Catherine LaCugna: "To be God is to-be-relationally."[78] Johnson continues with the Johannine statement:

> Being related is at the very heart of divine being. God's being is not an enclosed, egocentric self-regard but is identical with an act of free communion, always going forth and receiving in. At the deepest core of reality is a mystery of personal connectedness that constitutes the very livingness of God. The category of relation thus serves as a heuristic tool for bringing to light not just the mutuality of trinitarian persons but the very nature of the holy mystery of God herself. Divine unity exists as an intrinsic *koinonia* of love, love freely blazing forth, love not just as a divine attitude, affect, or property but as God's very nature: 'God is Love' (1 Jn 4:16).[79]

In another Trinitarian approach, John Milbank argues for a "postmodern Christianity" that values diversity as a central organizing principle. For Milbank, the Trinity is a sign of God as community, "even a 'community in process,' infinitely realized, beyond any conceivable opposition between 'perfect act' and 'perfect potential.'"[80] He writes:

Trinity and the Kingdom); Boff's statement: "In the beginning is communion" (*Trinity and Society*, 9). See also Macquarrie's rendering of the Trinity as primordial source, expressive dynamism and unitive Being in Love, in *Principles of Christian Theology,* 190–210; McFague's feminist trinity of mother-lover-friend, *Models of God*, 35.

76. Johnson, *She Who Is*, 192.

77. Ibid. 227–28.

78. Ibid. 228.

79. Ibid.

80. Milbank, "Postmodern Critical Augustinianism," 274.

> Christianity can become 'internally' postmodern . . . I mean by
> this that it is possible to construe Christianity as suspicious of
> notions of fixed 'essences' in its approach to human beings,
> to nature, to community and to God, even if it has never fully
> escaped the grasp of a 'totalizing' metaphysics. Through its be-
> lief in creation from nothing it admits temporality, the priority
> of becoming and unexpected emergence. A reality suspended
> between nothing and infinity is a reality of flux, a reality with-
> out substance, composed only of relational differences and
> ceaseless alterations (Augustine, *De Musica*). Like nihilism,
> Christianity can, should, embrace the differential flux. [81]

Milbank finds the expression of this Christianity not in creedal statements about God but in Christian practices of community.[82] Christian
community embodies a commitment to difference, but unlike nihil-
ism, envisions the possibility of difference with harmony—borrowing
from Augustine, a *concentus musicus*.[83] This idea echoes political and
liberation theologians' formulations of the social trinity, such as Jürgen
Moltmann's and Leonardo Boff's.[84] In Milbank's attempt to work within a postmodern framework, a subtle shift has occurred, however, in
which the implicit ethic is not justice based on equality[85] as much as a
nonviolence based on valuing differences.

The detailed arguments of Milbank's postmodern theology (including some internal contradictions, imported from postmodernist
philosophy[86]) cannot be adequately explored here. It is interesting,
though, in light of the focus here on consciousness and unconscious-

81. Ibid,. 267.

82. See also Graham, *Transforming Practice*.

83. Ibid., 268–69. This idea echoes Moltmann's "social doctrine of the trinity,"
e.g., Moltmann, *The Trinity and the Kingdom*. In Milbank's attempt to work within a
postmodern framework, a subtle shift has occurred, in which the implicit ethic is not
justice based on equality (cf., Irigaray's critique:"Equal to Whom?") as much as a nonviolence based on valuing differences. For a further discussion of Irigaray's critique
of equality, see also Jones,"This God Who Is Not One"; Jantzen,"Luce Iragaray."

84. Moltmann, *The Trinity and the Kingdom*; Boff, *Trinity and Society*, esp. 118–19; see
also Boff, *Holy Trinity, Perfect Community*.

85. Cf., Irigaray's feminist critique:"Equal to Whom?"

86. Milbank's theology imports one of the central problems of postmodernist philosophy—that of ethical criteria. In his own words, "postmodernism claims to refuse
dialectic, but this is the instance of its failure to do so; it is right to make the effort"
("Postmodern Critical Augustinianism," 270–71). Like many postmodern writers,
Milbank links violence with exclusion of the other but does not resolve the real social
and political problems resulting from the inclusion even of oppressors (e.g., ibid., 273).

ness, the known and the unknown (*das Unbewusste*), that another of Milbank's propositions is that desire (which for Milbank is the expression of the third person of the Trinity) and not "Greek knowledge" is the mediator of reality.[87] Desire for the other reaches across the gaps, across the "potential space,"[88] to create an intersubjective arena of creation. If we accept the concept of the relational dimension of consciousness and its construction, our theology can be similarly understood as a mutual, co-constructive, co-generative yearning between humans and the divine.[89] Luce Irigaray's postmodern creation statement is, "On the first day, the first days, the gods, God, make a world by separating the elements."[90] Irigaray emphasizes the act of creation as doubling and difference rather than unity, which can all too easily translate into totalitarian oppression, the subsuming of all otherness into the One. What binds and heals in a relational model is not a vision of ultimate oneness, as in homogenization, but mutual desire and love that bridges toward the other, embracing difference.

Christianity is at heart a praxis of diversity in love, not what Milbank calls a "gnosis, in the sense of a formulaic wisdom that we must just recite or magically invoke."[91] A relational theology both models and makes room for difference, for a multiplicity of ways of knowing, and a flux between sensation, hunger, emotion, and rational thought. It is a theology that is not set abstractly apart from bodies, but locates itself in and between them.

Such a view also works well with the idea from process theology that God is not monolithic or static but fluid, changing, and in process. "God is a verb,"[92] to quote the feminist theologian Virginia Ramey Mollenkott. Process theology offers us a vision of a God who does not interfere with the gift of human free will, but who is always present to transform suffering once again into healing, and each twist and turn of life into a new possibility, a new beginning.[93] Bernard Loomer speaks

---

87. Ibid., 275.

88. Winnicott, "Transitional Objects and Transitional Phenomena."

89. Cf., ibid., 274–75.

90. Irigaray, *An Ethics of Sexual Difference*, 7; also cited in Ward, *The Postmodern God*, xxvi.

91. Milbank, "Postmodern Critical Augustinianism," 274.

92. Mollenkott, *Godding*.

93. See, for example, Suchocki, *God, Christ, Church*; Cobb, *Christ in a Pluralistic Age*.

of the "size of God," large enough to contain everything in the universe, even our suffering.[94] This view is one that respects and honors the depth of suffering without trivializing or sugarcoating it, but also offers hope for transformation as always and eternally available, small resurrections possible every day.

A final caution regarding theology: a theology of multiplicity, like any theology, could under certain circumstances waft again into the realm of abstraction and disconnection from the body. In some postmodern constructions, cyberspace has been posited as a metaphor for not only the human mind but for the divine. Graham Ward writes of cyberspace:

> In this land of fantasy and ceaseless journeying, this experience of tasting, sampling and passing, truth, knowledge, and facts are all only dots of light on a screen, evanescent, consumable. This is the ultimate in the secularization of the divine, for here is a God who sees and knows all things, existing in pure activity and realized presence, in perpetuity. Divinization as the dissolution of subjectivity within the immanent, amniotic satisfaction, is the final goal and object of postmodernity. Cyberspace is the realization of a metaphor used repeatedly by [Jacques] Derrida, [Luce] Irigaray, and [Julia] Kristeva—the Khora, the plenitudinous womb, dark, motile, and unformed, from which all things issue.[95]

What is problematic in this view, however, and why for me the analogy between cyberspace and the womb is incorrect, is precisely that cyberspace is so *dis*embodied. The *Khora* signifies a profound origination in relation that cyberspace, for all its rapid-fire electronic connectivity, lacks. "Surfing the Web" can be as much an experience of profound isolation and alienation as one of connection. In the anonymous dis-

---

I am using process theology selectively here. Certain themes in process theology, especially a tendency toward binary formulations, are not so useful in constructing a theological model of multiplicity—e.g., Whitehead's polarities of conceptual and physical, and God's "primordial nature" and "consequent nature" (part 5 *in Process and Reality*, diagrammed by Suchocki as a *yin-yang*, [113]). See also Cobb's discussion of "binity" in Cobb, "Relativization of the Trinity." Such language in process theology as God's "feeling of the world" (Cobb, "Relativization") also—perhaps—ascribes an unnecessarily monistic and conscious subjectivity to God. Whitehead's category of subjective unity of "actual entities," including God (*Process and Reality*, part 3), does not encourage a normative model of multiplicity.

94. Loomer, "Two Conceptions of Power"; and Loomer, *The Size of God*.

95. Ward, *The Postmodern God*, xvi.

course of cyberspace, identity is not only fluid but disconnected from bodies and from any ongoing commitment or responsibility either for oneself or for others. It is also, as Ward himself notes, a realm that purports to offer universal access, but in fact is heavily tied to capitalist venture, and therefore available only to those with the financial resources to pay for the privilege of "surfing."

The image of the *Khora* does, however, speak to something beyond sheer complexity and motility. God is in the body, not disembodied. Numerous feminist theologians have challenged the Cartesian mind-body dualism as perpetuating the subjugation of women's experience and glorifying disconnected rationality at the expense of the lived experiences of childbirth, sexuality, dying, suffering, and surviving.[96] Womanist theology in particular celebrates the power of sheer survival as a source of power and knowledge to inform and sustain faith.[97] God is experienced both in the community of solidarity and within the self, as in Ntozake Shange's often-quoted line of poetry: "I found God in myself and I loved her / I loved her fiercely."[98] God is understood in the Black Church tradition as immanent, a source of strength in the face of concrete racial and economic oppression, the God "who makes a way out of no way."[99] This is a profoundly incarnational theology, in which God/Jesus/Spirit is recognized and celebrated as present and in motion in the world, in the dailiness of life, and in the body.[100]

The *imago Dei* we embrace inevitably influences our theological anthropology. Faith in an incarnational God conceived as fluid, multiple, in motion, and in perpetual relation both with us and within us, emancipates us from constraining, static, monolithic notions of both God and human beings. A multiple, relational theology, it seems to me, is hospitable to an embodied conception of mind and self that

96. E.g., Moltmann-Wendel, *I Am My Body*.

97. E.g., Williams, *Sisters in the Wilderness*; Townes, *Embracing the Spirit*.

98. Shange, *for colored girls who have considered suicide*, 63.

99. Cone, *A Black Theology of Liberation*, xix, claims experience alongside revelation as a critical source for doing theology. This claim is also made by Womanist theologians (e.g., Williams, *Sisters in the Wilderness*, 6; Baker-Fletcher, "The Strength of My Life" in Townes, *Embracing the Spirit*, 125). See also, from a Latina/mujerista perspective, Isasi-Díaz, *Mujerista*. Isasi-Díaz emphasizes "*lo cotidiano*" (the daily) as a source of theological wisdom and resistance to oppression.

100. Cone, ibid., claimed experience as an equal source for theology alongside revelation.

gives room enough for the human person to encompass a wide capacity for relationality, both with other people and with and among the *inner* selves that inhabit the time and spatial dimensions of one's own lived life. The rigid hierarchy of "higher powers" and "infernal regions" collapses, as we recognize that all of us contain spheres of both rationality and irrationality, knowability and unknowability, of abstract thought, emotion, and animal sense, both within ourselves and in our relations with one another—and even with the divine. Furthermore, these are not fixed positions, but are in continual flux as we move in and out of different internal and external states of pressure, desire, conflict, and union.

IMPLICATIONS FOR PASTORAL PRAXIS

In conclusion, what are the implications for pastoral praxis? Especially for those of us who are practitioners of pastoral care and psychotherapy, the archetype of the heroic explorer of "dark continents," while seductive, must be modified, especially in light of postcolonial theory and the recognition of how imperialism is implicated in "traditional" or "classical" Western thought and practice.[101] This is not to say that as helping professionals we can jettison all authority or erase the boundaries that create a safe holding environment for those who come to us for help. Drawing again from the relational school of psychoanalysis, it is possible, however, to move from a more hierarchical model of the therapist as knowing explorer (active) and the patient as continent (acted upon) toward a model that acknowledges an asymmetry of roles and responsibilities but at the same time honors that meanings are continually being co-constructed and reconstructed in the intersubjective space of the therapeutic relationship.[102]

New capacities are required of us in this emerging paradigm. First, *complexity*. Simplistic answers and once-for-all interpretations will not satisfy. They will tend again toward fixity, absolutism, and totalitarian force—even if only ideological. This will change the quality

---

101. For a good discussion of postcolonial theory in relation to pastoral theology, see Lartey, *In Living Colour*.

102. For more discussion of professional ethics in the relational paradigm, see Cooper-White, *Shared Wisdom*, 58–60; term from relational psychoanalysts, e.g., Aron, *A Meeting of Minds*, 87, 96–100; Hoffman, "Discussion: Toward a Social-Constructivist View," 92.

of our listening. Rather than listening only or primarily for unifying themes and overarching patterns, we will listen with greater attention for complexity and multiplicity.

Bromberg suggests a shift in the focus of our attention, involving a "dialogue between discontinuous domains of self-meaning held by a multiplicity of states of consciousness, some of which can be told and some only enacted . . . ['G]etting into a mood' represents a shift to a state of consciousness with its own internal integrity, its own reality, and sometimes its own 'truth.'"[103] He writes:

> A case could be made, for example, that the reason a state such as depression is difficult to alleviate even with medication is that it is not simply an 'affective disorder' but an internally coherent aspect of the self . . . with its own narrative, its own memory configuration, its own perceptual reality, and its own style of relatedness to others . . . So the 'curing' of depression must be a process that does not become an effort to cure the patient of 'who he is'. . . [but] a dialectic with a multiplicity of different self-narratives, perceptual realities, and adaptational meanings to the patient, each of which speaks with its own voice.[104]

This also suggests a shift in listening from content to process, especially shifts in states of self and the quality of relatedness between subjects, between the multiple "I's" and the "Thou's" that may be present to any given moment.

This calls for a second capacity, a *revaluing of subjectivity*: We are challenged to give recognition to more varied kinds of knowledge than just the positivist and argumentative versions of "truth" we were all taught to render from our modernist grammar-school curricula onward. In the words of Mary Belenky and her colleagues, we are called to "passionate knowing."[105] In their book *Women's Ways of Knowing*, these researchers describe "passionate knowers" as those who "seek to stretch the outer boundaries of their consciousness—by making the unconscious conscious, by consulting and listening to the self, by voicing the unsaid, by listening to others and staying alert to all the currents and undercurrents of life about them, by imagining themselves

103. Bromberg, "'Speak! That I May See You,'" 533.
104. Ibid., 522–23.
105. Belenky et al., *Women's Ways of Knowing*, 141ff.

inside the new poem or person or idea that they want to come to know and understand . . . [,] knowers who enter into a union with that which is to be known." Like their example, the geneticist Barbara McClintock, we are challenged not to look at the subjects of our investigation from the outside, but to get inside them as much as is humanly possible, to know one another and perhaps even God through experience and empathy, not just objective observation. The word *I* thus comes back into serious, even scholarly discourse.

This subjectivity, this passionate knowing, will lead us naturally, I believe, to a third necessary quality or qualities: *empathy and mutuality.* A relational image of God works together with a relational human- ity. Such a theology holds empathy and mutuality at the heart of an ethical stance toward one another. If reality is no longer imposed, but co-constructed in relationship, then relations among people require a higher level of intentional listening and intentional speaking. The "ideal speech situation," to use Habermas's language,[106] will be one of *inter*-subjectivity. I find resonance for this idea in the Judeo-Christian tenet of reciprocity of love of self and neighbor, the New Testament language of *agape* love, and the Catholic tradition's *caritas.* We can per- haps find an intersubjective interpretation in the narratives of Jesus's life. For example, Jesus allowed himself to be changed by his encoun- ters—as in the story of the Canaanite woman who dared to enter into a midrash-like debate with him on behalf of her sick daughter, and won his admiration: "Great is your faith! Let it be done for you as you wish" (Matt 15:21–28; Mark 7:24–30). Peter is able to walk on the water toward Jesus, upheld by his faith while held in a mutual gaze, but when he is distracted by his fear of the wind, the intersubjective moment is eclipsed, and Peter begins to sink. He is saved from drowning by Jesus's reaching out and restoring their relational connection (Matt 14:22–32).

A commitment to mutual engagement and intersubjectivity leads to a fourth capacity: *patience.* A recognition that the sacred and all life is a process, and a faith that God is in process with humanity (i.e., not just acting *upon* human beings from above), demands the capacity to allow time for changes to unfold. Nor can human beings simply act upon others. In this sense, even the most activist behaviors may participate in wrong if the activists seek to undo what they perceive as the wrongs of others with totalitarian moves themselves. Balance is

106. Habermas, *Legitimation Crisis* Also cited in ibid., 145.

required, and therefore patience is important, because time is needed for discernment and for process. When balance fails, patience will help in those times as well to be of good courage, to seek one other's forgiveness, to begin again, and to take the long view.

The last capacity I will mention, inspired by a postmodern, relational paradigm, is *commitment to emancipatory listening,* a form justice making based on respect for difference. Flax's formulation of a non-unitary self in the context of an emancipatory intersubjectivity leads to ethics, understood as the deconstruction of dominant discourses—even within the self, but certainly between and among selves, none of whom are conceived as static or monolithic. Selves are gendered, embodied, and embedded in contexts of culture, race, and class. Difference will emerge from the gaps and the margins. If God's own being is to be understood as multiple, fluid, relational, and in process, encompassing difference, then we will be attentive to finding God's own self/selves also in the gaps and on the margins.

This will involve silence as well as speech. We will need—often—to still our own voices (including the internalized voices of our own socialization and enculturation) in order to seek and discern beyond the tacitly accepted "knowns" and "truths" of any particular time and place, to what voices and realities may be excluded or not yet recognized. Our practice of silence will not be one of "neutrality" but of profound respect for the complexity that might emerge from the not-yet-known-or-knowable. In such a model, a fluid, multiple, dynamic God will be found in the interstices, the "transitional spaces" of domestic, social, political, and institutional life, and sometimes in the least expected places, even within the many continents and "infernal regions" of our own selves.

FOUR

Interrogating Integration, Dissenting Dis-integration

Multiplicity as a Positive Metaphor in Therapy and Theology

"INTEGRATION" AS HEGEMONIC DISCOURSE

The term *integration* has long been used as a metaphor for psychological health, healing, and wholeness, and as a goal for psychotherapy. It is usually posited in opposition to a variety of related conceptions of pathology, such as *disintegration*, *fragmentation*, and *splitting*—all the "schiz's." Paradigms for health from a variety of psychological schools value metaphors of oneness as posited against division, dividedness, or fragmentation. Popular conceptions of mental health such as "having it all together" are counterposed against "having a nervous breakdown" or "going to pieces." In self psychology, the metaphor of the "cohesive self" counters fragmentation and lack of psychic structure.[1] Developmental models value individuation as maturity, in contrast to forms of dependence, merger, or lack of autonomy, and Erikson's

1. Kohut, *The Analysis of the Self*.

100

"ego integrity" is posited again despair as the last crisis of the mature adult who faces mortality.[2] Rogerian therapists affirm "congruence." Ego psychology values "ego strength" against the various forms of removing mental contents from awareness, ranging from neurotic repression and the defense mechanism of denial, to pathological dissociation.[3] Jung's archetype of Wholeness is a universal metaphor for all as one, echoing imagery from world religions and mysticism.[4] Klein's emphasis on unconscious splitting as the source of psychopathology is a vivid metaphor for pathology as dis-integration.[5]

Christian theology has similarly valued oneness in the form of salvation as unification with God—"at-one-ment," and especially in depicting sin as alienation, separation from God, going astray, or missing the (one) mark (*hamartia*).

Thus the language of integration has functioned both as a central metaphor of mental health and as a goal of therapy in a variety of theoretical and practice orientations, and therefore, I would argue, has operated as a "paradigm" in the Kuhnian sense[6]—a social-scientific worldview that has shaped approaches to healing and influenced if not circumscribed the questions that can be asked within it. In other words, the paradigm of integration has become in some sense a form of hegemonic discourse.

INTEGRATION AND ITS DISCONTENTS

In contrast, contemporary psychologies have begun to contest the hegemony of the "One," leading to a number of paradigms of health that do not privilege integration as the primary model. For example, feminist developmental theorists have critiqued the privileging of individuation, placing emphasis on the capacity for interdependence and relationality.[7]

2. Erikson, *Childhood and Society*; and Erikson, *Identity and the Life Cycle*.

3. The concept of "ego strength" is emphasized in Ego Psychology, the psychoanalytic school of thought stemming from Anna Freud, e.g., Hartmann, *Ego Psychology and the Problem of Adaptation*.

4. E.g., Jung, *Answer to Job*, 469.

5. Klein, "Notes on Some Schizoid Mechanisms."

6. Kuhn, *The Structure of Scientific Revolutions*.

7. E.g., Gilligan, *In a Different Voice*; Belenky et al., *Women's Ways of Knowing*; writers affiliated with the Jean Baker Miller Center (formerly the Stone Center), founded

Feminist postmodern theorists (particularly Jane Flax), heavily influenced by Lacanian psychoanalysis, value multiplicity over models of a unitive self, asserting multiple subjectivities ("emancipatory subjects") as a form of political resistance.[8] (I will return to Flax later in this chapter.) This postmodern view is not unlike Homi Bhabha's postcolonial formulation of hybridity in relations between subjects.[9] Relational psychoanalysts, as described in the previous chapter, have drawn an important clinical distinction *between multiplicity and fragmentation,* and maintain the importance of multiplicity as a paradigm of self-knowledge and fluid agency.[10]

Moreover, the seeds of a positive view of multiplicity already are to be found in earlier psychoanalytic models as well. Jungian "Wholeness" is better understood not as a symbol of unification but as a dialectic that maintains the tension of opposites, as they are brought into consciousness from the Self and the collective unconscious. The theory of archetypes may even be better understood, as Don Browning and Terry Cooper have written, as a model of "instinctual pluralism"—"a veritable choir of instinctual voices all trying to sing their special songs, although not always at the same time."[11] Freud's positing of the "institutions" of ego, id, and superego already represents a view of multiple subjectivities inherent in the human personality, and the construction of conscious and unconscious domains of psychological functioning.

Object-relations theories, deriving from Klein, take this even further, with models of mind such as Fairbairn's encompassing multiple internal representations or "objects" that have their own dynamic life within the psyche as well as in relation to other persons in the external world. Bion's and others' formulations of multiple self states further elaborate this model of mind as mutable, fluid, and dynamically constituted.

---

by Jean Baker Miller, e.g., Miller, *Toward a New Psychology of Women*; Judith Jordan, *Women's Growth in Diversity*. For a detailed bibliography, see http://www.jbmti.org/content/view/1754/328/.

8. Flax, "Multiples," 93.

9. Bhabha, *The Location of Culture*; See also Brickman, *Aboriginal Populations in the Mind*.

10. The development of relational theory can be traced through the journal *Psychoanalytic Dialogues* beginning with volume 1 in 1991, and in Mitchell and Aron, *Relational Psychoanalysis*, ixff.; for further sources, see chapter 1n5, below.

11. Browning and Cooper, *Religious Thought and the Modern Psychologies*, 152.

A central argument of this volume of collected essays, then, is for the *valuing of multiplicity in psychotherapy,* as both a way of *conceptualizing health* and a *goal of treatment*—if not entirely as a replacement for the model of integration, then at least as an important counterpoint to it.[12] Multiplicity is the conceptual through-line or red thread that weaves through the work I have been doing most recently. I am interested in an anthropology, both psychological and theological, that explores the multiplicity of persons—not only in terms of pluralism and diversity of human beings in our relations with one another, but multiplicity as *internally* constitutive of each individual mind/self/subject, at both conscious and unconscious levels.

An appreciation for this multiplicity informs a corresponding pastoral psychotherapeutic praxis, as a method of working with all the varied, contradictory and creative parts of each patient in his or her many self states, identifications, and subjective moments. This model of psychotherapy differs a good deal from a traditional therapeutic model that holds *integration* as a goal. *Integration* as a term may be all too easily (mis?)understood as a kind of process of homogenization in which the unconscious is brought into consciousness somewhat as the contents in the bottom of a blender are brought up and whirled together into a pudding with those on the surface.

Note the verticality of this "blender" image, which corresponds to a classical psychoanalytic paradigm (Freud's "topographical model"[13]) of consciousness and unconsciousness, in which the unconscious is "deeper," pressed down and out of sight, beneath the repression barrier. As described in chapter 3, relational psychoanalysis has turned away from an exclusively vertical conception of consciousness and unconscious, in favor of a more spatially dispersed model of the mind, where conscious and unconscious coexist more fluidly, on multiple planes or axes. The therapeutic process of tapping unconscious material in such a model involves not only a cathartic release (upward) of repressed (pressed-down) mental contents, but exploration and increasing awareness of *all* feelings, thoughts, fantasies and sensations

12. For a lengthy discussion of this theme, and clinical application, see Cooper-White, *Many Voices.*

13. Freud, *The Interpretation of Dreams,* 541ff. For a graphic representation, see figure 3.1, above.

that have been dissociated, disavowed, projected, and split-off, in a potentially infinite number of inner and outer directions.

A MULTIPLE ANTHROPOLOGY

> *"What are human beings, that you are mindful of them, mortals that you care for them? Yet you have made them a little lower than God/the gods, and crowned them with glory and honor."*
>
> —Psalm 8:4–5

All theology, but especially pastoral theology, begins with human beings, and in particular, the pain and brokenness of the human condition (and indeed all creation). Pastoral theology takes suffering as its starting place.[14] This tradition runs deep in pastoral theology. It has significant 20th century precedent in the writings of Anton Boisen, a pioneering hospital chaplain and founder of Clinical Pastoral Education (CPE). Boisen's seminal text, *Exploration of the Inner World*, was informed by his own treatments for psychosis from the late 1890s through the early1920s. As a patient, Boisen recognized firsthand the importance of being treated as a whole person rather than as a textbook diagnosis. From this experience he wrote about the importance of pastoral caregivers attending not just to their theories and textbooks, but to"the living human document."[15] This concept was further expanded in a relational, feminist mode by Bonnie Miller-McLemore, as a"living human web,"[16] recognizing the basic human interconnectedness of caregivers and care recipients.

In my book *Many Voices* I develop a framework for a pastoral theological anthropology in which I describe human beings as created good, yet vulnerable (fragile; easily wounded, confused, and tempted by the complexity of the world; and susceptible to straying away from our own highest good); embodied; both alike and unique—including individually and culturally (as Lartey has highlighted: "like all others,

14. It is also part of a larger trend of correlational theology, attributed to Paul Tillich, *Systematic Theology* 1 (*Reason and Revelation*) introduction; and Tillich, *Systematic Theology* 3 (*Life in the Spirit*); further critiqued and developed in Tracy, *Blessed Rage for Order*; and Taylor, *Remembering Esperanza*.

15. Boisen, *The Exploration of the Inner World*. For more information on Boisen, see Holifield,"Anton Boisen"; and Asquith, *Vision from a Little Known Country*.

16. Miller-McLemore,"The Living Human Web."

like some others, and like no others"[17]); intrinsically relational (connected with all creation and with one another, knit into the entire fabric of creation, and interwoven in this unfathomably deep and wide "living human web"); multiple, not unitary; mutable, fluid, and in process; and finally both loved by the divine, and therefore also loving: as creatures made in the image of God, human beings are endowed with the capacity for love. In particular, a more multiple conception of the human person may open new horizons for empathic relating, both with the intricacy of one's own inner life and with others in the world beyond oneself (a theme that will be elaborated in chapter 7). But first, what are the arguments for this theological anthropology of multiplicity?

Human Beings Are Multiple[18]

One of my favorite quotations on multiplicity comes from the philosophers Gilles Deleuze and Felix Guattari: "The two of us wrote [the book] *Anti-Oedipus* together. Since each of us was several, there was already quite a crowd."[19] Contemporary relational-psychoanalytic theory, with its operating concepts of relationality, mutuality, and intersubjectivity has brought a strong critique of the classical Freudian model of mind based on a paradigm of inner conflict and repression. As discussed in the previous chapter, Freud's model of consciousness and unconsciousness has been conceived of vertically, following the "topographical model,"[20] in which *conscious, preconscious,* and *unconscious* reside in successive layers from top to bottom, with *repression* as the central mechanism for removing mental contents from consciousness. While this model represented a powerful metaphor for depicting the forceful influence and seeming independence of unconscious mental processes, its hegemony is now increasingly being challenged within psychoanalytic schools of thought. The challenges are arising from a number of separate theoretical and clinical spheres, generating ideas just now increasingly converging toward a new, more multiple, dispersed, and spatially (horizontally or three or even four! dimensionally) conceived

17. Lartey, *In Living Colour*, 34, citing anthropologists Kluckholn and Murray, *Personality in Nature, Society and Culture.*

18. This section is drawn from a more detailed version in Cooper-White, *Many Voices*, 51–61.

19. Deleuze and Guattari, *A Thousand Plateaus*, 3.

20. Freud, *The Interpretation of Dreams*, 541ff.

model of mind. Contemporary psychoanalytic theory is increasingly replacing Freud's vertical "depth" model of consciousness/unconsciousness with an even more sweeping reconception of the mind as a multiplicity of mental states—a "normal nonlinearity of the human mind,"[21] conceived as more spatially or horizontally dispersed and at varying levels of conscious awareness.[22] In relational-psychoanalytic theory, the traditional psychoanalytic focus on repression as a by-product of conflict has been replaced or at least set alongside an interest in *dissociation* as a nonpathological phenomenon.

Dissociation is no longer regarded in this model solely as a pathological outcome of trauma, or an irremediable state of alienation from one's self, as in Lacan's concept of the illusion of a unified self as seen in the mirror defending against the infantile experience of being a body-in-pieces (*corps-morcelé*), "sunk in motor incapacity, turbulent movements, and fragmentation."[23] As Philip Bromberg, another relational thinker, has observed, "The process of dissociation is basic to human mental functioning and is central to the stability and growth of personality. It is intrinsically an adaptational talent that represents the very nature of what we call 'consciousness.' . . . [T]he psyche does not start as an integrated whole, but is nonunitary in origin—a mental structure that begins and continues as a multiplicity of self-states that maturationally attain a feeling of coherence which overrides the awareness of discontinuity. This leads to the experience of a cohesive sense of personal identity and the necessary illusion of being 'one self.'"[24]

A way of explaining this more concretely might be that at any given moment, each of us experiences ourselves in one particular "self state," or state of consciousness that is laden with thoughts, memories, physical sensations, emotions, and fantasies. Our subjectivity is not monolithic. In this sense, none of us at any given point in time is a unitive "Self" or "Being." This accords better with non-Western conceptions of the self, which tend to understand selfhood and identity more in terms of one's belonging in community and not as an isolated

21. Bromberg, "'Speak! That I May See You,'" 529. See also Mitchell, "Multiple Selves, Singular Self."

22. From a self psychological background, see also Stolorow and Atwood, *Contexts of Being*.

23. Lacan, *Écrits: A Selection*, 3–7.

24. Bromberg, "Speak! That I May See You!'" 521. A longer quotation appears in chapter 3, above.

individual defined by his or her own consciousness or will.[25] In fact, as Clifford Geertz wrote, "The Western conception of the person as a bounded, unique, more or less integrated motivational and cognitive universe, a dynamic center of awareness, emotion, judgment, and action organized into a distinctive whole and set contrastively both against other such wholes and against its social and natural background, is, however incorrigible it may seem to us, a rather peculiar idea within the context of the world's cultures."[26]

We are more accurately understood in this theory as a conglomerate or web of self states, affect-states, personalities formed in identification with one or more of our inner objects or part-objects, and especially a multiplicity of "selves in relation."[27] At any given moment, we may experience ourselves as a Subject, an "I," but behind, beyond, or alongside every subject-moment, are all the other subject-moments that compose the whole of this web. This resembles what C. G. Jung referred to as the "Self" (capital *S*), which is greater than the executive "ego" that does the conscious knowing. Jung's Self incorporates all the disavowed and unknown parts of oneself. "As an empirical concept, the self designates the whole range of psychic phenomena in man [*sic*]."[28] But there is a distinction as well. For Jung, the Self is ultimately an archetype of unity, and the Self is always desiring the archetype of Wholeness: "It expresses the unity of the personality as a whole . . . it is a *transcendental* concept."[29] Further, as with Freud so with Jung, the direction of the unconscious is still imagined largely in terms of downward "depth" (as in the term especially favored by Jungian therapists, *depth psychology*.)[30]

In the relational-psychoanalytic model, by contrast, we experience ourselves as intersubjectively constituted both in our own internal relationship or "primary subjective experience"[31] of our multiple selves, and in relation to others—particularly as we are formed from

25. E.g., Roland, *In Search of Self in India and Japan*.
26. Geertz, "'From the Native's Point of View,'" 59.
27. Mitchell, "Multiple Selves," 105.
28. Jung, *Psychological Types*, 789.
29. Ibid.
30. E.g., C. G. Jung Institute of San Francisco, *Jung Journal*.
31. Stern, "The Self as a Relational Structure," 698.

infancy onward through identification with others' responses to us.[32] In a postmodern conception, what is outside consciousness at any given moment is not necessarily repressed, suppressed, or disavowed, as in other models of the unconscious. These are all potential parts of the web, but there are multiple varying degrees of accessibility and inaccessibility between and among the different parts.

Further, this web develops relationally, not in isolation. Like Gilles Deleuze's notion of the *implex*, development occurs in a mutual process of enfolding and unfolding, even, as we will imagine theologically, "God folded in all things and all things enfolded in God."[33] Relational analyst Ken Corbett has suggested that we reimagine Anna Freud's classical concept of "developmental lines"[34] in terms of a "weblike substance . . . a spiral web or tissue that can be stretched, twisted, elongated, folded in on itself—and that springs back . . . but is never quite the same . . . like taffy but each having a different tensile strength (some spirals are more flexible than others)."[35]

While Corbett does not take an explicitly theological turn, his words leave room for the pastoral theologian to conceive of multiplicity in quantum theological terms: "The lacework of a web articulates the confluence and coadaptive dependence of the interlacing on the context; it is not a Newtonian a priori structure, or a fixed form, but rather a structure that is never fixed and is always in transition, always moving in accord with the atmosphere."[36] The very illusion of seamless going-on-being from one self state to another, then, is a developmental achievement, and represents the fluidity of mental contents.

32. Ibid., 702, also citing Freud's views on identification in *Beyond the Pleasure Principle*; Fairbairn, *An Object-Relations Theory of The Personality*; and Loewald, "Instinct Theory."

33. The doctrine of panentheism, articulated by early and medieval church theologians such as Nicholas of Cusa in the fifteenth century (Nicholas, of Cusa, *Selected Spiritual Writings*) was a view of God in all things and all things in God; for a contemporary view, see also Clayton and Peacocke, *In Whom We Live and Move and Have Our Being*.

34. Anna Freud, "The Concept of Developmental Lines"; Anna Freud, "The Concept of Developmental Lines: Their Diagnostic Significance."

35. Corbett, "More Life," 328.

36. Ibid.

Thinking Rhizomes

Another image helpful in considering this multiplicity of the human person is Deleuze's and Guattari's image of the *rhizome*. A dictionary definition of *rhizome* is "a horizontal, usually underground stem that often sends out roots and shoots from its nodes."[37] It is different from a root in that it extends horizontally, in network-like fashion, and biologically carries on multiple functions—e.g., reproduction as well as nourishment. A root, by contrast, normally grows downward, and when used as a metaphor signifies such unitive meanings as depth, foundation, source, and origin (even though roots too, if not the taproot, can be multiple). Deleuze and Guattari use the metaphor of the *rhizome* to challenge the privileging in Western philosophy and in capitalism of images that tend to reinforce or justify hegemony, as if the natural order itself privileged "the One" or "unity" over multiplicity and difference.[38]

The principles or properties Deleuze and Guattari identify with the rhizome are useful in conceiving of the mind as similarly multivarious and complex. The rhizome is characterized by connection, heterogeneity, multiplicity, asignifying rupture, cartography, and something they term "decalcomania."[39]

1. *Connection*: "any point of a rhizome can be connected to anything other, and must be."[40] One of the reasons we do not experience ourselves from moment to moment as a disparate jumble of perceptions is that the mind—and neuroscience confirms this in the form of the networking of brain cells as well—is continually creating and renewing *connections* among mental representations and constructs. The "whole" is constantly shape-shifting, but usually the changes are so gradual as to be hardly noticed, as certain memories and percepts are stimulated by new experiences, while allowing other unused or unstimulated connections to decay.

2. *Heterogeneity*: "It evolves by subterranean stems and flows, along river valleys or train tracks; it spreads like a patch of oil."[41]

37. "Rhizome," in *American Heritage Dictionary*.

38. Deleuze and Guattari, *A Thousand Plateaus*, 3–25. An excerpt from pp. 7–13 outlining the principles of the rhizome appears at www.gseis.ucla.edu/courses/ed253a/kellner/deleuze.html.

39. Ibid., 3–25.

40. Ibid., 7.

41. Ibid., 7, citing Clément, Interview with Gilles Deleuze, 99.

3. *Multiplicity:* Here Deleuze and Guattari's theory corresponds most closely to the relational-psychoanalytic conception of mind as multiple, and spatially rather than vertically imagined:

> There are no points or positions in a rhizome, such as those found in a structure, tree, or root. There are only lines. When [pianist] Glenn Gould speeds up the performance of a piece, he is not just displaying virtuosity, he is transforming the musical points into lines, he is making the whole piece proliferate . . . The notion of unity appears only when there is a power takeover . . . All multiplicities are flat, in the sense that they fill or occupy all of their dimensions . . . [and] the dimensions of this "plane" increase with the number of connections that are made on it.[42]

4. *Asignifying Rupture*: "A rhizome may be broken, shattered at a given spot, but it will start up again on one of its old lines, or on new lines."[43] Here, perhaps inadvertently, Deleuze and Guattari's theory relates to the felt sense of dis-continuity that occurs in mental life because of trauma, crisis, or other acute disruption of one's habitual thought processes or modes of coping. One does go on thinking, except in cases of literal unconsciousness, as in a coma, but the ordinary illusion of continuity is broken. Even so, whether through dissociative coping patterns, or the attempted construction of a new subjectivity following amnesia, mental life continues. It springs up, like the shoots and tubers on a rhizome, from nodes of earlier wounding, or perhaps even from places of earlier creative potential. Such shatterings, while not desired, can even become places of new life for those who survive—"strong at the broken places."[44]

5. *Cartography*: Deleuze and Guattari contrast the metaphor of a map with a genealogy. Most if not all psychoanalytic theories until recently tended to frame self-understanding and insight in terms of tracing the "genetic origins" of neuroses and other pathology. While a *genealogy* attempts to fasten relations to particular origins in a hierarchical fashion, a *map* constructs relations

---

42. Deleuze and Guattari, *A Thousand Plateaus*, 8–9.

43. Ibid., 9.

44. This term is used frequently in the abuse-survivor literature. It was originally used by Hemingway in *A Farewell to Arms*: "The world breaks everyone, and afterward many are strong at the broken places. But those that will not break it kills" (chapter 34).

spatially and is continually "detachable, reversible, susceptible to constant modification."[45]

6. The last principle, *decalcomania*, relates to this critique of Lacanian genetic analysis: "A rhizome is not amenable to any structural or generative model. It is a stranger to any idea of genetic axis or deep structure."[46] (*Décalcomanie*, in French, referred to the nineteenth-century craze for transferring tracings or designs to glass or metal[47]—in other words, images that are traced on the surface, rather than something involving deep structure). Deleuze and Guattari invent the term "schizoanalysis"[48] in opposition to "psychoanalysis," to suggest a form of mutable, open, experimental exploration that "rejects any idea of pretraced destiny, whatever name is given to it—divine, anagogic, historical, economic, structural, hereditary, or syntagmatic."[49]

The rhizome presents an alternative model to the classical psychoanalytic assertion that all thought, all behavior, proceeds genetically and to some extent deterministically from a deeper root cause, in the past. With the rhizome image held in tension with the image of roots, we retain the psychoanalytic importance of tracing associations, but now we can see the possibility for a different kind of associational chain of events—horizontal, at times more randomly selected, and linked by present conditions as well as past. Deleuze and Guattari's rhizome provides a useful image to hold in tension with traditional psychoanalytic conceptions of the mind in terms of psychogenetics, tree-like tracings of pathology, and heroic metaphors of plumbing the depths of a single, vertically conceived unconscious.

The metaphor has its limits, of course.[50] Like many postmodern thinkers, Deleuze objects in general to modernist, binary oppositions,

45. Ibid., 12; Baudrillard works with a similar image in *Simulation and Simulacra*: "the cartographer's made project of the ideal coextensivity of map and territory." (2)

46. Deleuze and Guattari, *A Thousand Plateaus*, 12.

47. French *décalcomanie*, from *decalquer*, "to transfer a tracing" (*de-*, "off, from"; from Latin *de-*; see *de-* + *calquer*, "to trace"; see *calque*) + *manie*, "craze" (from its popularity in the nineteenth century) (from Late Latin *mania*, "madness." "Decalcomania," in *American Heritage Dictionary*.

48. Deleuze and Guattari, *A Thousand Plateaus*, 13.

49. Ibid.

50. Deleuze and Guattari's work should not be taken uncritically. For example, their image of the "body without organs" (*A Thousand Plateaus*, 149–66) is troubling in

but there is no doubt that the rhizome/tree dichotomy presents another logical dualism of its own.[51] By placing the rhizome in opposition to the root, Deleuze and Guattari again posit a kind of contest.
The humble potato wins out over the formerly exalted tree.[52] This,
too, however, is problematic in psychoanalytic thinking, it seems to
me, since some events, some behaviors and feelings, do appear to be
"generated"—"rooted" in early childhood experiences and wounds.
Yet, to assign *all* problems in daily living to a theory of infantile origins
may be too reductionistic as well.

It might therefore be most useful to take a both-and approach:
rhizome and tree, horizontal and vertical, spatial associational chains
and the repetition that can arise out of repressed early childhood experiences and wishes. At the same time, Deleuze and Guattari's caution
must be taken seriously: never to lose sight of the more uncontrollable
rhizome in favor of the seductively analyzable tree. Imagine mind and
self in terms of a three-dimensional multiplicity (or more)—neither
vertical "depth," nor purely horizontal "plane," but an infinitely di-
mensional, quantum substance, with internal indeterminacy and
some fluid external parameters. Imagine a subjectivity, a multiple self,
identifiable as both an "I" and a "Thou" simultaneously, as subject and
object, "self" and "other," and with a mobile consciousness that scans
and networks various parts of the "self," in an illusory but functional
sense of self-cohesion, self-regulation, and self-continuity.

This reconceptualization carries a political and ethical dimension
as well. Being open to a variety of "others" within the web that constitutes oneself, it seems to me, should potentiate a greater openness to
"others" beyond oneself. As noted in chapter 3 above, Jane Flax describes multiplicity and fluidity of subjects as emancipatory and even

---

relation to a feminist insistence on embodiment. While they are not referring literally
to the individual human body but rather to a corporate communal "body," the image
calls for some careful critique and qualification.

51. The authors anticipate this critique directly, and assert that "it is a question
of method: the tracing should always be put back on the map" (13). While continuing to privilege maps over the root-like metaphor of "tracings," they insist that as
soon as any theorist pursues a genetic line of thinking, "whenever desire climbs a
tree, internal repercussions trip it up and it falls to its death" (14). While still arguing
dichotomously, they are showing the rhizome as a continually necessary corrective to
the universalizing tendency of root-and-tree thinking.

52. "Where the potato is the hero of this story, the tree becomes the villain"
(Clinton, "Deleuze and Guattari, 'Rhizome,' Annotation").

as a remedy for hegemonic models of "one self" that may all too easily be co-opted by dominant paradigms of both self and society: "I believe a unitary self is unnecessary, impossible, and a dangerous illusion. Only multiple subjects can invent ways to struggle against domination that will not merely recreate it . . . [I]t is possible to imagine subjectivities whose desires for multiplicity can impel them toward emancipatory action."[53]

Postmodern writers highlight the ethical implications of a nonunitary conception of self and mind, especially as they influence the social construction of self and others, and a resulting creative fluidity and expansiveness in the social construction of categories such as gender, race and class, and the distribution of power.[54]

A PSYCHOTHERAPY OF MANY VOICES

As a model for pastoral psychotherapy, this valuing of multiplicity challenges the idea of integration as its primary therapeutic goal. The goal, rather, would be an approximation or process in which both patient and therapist would experience an increasingly harmonious awareness and constructive dialogue among all the disparate parts— conscious and previously unconscious—of the patient, rather than an integration of conscious and unconscious into one homogenized whole. Drawing both from postmodern understandings of the diversity of truths, and from the postcolonial notion of *hybridity* in which dialogue partners join together in new creative ways without losing their individual distinctiveness,[55] this model of pastoral psychotherapy seeks to help individuals come to know, accept, and even appreciate all the distinctive parts—the many voices—that live within them.[56]

Such an approach to psychotherapy is, in the final analysis, more orientation than method. Specific therapeutic techniques can be discussed and debated in relation to various psychoanalytic practice

---

53. Flax, "Multiples," 93. A longer quotation is given in chapter 3, above.

54. For further elaboration of the relationship between postmodernism and justice, including an appropriation of Winnicott's *Playing and Reality*, see Flax, "The Play of Justice."

55. Bhabha, *The Location of Culture*.

56. This is the foundation for the clinical approach detailed in Cooper-White, *Many Voices*, see esp. 59–63, 153–56.

theories.[57] But the main point is that this approach, finally, is an orientation toward multiplicity, toward embracing mystery and all that remains *beyond* knowledge, beyond certainty, beyond any singular Truth. By embracing such multiplicity, and honoring such mystery, the pastoral counselor or psychotherapist may help to facilitate a process by which the patient may discover a more expansive, appreciative, and generous way of living and relating with others, and even with the divine—the source of *all* loves, all mercies, all creativities, all truths, all voices, and all just relations.

MULTIPLICITY OF GOD

In considering *pastoral* psychotherapy in particular, this model of multiplicity has led me to explore what I have found to be fruitful parallels in doing constructive theology emphasizing the *multiplicity of God*.

A radical image of the multiplicity of God may be drawn from Gilles Deleuze's image, again, of the rhizome.[58] Deleuze's discussions of "difference and repetition" have prompted theological meditations, for example by John Milbank, on the nature of God's creativity as "nonidentical repetition."[59] Deleuze links difference to "original depth," a chaotic, plenary source from which all being does not so much emerge upward as it "unfolds." For Deleuze, the idea of "God" is constricted by such "deep" formulations as the "Ground of Being,"[60] since "ground" itself is not exempt from deconstruction—there yet must be a deeper deep or preceding *profond* ("deep" in French), a "*pro/fond*," a bottomless or groundless pre-origin, which precedes the stable "foundation" (*fond*) implied by the term "ground."[61]

This resonates well with the psychological construct of the unconscious as more a matter of horizontal or spatial multiplicities of subjectivity and affect than of Freud's vertical "depth," as discussed in

57. For a detailed discussion of therapeutic technique in relation to this model of multiplicity, see ibid., chapters 4–5 (135–238).

58. Deleuze and Guattari, *A Thousand Plateaus*.

59. Milbank, *Theology and Social Theory*.

60. Tillich, *Systematic Theology*, 1:155–57, drawing on his acquaintance with Eastern religious sources, and resonating with the biblical passage "God, in whom we live and move and have our being" (Acts 17:28).

61. Deleuze, *Difference and Repetition*, 229; also described in Keller, *Face of the Deep*, 168. Elsewhere, it should be noted, I have questioned aspects of Deleuze's work, e.g., *Many Voices*, 285n50 and do not believe he should be read uncritically.

the previous chapter and in this chapter, above. For Deleuze, depth itself is a matter of "extensity," heterogeneity, and the horizontal play of differences, not defined by any shared "root," origin, or ground: "the (ultimate and original) heterogeneous dimension is the matrix of all extensity, including its third dimension, considered to be homogeneous with the other two."[62] (In other words, what we perceive as the three dimensions, represented by a point, a line, and volume, are to be conceived in Deleuze's philosophy as spreading out spatially, and depth is therefore more than simply vertical. It is depth as in our *depth perception*.) Deleuze's rhizome is an image of such horizontal extensity.

The fluid multiplicity of the created universe is neither chaos nor cleaned-up composition, according to Deleuze, but a "chaosmos'"[63] This is a term borrowed from James Joyce, meditating on Aquinas's "wholeness,""harmony," and "radiance."[64] So, extrapolating from this discussion of a multiple, heterogeneous, bottomless origin, God, in a Deleuzian framework, must be similarly bottomless, *unfathomable* not in the sense of abdication from all attempts to relate to and with the divine, but superabundant. It is impossible to reach a (singular) depth and thus to objectify or possess it.

In a brilliant work titled *Face of the Deep*, Catherine Keller has argued that God did not create *ex nihilo*, as an act of mastery upon an external sterile void,"upholding transcendent power-structures,"[65] but in an unfolding, germinating, and forming out of an unruly primordial *chaosmos*. Creation, states Keller, is not a "function of power and order, upholding transcendent power-structures"; rather the ancient scriptures "imagine a messier beginning, with no clear point of origin and no final end:[66]

62. Deleuze, *Difference and Repetition*, 229. Also cited in Keller, *Face of the Deep* in connection with the chaotic depths of *tehom*.

63. Deleuze and Guattari, *What Is Philosophy?* 205, cited in Keller, *Face of the Deep*, 171.

64. Eco, *The Aesthetics of Chaosmos*.

65. Keller, *Face of the Deep*. For a similar discussion of chaos theory and creation theology, and a critique of the doctrine of *creatio ex nihilo* from a scientific perspective, see also Bonting, *Creation and Double Chaos*, 52–125.

66. Keller, *Face of the Deep*, i: "*Face of the Deep* is the first full theology of creation from the primal chaos. It proposes a *creatio ex profundis*—creation out of the water depths—both as an alternative to the orthodox power discourse of creation from nothingness, and as a figure of both bottomless process of becoming." Keller explicates: "The heteroglossic Deep—the Hebrew *tehom* or primal oceanic chaos—already marks

Keller has also discussed the multiplicity of God in terms of the "plural-singularity of creation."[67] Following Hebrew Bible scholars Danna Fewell and David Gunn, she explores the "curious slippage" in the grammar of Genesis 1:26a–27, literally: "Then God(s) ['Elohim—plural] said [singular] 'let us make humankind in our image, after our likeness'. . . So God(s) created [bara'—singular form of the verb] humankind in his own image, in the image of God(s) he created him, male and female he created them."[68] "God 'himself' is unsure whether he is plural or singular, echoing the narrator's grammatic confusion of a plural name ('elohim, which may or may not be a proper noun!) and a singular verb."[69] Keller cites rabbinic sources (e.g., Rashi) who suggested that God needed here to consult a heavenly court, the angels: "The role of the angels 'is to suggest a 'many-ness of viewpoints, a spectrum of opinions.'"[70] Keller reads philosopher of science Michel Serres, in his reflections on the "angelic swarm,"[71] to support a "divining" of "the multiple" as the "Manyone"[72] [many/one]—"an elemental power of creativity, articulate, humble, kenotic, almost democratic, in its delegations; and effusive in its delights."[73] This multiplicity is always in relation, both internally, as the plurality of god(s) and the angelic court, and in relation with the creation/humanity. Concluding a meditation on the multiplicity of God, Keller brings this "matrix of possibilities" back full circle to the multiplicity of creation, and what I would also describe in terms of the intersubjective relation between humanity/creation and the divine.

---

every beginning. It leaks into the bible itself, signifying a fluid matrix of bottomless potentiality, a germinating abyss, a heterogeneous womb or self-organising complexity, a resistance to every fixed order. It sweeps away myths of abstract potency—of the paternal Word—in a tumultuous jumble of neglected parts whose creation is material and laboured" (i).

67. Ibid., 172–82.

68. Translation from Fewell and Gunn, Gender, Power, and Promise, 23, quoted in Keller, Face of the Deep, 281n6.

69. Ibid., 172–82, quoted in Keller, Face of the Deep, 173.

70. Keller, Face of the Deep 174, citing Zornberg, The Beginning of Desire, 4ff.

71. Serres and Latour, Conversations, 118, quoted in Keller, Face of the Deep, 176.

72. Keller, Face of the Deep, 181.

73. Ibid., 177, also drawing from Serres, Genesis, 6.

Laurel Schneider's recent book *Beyond Monotheism: A Theology of Multiplicity*[74] extends Keller's reading of Deleuze even further, to contest the hegemony of the One in monotheism as a construct reinforcing a theo-politics of disconnected domination. She writes:

> When did the stories of God become a story of totality, of a closed system, of a One? To what corner of human longing does the story of the One belong? As the motors of fundamentalism in all of the religions of One God race on the fuel of battered bodies and broken hearts, the logic of the One chokes on itself like a stone in the mouth. The story of the One denies fleshiness and the stubborn shiftiness of bodies; it cannot abide ambiguities and unfinished business; it cannot speak syllables of earth. But in its failures are openings, for there are always gaps in the story of the One, fissures that widen and crumble at the edges. Through the gaps, rivers of divine faces flow, their eyes the eyes of children, hinting at depths of losses and possibilities, and of incarnate coming-to-senses. In bodies, both of the lost and of the living, multiplicity makes itself known, tumbling through the stories of the One, birthing worlds and confounding certainty at every turn. The story of the One cannot, finally, achieve the still point that it pretends to crave; the very stones cry out. [75]

As an Anglican theologian, I appreciate this trenchant critique of the One, and at the same time I want to mine ancient Christian sources for images to counter this hegemonic tendency in traditional doctrine. The Trinity, it seems to me, is a deeply evocative and compelling metaphor of multiplicity already present in ancient Christianity.[76] We have from the fourth-century Cappadocian theologians, including Gregory of Nyssa, Basil "the Great," Gregory of Nazianzus, and Macrina, the sister of Gregory of Nyssa and Basil,[77] an engaging, metaphorical image of the Trinity as *perichōrēsis*—the complete, equal, and mutual interpermeation of the three persons or dynamic dimensions of the Trinity. Catherine LaCugna gives a beautiful, clear description, as follows:

> *Perichōrēsis* expressed the idea that the three divine persons mutually inhere in one another, draw life from one another,

---

74. Schneider, *Beyond Monotheism*.

75. Ibid., ix.

76. Cooper-White, *Shared Wisdom*, 181–83; Cooper-White, *Many Voices*, 76–94.

77. Gregory the Great, *Life of St. Macrina*.

"are" what they are by relation to one another. *Perichōrēsis* means being-in-one-another, permeation without confusion. No person exists by him/herself or is referred to him/herself; this would produce number and therefore division within God, Rather, to be a divine person is to be by nature in relation to other persons. Each divine person is irresistibly drawn to the other, taking his/her existence from the other, containing the other in him/herself, while at the same time pouring self into the other . . . While there is no blurring of the individuality of each person, there is also no separation. There is only communion of love in which each person comes to be . . . what he/she is, entirely with reference to the other. *Perichōrēsis* provides a dynamic model of persons in communion based on mutuality and interdependence.[78]

This parallels Deleuze's concept of differences,[79] not arising as separate outcroppings or representations from some prior unitary Source or Ideal but constituting difference through mutual interplay in a web-like horizontal extending ("extensity") of relation. The Trinity is, then, a spacious room—even a *matrix*/womb, in which multiple metaphors can flourish, honoring simultaneously the relationality and the multiplicity of God.

As we embrace a model of greater complexity and multiplicity of the human mind, this will lead us to a more complex and nuanced appreciation for the diversity and mutability of human persons in the way we understand pastoral care, counseling, and psychotherapy. What is *pastoral*—that is, what protects and promotes human growth, and helps to heal psychic and interpersonal wounds—from this relational perspective, then, is not a vision of ultimate or reified *oneness*, as in a homogenization of all "patients" (as objects) into a single uniform model of health and wholeness, but rather the capacity for a pluriform and diversely just and loving human *creativity*. This creativity is grounded/surrounded/infused in the creative profusion, incarnational desire, and pulsing, living inspiration of the Trinity/loving God, which is the "source, wellspring and living water"[80] of mutual desire that bridges, through the very embracing of difference, toward the creative multiplicity of the other. This, then, becomes the new starting point for

78. LaCugna, *God for Us*, 270–71.
79. Deleuze, *Difference and Repetition*.
80. Cunningham, *These Three Are One*.

an emancipatory praxis of pastoral care, counseling, and psychotherapy, wherein the goal of care is to provide a space in which the person
can be freed from the constraining myths of oppression (whether individual, intrafamilial, or social and cultural) toward a freer exploration
of his or her own multiform creative potential.

In my own constructive theological work I have proposed the following Trinitarian image—*God as Creative Profusion, God as Incarnational
Desire,* and *God as Living Inspiration*—as a theological framework for
interrogating "integration" and even claiming "*dis*-integration" as a
form of psycho-spiritual dissent, and creativity.[81] Beginning with *God
as creative profusion,* the creation is no longer conceivable as a cleanly
ordered, unified world, but as an irrepressible fecundity. This fecundity, this turbulent swarming of creation, it seems to me, is a much
more consoling, liberating, and empowering image for pastoral relations, which further opens passage to understanding the divine as
incarnational desire: the yearning of the creatures for one another and
the source of their creative life; and *living inspiration*: the erotic embodiment, and life-breath, through which we prayerfully breathe in
each other, in and through mindful community. The elaboration of this
pastoral Trinitarian theology is the subject of the next chapter.

Such Trinitarian imaginings perhaps can open the way toward
affirming the dappled, fickle, freckled multiplicity both of ourselves
and the real human persons who come to us for care and healing. It is
not the attainment of a shiny, polished *integration* that heals and empowers, but increasing consciousness of our own intricacy as we are
continually, fluidly, and multiply constituted in the complexity of all
our relations.

To quote from Laurel Schneider once more in closing: "The One
is not lost, therefore, in multiplicity; it is just *ruined* in the way that
stars fall, which is not falling but becoming-other in the attractional
flight of planetary bodies. The ancient stories of One God are full of
just such desire, such gravitational pull toward bodies. The Divine
has been there all along in the story of the One, spelling its end and
beginning-again like a DNA script at the core of the living cell, like a
star falling into brilliant ruin in the arms of the nearest body."[82]

---

81. In its most detailed form, this appears in Cooper-White, *Many Voices,* 76–94.
82. Ibid., xi.

FIVE

Dancing Partners

Trinitarian Theology and the Use of the Self in Pastoral Care and Counseling

One of the most compelling images of God, from the fourth-century Cappadocian theologians, is the image of the Trinity as *perichōrēsis*—"being-in-one-another, permeation without confusion."[1] Catherine LaCugna's description, quoted in full in the previous chapter, provides a poetic, detailed description of the Cappadocians' vision of the three-in-one: "*perichōrēsis* expressed the idea that the three divine persons mutually inhere in one another, draw life from one another, 'are' what they are by relation to one another . . . communion of love in which each person comes to be . . . and at the same time . . . what God is: ecstatic, relational, dynamic, vital."[2] She goes on to claim *perichōrēsis* as an example for Christian living and community: "a dynamic model of persons in communion based on *mutuality and interdependence*."[3]

Although technically not a translation for *perichōrēsis*,[4] the popular rendering into English of *perichōrēsis* as the divine dance is also a

1. LaCugna, *God for Us*, 270. This discussion of *perichōrēsis* is elaborated in Cooper-White, *Many Voices*, 76–82.

2. LaCugna, *God for Us*, 270–71.

3. Ibid., 271.

4. *Perichōrēō* means "to encompass"; *perichōreuō* means "to dance around" (ibid., 312n94).

compelling image for the dynamism, energy, and multiplicity-in-unity inherent in the symbol of the Trinity. As LaCugna writes, again:

> Choreography suggests the partnership of movement, symmetrical but not redundant, as each dancer expresses and at the same time fulfills him/herself towards the other. In interaction and inter-course, the dancers (and the observers) experience one fluid motion of encircling, encompassing, permeating, enveloping, outstretching. There are neither leaders nor followers in the divine dance, only an eternal movement of reciprocal giving and receiving, giving again and receiving again . . . The image of the dance forbids us to think of God as solitary. The idea of Trinitarian *perichōrēsis* provides a marvelous point of entry into contemplating what it means to say God is alive from all eternity as love.[5]

Perichōrēsis has been adopted in feminist theology as an image for "an ethics that upholds three central values: inclusiveness, community, and freedom. Since these ways of relating are the hallmarks of divine life, they should characterize the patterns of human persons in communion with one another."[6]

The image of the dance is not an image of an exclusive club or divine committee of three. The imagery of motion and spontaneity would seem to invite others—humanity, creatures, all living beings—to join in the "dance of all creation."[7] In Andrei Rublev's fifteenth-century icon (Figure 5.1), which depicts the Trinity as the three mysterious visitors to Sarah and Abraham under the tree at Mamre, the three figures incline democratically toward one another, but also there is a space at the table for us, as we gaze on the icon.

Elizabeth Johnson's description of the image of the Trinity (quoted in full in chapter 2 above) is one that refutes all monolithic, totalizing tendencies of theology to define God: "At its most basic the symbol of the Trinity evokes a livingness in God, a dynamic coming and going with the world that points to an inner divine circling around in unimaginable relation . . . Not an isolated, static, ruling monarch, but a relational, dynamic, tripersonal mystery of love."[8]

5. Ibid.

6. Wilson-Kastner, *Faith, Feminism and Christ*, cited in LaCugna, *God for Us*, 272–73.

7. Line from the hymn by Arthur, "This Is the Feast."

8. Johnson, *She Who Is*, 192–93.

Figure 5-1. The Rublev Icon

The Trinity is not a concrete representation of a static, or even knowable God. It is, rather, as noted in the previous chapter, a "potential space"[9] for multiple images and metaphors for God. "Father," "Son," and "Holy Spirit" are not the proper names of three reified persons, like human persons only bigger (although these terms come to be used in just this concretizing way in some theological circles). From

9. Winnicott, *Playing and Reality.*

a contemporary and even postmodern perspective, the Trinity is an image that continues to empty itself of fixed essences, not cascading into a nihilistic nothingness of divine absence, but rather, ever shifting in a kaleidoscopic pattern, whose broadest parameters are defined only by an ever expanding and eternal relationality—parameters that shape but never limit the bright multiplicity of divine love. The Trinity as image and metaphor is like a waterfall, *full* of light, color, and dancing shapes that provide continual refreshment, a long cool drink for parched feelings and hardened thinking, cleansing for the perceived wounds and stains, cooling for fevered human hubris, and the occasional deluge for those who become too comfortable with the delights of any particular tributary of sacred ideology. Who would dare to enter into such dangerous, wet, creative contemplation? And yet, who would not be drawn by the beauty of such overflowing abundance? Moreover, as a pastoral theologian, who would not be drawn by the promise of growth, healing, and empowerment that springs from such a multiple image? What, then, are some implications for a relational pastoral theology?

A TRINITARIAN PASTORAL THEOLOGY

If we are willing to explore these multifaceted efforts toward a multiple concept of God, and a corollary construction of a mutual, co-constructive, co-generative yearning *between* humans and the divine,[10] then we are led to a pastoral construction of human beings, consciousness, and its construction in mutual relations (potentially resonating with a variety of faith traditions, not just orthodox Christianity), and to an appreciation of this multiple, fluid, relationality of both God and human persons as underpinning all relational approaches to pastoral praxis— through the spectrum of care, counseling, and psychotherapy.

What might the three traditional aspects of the Trinity say, in a *non-essentialist* key, particularly as a source for a healing and liberative pastoral praxis—with an ear toward metaphors that resonate with the pastoral functions of healing, sustaining, guiding, reconciling, and empowering? I have proposed the following Trinitarian language to serve as one possible pastoral Trinitarian formula among the many

10. Johnson, *She Who Is*, 274–75.

that might be creatively imagined: *God as Creative Profusion, God as Incarnational Desire,* and *God as Living Inspiration.*[11]

God as Creative Profusion

> GLORY be to God for dappled things—
> For skies of couple-colour as a brinded cow;
> For rose-moles all in stipple upon trout that swim;
> Fresh-firecoal chestnut-falls; finches' wings;
> Landscape plotted and pieced—fold, fallow, and plough;
> And áll trádes, their gear and tackle and trim.
>
> All things counter, original, spare, strange;
> Whatever is fickle, freckled (who knows how?)
> With swift, slow; sweet, sour; adazzle, dim;
> He fathers-forth whose beauty is past change:
> Praise him.

The English poet Gerard Manley Hopkins captures the multiplicity and fecundity of creation in this poem *Pied Beauty.*[12] Hopkins's nineteenth-century "father" language recedes in importance, amid the swirling alliterations and the crunch of consonants that capture the wildness, unpredictability, and perfect imperfection, "dappled . . . fickle, freckled," of creation. The tenacity of life gives further evidence of the irrepressible nature of God's creativity. One of my own most powerful experiences of the realization of God's presence was in the Oakland, California, hills one late afternoon. I suddenly "saw," in a nonordinary way of seeing, the tremendous force and thrust and determination of the trees jutting out of the soft, seemingly precarious hillside soil and leaning vertiginously out over the landscape far below. The terrible scarring of those same hillsides by fire a few years later, and the rising again of tiny trees out of the seeds broken open by the ferocious heat of the fire, was a powerful sign of the force of new life, even resurrected life. What a deep symbol for the process of healing—from both loss and illness! Yet every day, if I pay attention, I am given the gift of reminders of those moments of seeing—in my urban setting in Philadelphia, and growing around the historic walls

11. Condensed from Cooper-White, *Many Voices*, 82–94. For further elaboration on the broader theological themes presented here, see "A Relational Understanding of God" (chapter 2 in *Many Voices*, 67–94).

12. Hopkins, *The Poems of Gerard Manley Hopkins*, 69.

of my Gettysburg home, I see it again: another tiny green spike or ten-dril, seemingly frail and tender, but with the force to gnaw and snake its way through concrete and brick until it finds the sun and opens.

I love the fact that even if I accidentally dig up a daffodil bulb in my garden while planting summer flowers, and stick it in upside down, again by accident, it will figure out how to send its shoots down and around and up again, and in the spring, the daffodil will rise once more to animate and color its own tiny patch of winter-deadened space. Here is the unstoppable force of both tree *and* rhizome—on flat sidewalks, on vertical walls, on the ridges and cliffs overlooking the San Francisco Bay, or curled upside down in the dirt of my garden: who can say where vertical ends and horizontal begins? Life, in all its fecundity, is three-dimensional, unruly, not bound by any compass but God's own green-ward direction: Up! Out! Forward! Sideways! Heal! Grow!

God, then, *is* creative profusion, and the creation is not understood in this theology as a pristine product by a distant supernatural maker, but a wild, dazzling, and virtuosic fecundity. This irrepressible, unruly image of God *as* limitless creativity[13] offers a metaphor for divine and human flourishing and diversity that far exceeds the possibilities of the image of a singular, authoritarian God the Father. To liberate the first "person" of the Trinity from a concretized identity as "Father," or even "Creator," opens the way to affirming the dappled, fickle, freckled multiplicity of the real human persons who come to us for care and healing. We are accepted, confirmed, loved in our complexities and contradictions. Tidy perfection will not save/*salve* (soothe and heal) us: we will, rather, find greater health and empowerment through growth in consciousness of our complexity—as Annie Dillard puts it, in our "intricacy": "Intricacy is that which is given from the beginning, the birth-right, and in intricacy is the hardiness of complexity that ensures against the failure of all life."[14] Our own inner landscape, like the land-scape Dillard describes, using poetic biblical imagery, is "'ring-streaked, speckled and spotted,' like Jacob's cattle culled from Laban's herd."[15]

This theology has resonance with an expansive and noncon-demning view of the human person as messy, multiple, in process, loved (in spite of and/or because of all his or her chaos) and therefore

13. Cf., Kaufman, *In the Beginning—Creativity*.
14. Dillard, *Pilgrim at Tinker Creek*, 145.
15. Ibid.

also loving. This is where all pastoral praxis has its beginnings and its endings: in learning to know and love *all* the messy, conflicted, chaotic parts of ourselves, even as God has loved us from our beginnings "made in secret and woven in the depths of the earth" (Ps 139:14b), and springing from that knowledge of being so deeply loved, growing in the capacity to love others. So the creation stirs in us and brings us into the awareness of God-with-us in our daily lives: God as incarnational desire.

God as Incarnational Desire

In all three aspects of the Trinity, God is love: the power of the erotic of life breaking through and insisting upon newness, change, growth. This is true in a particular way as God is imaged in the second dimension of the Trinity—God willingly and lovingly present, *in* the flesh, fur, feathers, sea, and soil of the creation. The name *Emmanuel* ("God-with-us") signifies God's own promise to be *with* us, even "to the end of the age" (Matt 28:20), and more, to be *in* us and in all creation. Just as *perichōrēsis* was used by the Cappadocians to describe the interpenetration of the three persons of the Trinity, *perichōrēsis* also applies to the relationship between God and the *world*. God is in us and we are in God—not on some disembodied or theoretical or "spiritual" plane apart or above from daily life, but deep in our blood and our bones. As we walk forward in time and space, loving, working, watching, weeping, rejoicing, God is the whole energy of both justice and mercy, struggling forward through us and in us, in the historical movement of the world. God walks with us and in us, incarnate in history, and intimately involved with us through the very human (and hence animal) experience of living and suffering in the body.

This is the miracle of incarnation, most clearly embodied for us in the Christian tradition in the life, passion, and resurrection of Jesus of Nazareth. The particularity of the astonishing revelation to the early Christians, that *this Jesus* was God, further tells us about what God is like. Jesus's character, as depicted over and over in the palimpsest of multiple Gospels and overlapping stories, was preoccupied with two central aims: to heal and restore to community those who were ill and/ or outcast; and to reverse the social order so that the oppressed would be liberated and the poor lifted up. In the belief that spread from the earliest eyewitnesses to the appearances of Jesus after his crucifixion,

Christians even came to the astonishing conviction, read through the prophesies of Scripture and the messianic fervor of their times, that Jesus had been raised from the dead.

Whatever one believes about later dogmatic arguments about sub-stitutionary atonement, or the imagery of God sacrificing "His" son, a Trinitarian understanding of the cross points to the astounding asser-tion that the God who created the universe was so intimately bound up in the fullness of human experience that God allowed *God's own self* to experience excruciating torture and to die, and in so doing, conquered death. Christians thus discern through God's actions in the person-ality of Jesus of Nazareth that God's own nature is to stand in solidarity with all who suffer, and that God not only created the world but offers a continuing promise of transformation from death to new life.

This promise of resurrection is not only a promise about the end of our lives, but is a promise that permeates all the deaths, the setbacks, the illnesses, and the losses we experience, big and little, with the hope that new life can and will come out of even the most desolate and wounded places in our lives. God, as revealed in the second dimension of the Trinity, comes to be known by us as the power of life—*eros*—which infuses our lives, our bodies, with new energy, zest for living, healing for wounds and diseased bodies, and hope for the future.

The Gospel narratives, and Christian images of Jesus in the man-ger, in his mother's arms, and later on the road to Golgotha, on the cross, and in his mother's arms again in the Pietà, also emphasize that God, like us, is vulnerable, is wounded. This is perhaps the greatest mystery of the incarnation. For Christians, there is no clearer depic-tion of God's vulnerability than that of God being born in a manger, on a dusty straw bed surrounded by the breath of curious animals and frightened, uprooted human parents. And for Christians, there is no clearer depiction of God's woundedness than that of God hanging, tor-tured, on a first-century imperial Roman cross, betrayed and murdered by earthly powers and principalities. This is one of the more remark-able features of the Christian faith—that the God of the universe is not a God who lords it over us, but who participates in the bloody realities of concrete, fleshy living and dying. Further, God's vulnerability is not an illusion, or greatness stooping to meet us, a condescension, as many classical traditions assert in order to preserve the greatness of God's sovereignty. This vulnerability is what God is, as God is revealed to us in the second dimension of the Trinity. And it is in and through such vulnerability, such at-oneness with the creation, that God continually acts to bring healing, justice, and transformation—new life!

This promise of transformation is at the heart of the pastoral enterprise. It heralds that change, however improbable, is never impossible. Much of what impedes growth, healing, and reaching out for new possibilities, new life, is fear. A Trinitarian-informed pastoral psychotherapy holds out the belief that hope is possible, and that fear does not need to have the last word. The great spiritual writer and theologian, Henri Nouwen, posed the question, "How can we live in the midst of a world marked by fear, hatred and violence, and not be destroyed by it?"[16] The message of the Gospels over and over is that, even at the times of our greatest fear and need, "Do not be afraid." In Nouwen's words, if we make the "house of fear"[17] our permanent dwelling, we find our choices narrowed, and our capacity for love constricted until we can hardly breathe. Staying in our fear of change causes us to try to control everything, to become preoccupied with ourselves, our safety, until we may even come to hate others because of threats we vaguely perceive. The rhythm of hope is the movement of pastoral care and psychotherapy—it is the movement out of this house of fear, this house of bondage, to a "house of love."[18] If we internalize this Good News, we will be led in the dance from fear and trembling to joy and freedom. This is the central aim of pastoral psychotherapy—not to be healed for our *own* contentment or a solipsistic "self-actualization," but to be fully human, even as God-in-Jesus was *fully* human, which is to-be-for-others. As pastoral theologians we cling to the belief that we can live again for others, in the power and the mystery of the risen life, which is Love.

The incarnation, finally, is about God's desire. Not condescension, but love of the creation, draws God to us, "as close to us as our own breath"(Augustine of Hippo). The promise of the incarnation, the promise of the transformation from fear to love, and from death to new life, lived vigorously, joyfully *in* the body, the promise of God's desire to be "as close to us as our own breath," leads in turn to the third aspect of Trinitarian imagery: that of the Holy Spirit as living inspira-

---

16. Nouwen, *Behold the Beauty of the Lord*, 19.

17. Ibid., 20.

18. Ibid.

tion, the ongoing energy that infuses and empowers the wonder of our relationships.

God as Living Inspiration

If the second dimension of the Trinity depicts God incarnate, the erotic, living presence of the Holy in our embodied lives, the third dimension brings God to us in the very rhythm of our breath. The "Holy Spirit" is what we experience as the movement of God in our lives, simultaneously in us and among us, binding us together with each other and the whole created world. The Spirit has been variously thought of as breath, power, energy, wind.

Not coincidentally, human practices of prayer often involve a deepening and calming of the breath (whether intentionally or unintentionally through the physical relaxation that often comes with a shift in brain state during the focusing or clearing of the mind in prayer). The combination of calm, cleansing breathing, and intentional focus on God or bringing one's life, one's questions, one's feelings, one's problems before God, helps us to become more clearly aware of the presence of God/Spirit in us and in the various concerns and actions of our lives.

Not all forms of prayer are quiet and contemplative. Prayer may be any activity in which we practice awareness of the presence of God. This is the Benedictine rhythm of prayer and work, in which work itself becomes a form of prayer—going about our daily tasks, even seemingly "mindless" chores such as washing the dishes, in a state of "mindfulness" of the presence of the sacred, as Thich Nhat Hanh described: "washing each dish as if it were a baby Buddha."[19] Whatever form it may take, prayer enhances our awareness of our relationship with God, which is always in motion, but not always something to which we attend fully. Prayer is the human practice of attending to the inspiration of the Holy in our daily existence—as lived in community.

Because the Spirit is not an isolated manifestation of the divine but conceived as one partner in the Trinitarian dance, the Spirit is in its own distinctive way yet another symbol of the *relationality* of God, and of our life in and with God. As we breathe in, we know that we are not isolated. We do not live in bell jars; we breathe in the entire world. And as we breathe out, if we are aware, we realize that we are reaching

19. Hanh, *Peace Is Every Step*.

even with our breath beyond the confines of our own physical being. Our very existence affects others. Our very breath ties us to one another, and to the planet. Even our breath, then, is unavoidably a matter of ethics. We cannot extricate ourselves from the very atmosphere in which we and all others live. Breathing reminds us that our very lives are intrinsically ec-static. We cannot live only for ourselves, but in and for one another, even as the Spirit swirls around and in and through us and all living beings in one great dance—a dance so great that it encompasses the entire cosmos and beyond.

The relational sign of the Spirit, then, is this motion of God, around and in and through, because it invisibly binds us together in one life, one community of creatures. Like it or not, believe it or not, we cannot help but participate in the dance of creation. And so our actions have consequences, not only for our own lives and those closest to us, but for the whole planet. The Spirit infuses all relationships, then, with God's own care, God's creativity, God's incarnational presence. We stand in relationship with this dynamic presence. The Spirit urges, whispers, prompts, and occasionally shoves us in the direction of God's priorities of love and justice. The image is a fluid one, like the air, not dominative and coercive but in-fluential—always in-flowing. This flow of urgent love can be impeded by human sin or the thick scar tissue of woundedness, but can it ever be entirely blocked?

The pastoral relationship, then, encompassing the full spectrum of care, counseling, and psychotherapy, is no less fundamentally infused with this energy of God to help heal, grow, strengthen, and promote just flourishing of all persons and creatures. As are all relations among living beings, the pastoral relationship is characterized by a fluid intersubjectivity, where each partner in the relationship is simultaneously both "I" and "Thou" to both self and other, and where meaning is co-constructed, not on either "pole" of the I-Thou duality, but in the "third space" that exists as a bridge of communication, a "potential space" to quote the British psychoanalyst D. W. Winnicott—a place of possible but as yet unformulated understandings, and a continuum of shared experience between them. In the pastoral relationship, given the asymmetry of roles between "helper" and "helpee," the psychoanalytic categories of transference (the helpee's subjective experience of the relationship and projections upon it) and countertransference (the helper's similar experiences and projections) become but one symbol of this dynamic interrelation, filtered through the separate subjective experiences and the asymmetry of responsibilities of each partner.[20]

The psychoanalytic perspective adds the significant insight that this mutual relation never operates only at the conscious, interpersonal level of ordinary communications and transactions, but encompasses the full range of unconsciousness in and between the participants as well—and encompasses the "unformulated experiences"[21] and co-constructed meanings that lie only in potential (Bollas's wonderful phrase, cited above in chapter 3, the "unthought known"[22]). This is the foundation of relational-psychoanalytic therapy. But in pastoral psychotherapy in particular, we are further convinced that we do not do this merely by our own powers of reason or intuition, but with the help of the pulsing, energizing breath of God dwelling in both partners in the therapeutic dance, and dwelling in the intersubjective space *between* us, which then opens up as a further space for God's creative profusion, God's incarnational presence, and God's living inspiration.

COUNTERTRANSFERENCE AND THE USE OF THE SELF[23]

A relational, pastoral Trinity leads us back to a pastoral praxis of relationality, in which the "between" of our encounters with one another urges us to consider all our pastoral relations in terms of a mutual knowing, a perichoretic dance of "intersubjectivity." The theory behind this intersubjective, relational approach to pastoral care, counseling, and psychotherapy has been elaborated in the previous chapters in this volume. To be more concrete about practice, however, we need to turn to the importance of self-awareness, and to the use of oneself as an instrument for empathic listening and understanding in the pastoral relationship. How do we bring both theory and theology back

20. For a much more detailed discussion of transference and countertransference from a relational, intersubjective perspective, and its ethical implications for boundaries and care, see Cooper-White, *Shared Wisdom,* esp. chapter 3, "The Relational Paradigm: Postmodern Concepts of Countertransference and Intersubjectivity," 35–60.

21. Stern, *Unformulated Experience.*

22. Bollas, *The Shadow of the Object.*

23. This section is adapted from Cooper-White, *Shared Wisdom,* 54–58. For a much more in-depth discussion of the concept of countertransference and the pastoral "use of the self," from both classical and contemporary psychoanalytic understandings, see Cooper-White, *Shared Wisdom,* chapters 1–3 (pp. 9–60).

to concrete practice, particularly in terms of our own subjectivity as caregivers?

I have long emphasized the importance of "countertransference" in pastoral ministry, and most students of Clinical Pastoral Education (CPE) and pastoral counseling will already be familiar with it as the crucial attention to awareness of one's own feelings and issues when in the helping role. Such self-knowledge has been at the heart of the pastoral care and counseling training mission for many decades. The term *countertransference* refers, most simply, to our subjectivity when we are in the helping role. In Freud's classical model it was already understood as such. However, in the classical model, *subjectivity* was not viewed as a good thing. In the scientific belief system in which Freud and most subsequent theorists were embedded, the helper was automatically conceived as the expert who observed and knew, and the helpee was the object to be observed and known. Objectivity was what was strived for. Subjectivity was devalued as contaminating the helping role and so the therapeutic relationship with emotionality, irrationality, and unconscious acting out. Thus, in the classical model—including the classic training models of both CPE and pastoral counseling—countertransference has been taught and understood mainly as a *hindrance* to the helping process: something to be analyzed so that it could be done away with or at least set aside while engaged in the work of helping.

In the relational paradigm, by contrast, subjectivity is *re*valued as representing the whole spectrum of ways in which both one's own and the other's reality(/ies) can be understood. Relational subjectivity does not exclude our rational, thinking function,[24] but it also pays attention to our affect (or emotion) and our felt bodily sense as ways in which both self and other can be known. The relational paradigm also replaces the positivist, one-sided relationship with something vastly more reciprocal. *Both* helper and helpee in this new model are *subjects.* They *both* observe and are observed, know and are known. Even more exciting, I think, in this paradigm, is that what becomes knowable, not only exists in each individual, but is made most fully accessible in the potential space that grows up *between* the two—already depicted early on in psychoanalysis by Carl Jung using the medieval image of the

---

24. Even this might be challenged—the postmodern suspicion of rational cognition goes deep. See Cooper-White, *Shared Wisdom,* 214n75.

alchemical bath. Knowledge, including the rational, the emotional *and* the embodied, is now understood as a shared and *co*-constructed pool in which the two participants are equally immersed, at both conscious and unconscious levels, in the "between" of their shared interaction.

Countertransference and transference (the helpee's conscious and unconscious views of us) become a continuum in this model, a continuum upon which our mutual projections *onto* each other, and even *into* each other (which is called "projective identification"[25]—when we begin to take in and behave out of what is unconsciously projected by the other onto and eventually into us, as described in chapter 2, above) mutually shape our growing sense of understanding. Because we are professional caregivers, chaplains, and counselors, of course our focus on what we understand about the parishioner or patient or client is uniquely lopsided; in the helping relationship, unlike in friendships, colleagueships, intimate partnerships, or parenting relationships, the focus of knowing is always in the service of care and is not reciprocal.

From a theological perspective, such shared knowledge participates in the "infinite conversation"[26] of which Buber wrote: "Extended, the lines of relationships intersect the eternal Thou."[27] In this model, we can see that as much or more is "going on" in the *middle* of the spectrum than at either end. In the relational model, insight—or, perhaps in its literal sense, *re-cognition* (thought that goes out and returns influenced, to be rethought again)—flows back and forth between both participants. Glimmers of meaning may spark at any point along the spectrum at any time. Recognition may bubble up initially not only as a verbal thought, but often in the form of an emotion or a bodily sensation or a behavior—or even as a holistic flooding of all of our perceptions. Thus, the helper *uses his or her own self*, not only as a channel of information about his or her *own* knowledge and experience, but equally as an empathic *receiver* of the *other's* affective state, and of the shared meaning that is emerging between them. This is the meaning of intersubjectivity in pastoral care—that we use all our senses not only to perceive what may be coming up inside us that could be getting in the way of our understanding of the other, but to "tune in" more deeply and empathically with the other's experience.

25. Klein, "Notes on Some Schizoid Mechanisms."

26. Buber, *I and Thou*, 114.

27. Ibid., 123. (NB: Kaufman's translation reads, "the eternal You.")

Therefore intersubjectivity is a tool that can sensitize us even more profoundly to the sacred multiple truth, the *logos*, the "I am" of each person in our care.

CONCLUSION: PASTORAL THEOLOGY AND PRAXIS

A pastoral perspective, "oriented" (paradoxically not just toward a singular "east," but toward a multiplicity of compass points and unfixed directions) toward a God conceived as fluid, vulnerable, multiple, in motion, and in perpetual relation both with us and within us, emancipates us from constraining, static, monolithic notions of both God and human beings. A multiple/Trinitarian, relational pastoral theology makes new breathing space—space for each human person that can heal narrowness of vision and the constraining hardness of psychic scars, to encompass an ever-widening capacity for relationality, both with other persons in the outer world of human relations, and internally among the many "persons" inhabiting the messy, intricate landscape of our own desiring, creative selves.

Theology and psychology meet in this pastoral "potential space" between certainty and unknowability, where rigid hierarchies of both deity/humanity and consciousness/the unconscious begin to collapse, as we recognize that our creativity, art, and human nature itself, contain spheres of both divinity and humanity, both rationality and irrationality, both knowability and unknowability, of abstract thought, emotion, and animal sense, both within ourselves and in our relations with one another and with God. In the words of T. S. Eliot's "Dry Salvages" from *The Four Quartets*:[28]

> . . . Or the waterfall, or music heard so deeply
> That it is not heard at all, but you are the music
> While the music lasts. These are only hints and guesses,
> Hints followed by guesses; and the rest
> Is prayer, observance, discipline, thought and action.
> The hint half guessed, the gift half understood, is Incarnation.

28. Eliot, "Dry Salvages," in *The Four Quartets*, 44.

SIX

Com|plicated Woman

Multiplicity and Relationality across Gender, Politics, and Culture

At the entrance to our house [when I was growing up] there was a Rosetta quilt. Each piece was a rose sewn from two folded circles—it took a lot of folds. Each rose was made of scraps of fabric, many colors, polyester, anything and everything, woven together by delicate threads. My grandmother and I would do things like that together. I have one now in my house—4 x 5 feet square. It makes me think of her, doing all these things—cooking, cleaning, helping people, being active in her church . . . She influenced me to be a fluid person who can move in different spaces and be comfortable.

—Sara[1]

What always matters is folding, unfolding, refolding.

—Gilles Deleuze[2]

---

1. Interview/conversation with Sara Calderón, January 18, 2008, used by permission. Note: This Sara is not the fictional composite "Sara" who appeared as a case study in my book *Shared Wisdom*.
2. Deleuze, *The Fold*, 137.

135

Figure 6-1. Sara and the Rosetta Quilt

My friend Sara's life looks a lot like the beloved Rosetta quilt that hangs on the wall of her house today. Sara's grandmother taught her to quilt, to take brilliant multicolored scraps of cloth, to cut them in circles, and then to fold them together into bunches and pleats until they took on the shape of a rose, and then with "delicate threads" to weave them all together in an ever-widening pattern that would dazzle and delight.

Sara's life, too, is a weaving and folding together of many parts. Born in Puerto Rico in 1962, she grew up bilingual, and it was her spirit of adventure in her twenties that prompted her and her husband of one year, Nelson, to move to the continental United States to pursue his Master of Divinity. As they returned together to Puerto Rico for Nelson's first pastorate, Sara began a Master of Arts in comparative literature, devouring postmodern French philosophy while encouraging Nelson in his ministry. After seven years of being told by doctors that she was infertile ("the seven lean years, like the seven lean cows in the Bible!"), she became pregnant. Her first child, Noelia, was born, and life began to change radically as she fell in love with her baby and then had a second little girl, Paula. The family moved back to the States where Nelson began his doctorate. Two more children, Celeste and Laura, were born in short order.

Today, Sara describes her activities in terms of "devotion:" in the order in which she herself describes her many commitments, she creates a warm and aesthetically beautiful home fragrant with wonderful meals for her four daughters and her spouse (now a seminary professor); she is very active in her church in both liturgical and programmatic ways; she makes meals and volunteers for the local interfaith homeless network; she is a member of the board of a shelter for battered women and their children; and she works full time as the administrator for the graduate degree programs of the seminary (where she also frequently volunteers in a variety of tasks that call upon her artistic, creative, and organizational talents). In addition, she does translating for the national Evangelical Lutheran Church in America and still somehow finds time to read everything from the Harry Potter books to Jacques Derrida. Her friends marvel at her capacity for multitasking and wonder if, like Hermione in *Harry Potter and the Prisoner of Azkaban*,[3] Sara has mastered the magical art of being in two places at the same time!

When I ask her how she herself understands all her multiple commitments and identifications, she demurs, saying, "One does these things—I don't think about how. It just flows—it just happens." But then, on reflecting, she credits her grandmother with a gift for moving seamlessly from one activity and set of relationships to another:

> I grew up in a family, somewhat traditional in the Latino context, where my mom and I lived with her parents and an uncle and two aunts. We lived in a small town with one of everything except markets—one barber, one seamstress. The Catholic church was at the center of town, on the plaza, and I went to Catholic school there . . . Before I started school, even, I would go with my grandmother on her rounds. She was a traditional country woman who went to the market each day to buy the food to cook for that day. And she was a big influence on me concerning relationships. She would negotiate, but also *visit*. Sometimes we would stop in at a merchant's even if she had no business there that day, just to ask about a family member or how someone was doing. She went to the funeral home around three times a week, just to see who had

3. Rowling, *Harry Potter and the Prisoner of Azkaban*.

died and to pay her respects! She would walk around town just to see people. This influenced my own desire to move in different spaces. The next generation, my parents and aunts and uncles, settled into jobs. They were settled in one place. But my grandmother *navigated*.

VALUING MULTIPLICITY

The purpose of this chapter is to argue that multiplicity is a more generous and apt description of women's lives, and indeed a better metaphor for women's hearts and minds, than the logic of "integration" that pervades much of modern psychology (see the previous chapter). Women, I argue, are "com|plicated"—literally, we are a folding together (*com-plicatio*) not only of multiple roles and relationships, but of multiple internal states of emotion and identity. Sara's Rosetta quilt offers a rich image for conceptualizing women's psychology and women's pastoral needs in the context of our postmodern, multicultural world today. "Selfhood," particularly ideas of what constitutes a healthy self, has been regarded in terms of "congruence," "cohesiveness," "integrity"—or, more popularly, "having it all together." Yet at least as far back as Freud's writings, psychology (especially psychoanalytic psychology) has pointed to a more complex, messier understanding of how human persons—and particularly human *psyches* (minds or souls)—are constituted. Our very selves might be understood as quilts in which our thoughts, feelings, memories, deeds, and desires are woven throughout our lives into an ever more complicated and colorful pattern of consciousness and identity.

The idea that we are not monolithic—that our minds encompass both conscious and unconscious domains—was at one time revolutionary, particularly to the Enlightenment rationalists, for whom the very act of thought was the defining moment of selfhood: "Cogito, ergo sum"—"I am thinking, therefore I exist" (Descartes). Such complexity, however, has become almost commonplace and is the prevailing paradigm in most models of human psychology. In Freud's classical division of the mind into the "institutions" of ego, id, and superego,[4] the unconscious was understood to be created by the child's internalization of paternal/parental and societal prohibitions (around the age of five,

4. Freud, *The Ego and the Id*.

during the "oedipal crisis"), creating a repression barrier in the mind between the id's instinctual desires and the superego's moral dictates.

We have come to think of this model in terms of vertical "depth," in which our understanding of ourselves is achieved by plumbing downward, digging like an archaeologist or continental explorer for "deeper" truths (see chapter 3 above). While elusive, the contents of the unconscious (at least in part) may be carried up into consciousness on such vehicles as dream symbolism, accidental actions (slips of the tongue and the like), and therapeutic conversation (especially as manifested in the "transference"—the projections onto the therapist of childhood feelings toward original caregivers, which are "caught in the act" to be analyzed, yielding new insights[5]). In relational-psychoanalytic theory, however, as described in earlier chapters, this vertical-depth model is increasingly accompanied and even replaced by an appreciation of an even greater multiplicity. As noted in chapters 2 and 3, above, the human mind is understood more horizontally or spatially in this model of multiplicity, and encompasses a wider spectrum of states of consciousness and accompanying emotion (often called affect states or self states). In contrast to Freud's conflictual model of repression as the mechanism for removing certain mental contents from awareness, the relational-psychoanalytic theorists cited above regard *dissociation* as a significant, even normative means by which a multiplicity of self states is generated.[6] Unlike Freud's theory of repression, which could be imagined to resemble a hydraulic system of pressures and counterpressures, dissociation is understood as a more organic process, occurring naturally as consciousness moves across a web of mental states and contents. The mind develops through ever-increasing organic associations among bodily experiences, memories, desires, moods, and fantasies—as described by Jody Messler Davies: "a multiply organized, associationally linked network of parallel, coexistent, at times conflictual, systems of meaning attribution and understanding."[7] *The* unconscious itself becomes multiple in this understanding: "Not one unconscious, not the unconscious, but multiple

5. Freud, "The Dynamics of the Transference."

6. For a more detailed summary in relation to pastoral care and counseling, see Cooper-White, *Shared Wisdom*, esp. chapter 3, "The Relational Paradigm: Postmodern Concepts of Countertransference and Intersubjectivity," 35–60, and Cooper-White, *Many Voices*, esp. chapter 1, "A Relational Understanding of Persons," 35–66.

7. Davies, "Multiple Perspectives on Multiplicity," 195. See also chapter 3 above.

levels of consciousness and unconsciousness, in an ongoing state of interactive articulation."[8] As part of this conceptualization, dissociation, then, is no longer being regarded primarily as pathological, solely as the outcome of trauma, but (as quoted above), as "basic to human mental functioning and . . . central to the stability and growth of personality . . . an adaptational talent that represents the very nature of what we call 'consciousness.'"[9]

Healthy subjectivity, then, is far from monolithic, but as described above in chapter 3, is more like a seamless weaving together of disparate experiences and subjective states to create the sense of being an "I," or in Philip Bromberg's words, "the *necessary illusion of being 'one self.'"[10] To explain this more concretely, each of us experiences ourselves at a given point in time as being in one particular state of consciousness ("self state"). Each self state comes laden with its own thoughts, memories, physical sensations, emotions, and fantasies. In this sense, none of us is a wholly unitive "self" or "being." This nonmonolithic understanding of self/selves as more than a singular individual with an isolated consciousness or will accords well with non-Western conceptions of persons. In fact, as noted in chapter 4 the anthropologist Clifford Geertz pointed out that the Western notion of the person as a "bounded, unique, more or less integrated motivational and cognitive universe" is viewed as "quite a peculiar idea" in most of the world's cultures,[11] in which identity is often conceived more communally.

Further, this web of ourselves develops, not in isolation, but always *in relation*. Contemporary infant-observation studies confirm earlier "object relations" theories that the earliest experiences of self appear to be organized around a variety of shifting self states formed through the internalization of affect-laden experiences of primary caretakers and others in the early environment.[12] The very capacity to move smoothly and seamlessly from one self state to another and to

8. Davies, "Dissociation, Repression, and Reality Testing in the Countertransference," 197. For longer quotation, see chapter 3 above.

9. Bromberg, "'Speak! That I May See You,'" 521. For longer quotation, see chapter 3 above.

10. Ibid., emphasis original.

11. Geertz, "From the Native's Point of View," 59. For a longer quotation see chapter 4 above.

12. Stern, *The Interpersonal World of the Infant*; Emde, "The Affective Self"; and Stern, "The Prerepresentational Self and its Affective Core"; Beebe and Lachmann, "The Contribution of Mother-Infant Mutual Influence."

regulate one's own bodily affect states is facilitated—or not facilitated —by primary caretakers' responsiveness—or unresponsiveness. The quality of the boundaries between self and other is gradually established through mutual recognition and regulation, or, in less desirable scenarios, impaired by parental nonrecognition or intrusion.[13]

We might be better understood, then, as a *folding together* of many selves—personalities formed in identification with numerous inner objects or part-objects (not just id, ego, and superego). Each of us is in ourselves a multiplicity of "selves in relation."[14] We are made up of many parts, with varying degrees of accessibility between and among them as our consciousness shifts more or less seamlessly from one to another, without our paying particular attention to the flux. It is precisely this subjective feeling of seamlessness that creates the illusion of being "oneself," but this very illusion of seamless going-on-being from one self state to another is in itself a developmental achievement.[15]

Imagine yourself for a moment as more multiple than you had ever considered before—a complex quilt of subjectivities, flexible enough to bend to new circumstances, to form new relationships drawing on an inner world of memories, experiences, and identifications. In a postmodern world, with its ever-burgeoning flow of information—verbal, visual, aural—and instantaneous communication around the globe, is it any wonder that contemporary psychologies are exploring and celebrating this possibility of a more fluid and variegated construction of self and identity? Perhaps it is such "identity complexity"[16] that is the healthiest and most responsive form of "selfhood," and the most able to cope with the continual flux of the world in which we live.[17]

COM|PLICATED WOMAN

The challenge to unitive notions of self is, *theoretically*, gender-neutral. In relational theory, consciousness is understood, in both men *and* women, to be multivalent, fluid, their realities continually constructed

13. For further discussion of these dynamics, see chapter 2 above.

14. Mitchell, "Multiple Selves," 105.

15. Bromberg, "'Speak! That I May See You,'" 521.

16. Saari, "Identity Complexity as an Indicator of Mental Health."

17. For more on the implications of a postmodern subjectivity/intersubjectivity, see also Cooper-White, *Shared Wisdom*, 52–54.

and reconstructed in the matrix of individual and social relationships. Why, then, include multiplicity in a pastoral-care anthology specifically about women?

The first and more pragmatic answer is that women probably more readily identify with multiplicity as having an intuitive resonance with our own experience. Our lives often *feel* complicated. The popular book *I Don't Know How She Does It*[18] pointed to the challenge of multitasking that confronts middle- and upper-middle-class women, especially those of us who embraced the liberal feminist battle cry of the 1960s and 70s that we could "have it all." "Having it all" has been repudiated by some younger women of similar economic means, because of the stress, and the separation from home and children, that "having it all" seemed to demand. However, women's personal declarations of liberation from sexism never could produce genuine liberation, unaccompanied as they were by a parallel liberation of men. The socioeconomic structures of white-male political power and monolithic, stoic constructions of masculine identity continue unabated. So "women's liberation" increasingly came to mean economically privileged women's running faster on the hamster wheel of multitasking, and increasing pressure to master multiple roles as equally true and full-time identities—wife, mother, daughter, professional, volunteer. Of course, such multiple roles, touted as new pressure by the publishing classes, were not at all new to working-class and poor women, who for centuries had already been doing it all—and having none of it!

The extent, then, to which we can readily identify with multiplicity of identities as women may have as much to do with externally imposed (and sometimes internally embraced) expectations about juggling multiple roles—involving multiple personas (the faces we show to others in various arenas of our lives)—as it does with the creative, dynamic potential of our true inner complexity and diversity. Sara says, "I don't think there is a woman or girl who can say she does just one thing or is just one thing . . . Women are more open to 'go with the flow.' Maybe because we're forced to do that, because of expectations on us. I try to fight them, but they are so ingrained. I can't resist." Such socially imposed external demands for increasing flexibility in our lives and relationships, it might be argued, may even be inhibiting the flowering of our internal potential, because we have been so well

18. Pearson, *I Don't Know How She Does It.*

socialized to inhabit the scripts others have written for us rather than to explore freely the stories of our own unlimited becoming.

Multiplicity therefore has resonance with women's lives at a more complex psychological level—of *inner* creativity and flux. This level of multiplicity is better illuminated by a postmodern feminist analysis that addresses the social construction of gender, and the linguistic mechanisms of reinforcement of patriarchalism embedded in the very language by which we come to know ourselves and others. Although women have made great strides in some arenas, especially as measured by a liberal feminism that demands political and economic equality for women (such as the first viable campaign of a woman presidential candidate in the United States), the social construction of gender difference(s) and the psychosocial category of "Woman" continue to pose problems for individual women's lives, as feminist psychoanalytic and postmodern theorists have shown.

It is by now a commonplace among liberal feminists, from the psychologist Carol Gilligan[19] to presidential primary candidate Hillary Clinton,[20] to speak about the importance of women's "finding their own voices." As part of a larger liberationist movement, feminist pastoral theology has warmly embraced this ideal of helping to give voice to the voiceless, and to "hear" the marginalized, including women, "into speech."[21] However, as French feminist philosophers have pointed out, language itself is part and parcel of the patriarchal infrastructure of Western societies, following Jacques Lacan's linguistically focused version of Freudian theory.[22] Lacan proposed that as babies we all experience a certain shock and alienation upon realizing that the image of ourselves in the mirror is false—a chimera of seeming wholeness, agency, and integrated motion that exceeded our infantile experience

19. Gilligan, *In a Different Voice*.

20. Victory speech after winning New Hampshire Democratic Primary, January 8, 2008: "I come tonight with a very, very full heart. And I want especially to thank New Hampshire. Over the last week, I listened to you, and in the process, I found my own voice" (quoted in "In Their Own Words," *New York Times*, January 29, 2008). Online: http://nytimes.com/.

21. Morton, *The Journey Is Home*. Teresa Snorton points out an additional caution: "hearing into speech" can be romanticized when other variables, such as culture, race, and class are not taken into consideration (personal communication).

22. For a wonderful introduction to the implications of French postmodern feminism for feminist theology, see Kim et al., *Transfigurations*.

of fragmentation and our erratic sense of control. We are plunged into an irremediable state of alienation from ourselves as we identify with the illusion of the unified self seen in the mirror. We trade our embodied selves for a false and inverse identity in the glass, in order to defend against the infantile experience of being a "body in pieces" (*corps-morcelé*), "still trapped in his motor impotence and nursling dependence."[23] This unconscious trade-off comes at a price—our first sense of self is inextricably linked with an experience of alienation and lack.

This "mirror phase" of development coincides with the recognition of the mother as a separate subject in her own right, with her own thoughts and feelings. The differentiation from the mother also occurs increasingly alongside the encounter with the father as an "other" whose "Law of the Father" (and the "symbolic Phallus") enforces the oedipal rule of further separations, and suppression of spontaneity in favor of survival in compliance with the norms and demands of civilization. Culture itself is the vehicle of the Law of the Father; and as language is intrinsic to culture, so patriarchal social structures are imbued with the very acquisition of language itself. There is consequently no coming to speech, or even *thought*, apart from patriarchy, because there is no thought apart from the "Symbolic" (Lacan's term for the world of language and culture by which all operative reality is constituted). Lacan considers this to be absolutely and universally determined, based on biological gender characteristics. In particular, the penis as Phallus—the symbolic role of principle social organizer—en-gendered what Lacan believed to be a universal phallo-cracy.

It is in this regard that Luce Irigaray, a French postmodern feminist philosopher and psychoanalyst, raised the question, "Can women speak?"[24] Irigaray, however, leaves room for a possible—albeit as yet unknown—construction of femininity, a "feminine god" for "divine women" that would not be so thoroughly conditioned by patriarchal sociolinguistic structures.[25] Irigaray's work entertains "the divine [as] a movement . . . a movement of love."[26] How can we imagine subjects/subjectivities that are no longer sub-jected (thrown under) by phallocentric language and culture? Such an "imaginary" would require

23. Lacan, "The Mirror Stage," 76. See also chapter 4n24 above.
24. Irigaray, in numerous writings, e.g., in *This Sex Which Is Not One*, 83, 89, 111.
25. Irigaray, "Divine Women"; see also Jantzen, *Becoming Divine*, esp. 1–58.
26. Grosz, "Irigaray and the Divine," 210.

somehow circumventing the patriarchal stamp of language and of civilization itself. Irigaray's writing style itself is full of circumlocutions, poetic images, and suggestive gaps in logic as an attempt to inscribe women's resistance to phallocentric language and culture.

As part of this effort at resistance, Irigaray writes frequently of images and themes that appear to derive from female bodily existence—fluidity, flux, folds, lips,[27] even mucous membranes[28] as a counterpoint to the masculinist "logic of the Same,"[29] in which truth is equated with linear, rational thought and the straight-ahead movement of progress informed by Enlightenment ideals.

Another postmodern philosopher, Gilles Deleuze, has offered an extensive meditation on the aesthetic theme or image of "the fold."[30] Elsewhere I have already shown how Deleuze's work provides useful metaphors for the embracing of multiplicity, both in reference to human subjectivity and theology—especially in his revaluing of the image of the *rhizome* as a counterpoint to the frequent "depth" psychological and theological metaphor of "trees" and "roots."[31] This resonates well with conceptions of the unconscious in terms of horizontal or spatial multiplicities of subjectivity and affect, as an alternative to Freud's and Jung's unconscious "depths."[32]

Deleuze links the process of creation to a chaotic, groundless pre-origin from which all beings do not so much emerge upward as they "unfold." Deleuze describes this bottomless origin or "chaosmos" as a "matrix" (literally, womb)[33]—a maternal image for the divine. Deleuze contests the linear logic of Enlightenment conceptions of space and time, posing a trinitarian dynamic of "folding, unfolding, and refolding"[34] as an alternative vision of creative process that, literally by

27. "Lips" provide a rich metaphor for Irigaray in discussing both touch and reciprocity in "This Sex Which Is Not One" and "When Our Lips Speak Together," in *This Sex Which Is Not One*, 23–33 and 205–17; and in "The Limits of Transference," in *To Speak Is Never Neutral*, 237–46; see also Meyers, *Subjection & Subjectivity*, 96–91.

28. Irigaray, "The Limits of Transference" in *To Speak Is Never Neutral*, 237–46.

29. Irigaray, "Così fan Tutti," in *This Sex Which Is Not One*, 90.

30. Deleuze, *The Fold*.

31. Cooper-White, *Many Voices*, 56–60, 73–74, 81.

32. See chapter 3 above.

33. Deleuze and Guattari, *A Thousand Plateaus*, 313. Also discussed in Keller, *Face of the Deep*, 167–70.

34. Deleuze, *The Fold*, 137, also see p. 24.

im-plication, is less phallocentric and patriarchal. Feminist theologian Catherine Keller (cited above in chapter 4 on the multiplicity of God) also draws on Deleuze and the fifteenth-century theologian Nicolas of Cusa to propose an "origami of creation":[35] "Deleuze cannot resist [the] formula: 'the trinity *complicatio-explicatio-implicatio.*" This is a trinity of folds, *plis*, indicating a relationality of intertwining rather than cutting edges. *Complicatio*, "folding together"; in Cusa, folding of the world in God signifies "the chaos which contains all; . . . *explicatio*: that which 'unfolds' what otherwise remains 'folded together;' . . . and that relation, the 'relation of relations,' may be called by *implication* the *spirit of God* . . . So the third capacity thus signifies the relationality itself."

Keller cites Elizabeth Johnson's affirmation of divine love as "the moving power of life, that which drives everything that is toward everything else that is."[36]

The fluidity of the fold, like the roses on Sara's quilt, offers a compelling image for the multiplicity of women's lives, both outwardly as we live between and among various spheres of activity and relatedness, and inwardly, as we contemplate the nonpathological—and even life-giving—fluidity of movement within our psyches. We are *complicated* (folded-with)—an inner folding together and togetherness of folds. We are inwardly constituted by an ongoing "folding, unfolding, and refolding" as various emotions and ideas unfurl to meet the challenge of each new moment.

Sara comments, "I like reading Derrida. And I think a woman must have come up with it—reading his autobiography, I see his mom's influence!"

I ask, "Why do you think his ideas are like a woman's ideas?"

"Because he has to undo and redo things. That's what I have done. I had expectations—I thought life was one way. Life takes turns. You have to redo and keep going." Reflecting back, she says, "When Noelia was born I just wanted to be with my baby and enjoy. I didn't feel like I was less of me. I had to make choices—conflicting choices—but I felt it was right. I had to rebuild myself . . . And I just said, 'Let's keep going! No regrets!' Now the first one is in college and it feels awesome! I am rejoicing in that." Of course regrets, or the specter of regrets put away, and the weathering of hard losses also are threads within the

---

35. Keller, *Face of the Deep,* 232 (emphasis original).

36. Johnson, *She Who Is,* 143, cited in Keller, *Face of the Deep*, 232.

texture of Sara's sense of self. But it is precisely this complexity, this ability to weave strands of experience together, that contributes to her resilience and determination:

> My creativity is always hands on . . . I find time to cook an extra meal for Northwest Interfaith. I find creative ways to manage my time. I teach Sunday school—it's an outlet—you always have to have one more trick under your sleeve . . . And being involved in other places, and with my own children— it pushed me to think outside the box: You have to use what you have. I could sit down and complain, I didn't have this opportunity, but this is what I have, how can I use it? This is a thread in everything I do. And, lo and behold, you can do a lot of stuff! Could I do more with more resources? Yes, but I can *do lots* with what I *have!*

Furthermore, as liberal feminism has insisted for decades, the personal is also political. Multiplicity becomes a feminist model of resistance to the phallocratic logic of the One or the Same. Deleuze's image of the fold has political implications. As cultural historian Gen Doy has written: "For Deleuze, [the image of the fold] is not confusing or disorientating, but empowering . . . the methods of thinking and being of 'possessive individualism' are destroyed . . . Indeed, the trope of 'the fold' seems to be in the right place at the right time in our postmodern era, where liberal humanist hopes of progress and freedom for all are confronted by wars, famines, indeed barbarism of all kinds."[37]

Jane Flax, drawing on Irigaray, articulates how a concept of multiplicity of selves/subjects is not merely a boon for individual women (and men) but also, as noted in previous chapters in this volume, opens space for an ethic that contests the failed promises of Enlightenment oneness with a new promise of social and political liberation. Irigaray's language of fluidity, echoed also in Sara's desire to "go with the flow," is apparent in Flax's statement: "It is possible to imagine subjectivities whose desires for multiplicity can impel them toward emancipatory action. These subjectivities would be fluid rather than solid, contextual rather than universal, and process oriented rather than topographical. Emancipatory theories and practices require 'mechanics of fluids.'"[38] Michel Foucault translated the need for multiplicity

37. Doy, *Drapery*, 150.
38. Flax, "Multiples," 93, also quoting Irigaray.

into just such political terms when he wrote, "We must not imagine a world of discourse divided . . . between the dominant discourse and the dominated one; but as a multiplicity of discursive elements that can come into play in various strategies."[39]

This postmodern view resonates well with Homi Bhabha's postcolonial formulation of hybridity in relations between subjects, where *hybridity* is defined as the capacity of two partners or two subjects to join together without losing the distinctiveness of either.[40] Unlike a dialectical relationship, in which each subject must somehow be transformed or even dissolved into a transcendent solution to the problem of difference, hybridity suggests the possibility of a new, more egalitarian intersubjectivity in which particularities, differences, and even conflicts are retained and respected. This image of multiplicity has not only to do with the gendered nature of relationships, both social and political, but the way the "other" has been constructed in global relations of domination, war, racism, and colonization of indigenous peoples.

Gayatri Spivak asks the parallel question to Irigaray's question about women: "Can the subaltern speak?"[41] Where the *subaltern* (the subjugated other) has been constructed through colonial conquest, is there space for resistance? Postcolonial writers have argued that there is no going back or romanticizing earlier, precolonial times, but resistance to the hegemonic influence of the dominant colonizing cultures becomes possible through creative strategies of reassertion of indigenous cultural values and identities. Hybridity becomes a resource for claiming the threads of multiple cultural inheritances, (*post*colonialization) without the need to surrender to dominance via assimilation. While the term *postcolonial* itself represents a hoped-for future that is not yet achieved,[42] postcolonial theorists offer a strategy of multiplicity through which new forms of life may flourish both locally and globally.

---

39. Foucault, *The History of Sexuality*, 100; also cited in Jantzen, *Becoming Divine*, 57.

40. Bhabha, *The Location of Culture*, 114; see also Bhabha, "The Third Space"; for a summary of how Bhabha's formulation of hybridity differs from a romanticized ideal of "diversity" free of conflict, see Cooper-White, *Many Voices*, 45.

41. Spivak, "Can the Subaltern Speak?"; see also Spivak, *A Critique of Postcolonial Reason*; and Spivak, *The Spivak Reader*.

42. Rivera-Pagán, "Doing Pastoral Theology in a Post-Colonial Context."

FOLDING, UNFOLDING, REFOLDING—MAKING THE QUILTS OF OUR LIVES

I have attempted in this chapter to argue that multiplicity is a more generous and apt paradigm for understanding women's lives, both social/relational and internal/psychological. This argument depends, in part, on the assertion that gender is socially constructed. There will always be an objection to this, that the biologies of male and female bodies (however uniquely constellated in individual human beings) cannot be ignored. Hormones are powerful. Men's psyches may be no less characterized by multiplicity and unfolding/refolding than women's. But we are differently constituted by the sheer biological distinction that while women and men are both birthed from the womb of a woman, only women have a womb like hers (whether we become biological mothers or not). Irigaray draws considerably in her theories from women's more diffuse bodily sources of desire and sexual pleasure.[43] Nevertheless, as "gender" participates in language, it is already embedded in culture. There is no pure biology of gender—all notions of gender are *already interpretations* of biological experience. And these interpretations are laden with implications for power and domination.[44]

However, as Elaine Graham, Judith Butler, and others have pointed out,[45] it is precisely because these categories are finally constructs, and not immutable facts of nature, that gaps and inconsistencies within them may provide spaces from which both women and racialized, subaltern, and queered subjects can speak. Subjugated voices can erode and "jam the machinery" of dominance much the way fluids can erode seemingly solid rock.[46] "If the regulative fictions of sex and gender are themselves multiply contested sites of meaning," Butler writes, "then the very multiplicity of their construction holds out the possibility of a disruption of their univocal posturing."[47] There are spaces within multiplicity from which subversion and critique can still unfold. Deleuze's "fold" and Irigaray's powerfully seductive writings about the fluidity of women's experience lived in the body can

43. E.g., Irigaray, "This Sex Which Is Not One," in *This Sex Which Is Not One*, 28.

44. For further discussion of this theme, see Graham, *Making the Difference*, 221.

45. Ibid., 223; see also Butler, *Gender Trouble* and Butler, *Bodies That Matter*; Flax, e.g., "The Play of Justice," 111–28; Jantzen, *Becoming Divine*, 57.

46. Irigaray, "Mechanics of Fluids," in *This Sex Which Is Not One*, 99.

47. Butler, *Gender Trouble*, 32; also cited in Keller, *Face of the Deep*, 179.

be invoked as alternative interpretations to dominant discourses, in which gender, race, and sexuality are constructed and assigned lesser political power and social worth through hierarchical, linear polarities and binary oppositions (male-female, straight-gay, and by extension, white-black, Christian-Muslim, and so on).

A distinction must now be drawn between this new "imaginary" of multiplicity, folding, and flux—which indeed may serve as a helpful corrective to patriarchal insistence on an ideal of the (male) One—and an essentialist rendering of gender difference as innate and biologically determined. Words like "matrix" (womb), "flux," *jouissance* (an untranslatable term used by Irigaray to refer to female pleasure, including orgasm, but also a superfluity of internal pleasure, a "reservoir yet-to-come" that may spill over into artistic creativity, writing, or play[48]), and even "fold" (especially when juxtaposed with phallic imagery that is "hard," "straight," and "penetrating") have clear associations with characteristics of the female body. Femininity itself has been associated with the internal in contrast with the masculine as external, although there is certainly a danger here in reinforcing sexist stereotypes.

A too-glib reading of Irigaray could locate her with essentialist feminists, who believe that women are inherently or "essentially" different from men, and that the feminist task is not to contest femininity as an immutable "truth" so much as to advocate its being valued equally alongside masculinity. While this may be a temporary strategy for living within patriarchy, Irigaray's appropriation of the postmodern tool of "deconstruction"[49] reveals a more revolutionary agenda in which the falsity and poverty of patriarchal culture itself is uncovered and repudiated through the play of linguistic analysis.

An additional metacaution should also be raised—against overtheorizing! The more abstract our discussion of gender becomes, the more it finally flows into an *aporia*—a philosophical impasse. As Jacques Derrida has pointed out, there is no construction of gender (or race or anything, for that matter), dominant or otherwise, that does not already contain the seeds of its own deconstruction.[50] Precisely because

48. Irigaray, *Speculum of the Other Woman*; see also Kristeva, *Revolution in Poetic Language* ; for further references to the use of this term see http://science.jrank.org/pages/9861/Jouissance-Feminist-Political-Applications-Jouissance.html/.

49. Term from Derrida, *Of Grammatology*.

50. Derrida, *Writing and Difference*.

gender is socially constructed, as soon as any certainty is claimed about it, the exceptions will sprout up—or unfold!—to undo it. The only way out of this dead end, then, is not finally through further theorizing but through *practices*. As Graham writes,

> The impasse of postmodernism is resolved not by turn-ing away from the critique of metaphysics and dominant rationality, but by insisting that purposeful, coherent and binding values can be articulated from within the core of human activity and value-directed practice. Such a perspec-tive translated into theology would speak of the contingency and situatedness of human existence and knowledge, and the provisionality of our apprehension of the divine. 'Truth' would be understood as realized within and through human practices and material transformation . . . Thus, the central-ity of practice—as self-reflexively reflecting and constructing gender identity, relations and representations—is confirmed as the focus of critical attention for a theology of gender. It would however add a feminist critique of such claims to truth and value by attending to latent aspects of domination and exclusion in the formulation of such values.[51]

PRACTICAL IM|PLICATIONS—THE QUILTS OF OUR LIVES

Although I am a strong advocate for the value of theory (as chapter 1 elaborated), and much of my own writing is admittedly very theo-retical, I am convinced that finally it will not be through new and bet-ter theoretical formulations but through *practices* of multiplicity that women's creativity and authentic power will come to fruition. What in this postmodern time *practically* keeps us com|plicated women from just flying apart or falling to pieces? If a psychological model of *integra-tion* comes too close to homogenization and a suppression of creative inner voices, what, if anything, holds our internal diversity together?

It should not be stated that there is no reified "*wholeness,*" or sense of cohesion, in this model of multiplicity. Far from being an image of endless iterations of existence without any sense of connectedness (which *would* be fragmentation), the figure of the fold is illustrated by Deleuze by an image of a labyrinth—a whole that is constituted *by*

---

51. Graham, *Making the Difference,* 227; also citing Benhabib, *Situating the Self;* and Browning, *A Fundamental Practical Theology,* 2–10. For a further elaboration of Graham's "theology of practice," see Graham, *Transforming Practice.*

the multiplicity of its folds: "A labyrinth is said, etymologically, to be multiple because it contains many folds. The multiple is not only what has many parts but also what is folded *in many ways*."[52] Our sense of wholeness, then, as distinct from a monolithic oneness, depends upon our being able to move fluidly and gracefully, *in many ways*, among all the many parts of ourselves, continually drawing from our complexity new strengths for the journey.

In Sara's words, "There is a thread that pulls it all together. And that is very spiritual. I have a sense of gratitude to God that pours out in different ways for different things. In my upbringing, it was important to give to others who are not your family, not just your obligation." Sara's spirituality is a crucial source of strength and has a strongly relational quality:

> I think: This life is our one chance—make it or break it! I believe in a promise of eternity, a reconciliation with God, some unity where wrongs are made right, a reunion of believers, people you will see again. I hold on to that—even if it's not true—because it helps. I expect to see my grandma, my grandpa—even my dog! I have a sense of God's creation [gesture of her arms encircling]—there's got to be something like that . . . The God I'm praying to—I have to meet some way. There is this force or power I've seen in my life—there has to be a point of looking and recognizing that, in a more tangible (can I say tangible?) way. We expect, we look, we see . . . in prayer. . . good things happen that we didn't expect, and we attribute that to God's good hand and help.

A Threefold-Braided Thread

There is still a thread that holds the quilt of our lives together, but I would argue that it is not the thread of *the* executive ego, although that is usually present as an aspect of subjectivity that very usefully carries the mature illusion of being one-self,[53] seaming all our disparate parts and self states together in a continuous sense of "me" going on being. Rather, I would propose that there is a *threefold-braided thread*—the experience of *inhabiting one body* in relation to other bodies, a mature sense of *spirituality*, and a commitment to a coherent set of *embodied ethical practices*—by which the roses of the quilt are bound together.

52. Deleuze, *The Fold*, 3.
53. Bromberg, "'Speak! That I May See You,'" 521.

I would even venture further to suggest that this threefold braid is not a single straight line, but like the filaments tying each Rosetta to the next in Sara's grandmother's quilt is itself *a network, a weaving*. It is not, finally, *one* thread or braid, but a web of threads that, taken together, constitute a "whole"—but a whole whose very coherence and binding power is made up of our embodied relationships (including our multiple cultural inheritances and our internalization of others across the lifespan), our spiritualities, and our moral commitments. Each woman (each person, I would argue) is thus a complex community within her- or himself. By recognizing and valuing this communality of self/selves, we are all the more likely to be able to value the pluralism of the many communities with which we intersect, and even those "others" beyond our immediate safe, familiar context.

Weavers of Connection

As women familiar with navigating the web of connections both within and without, we can become weavers of connection and empathy, not only creating personal ties, but building political coalitions through relational acts of *capacitación* (= creating capacity/empowerment). Sara describes her own role in such a moment of weaving, which engaged her at the inner level of emotions and multiple identifications, while externally evoking her best political, cross-cultural, and linguistic skills:

> It had to do with some awareness of "crossing" identifications or something like that. I kept thinking about that and remembered this experience. Last year I attended a MLK day of service at New Creation Church in North Philly . . . [One of the groups] at New Creation was Rebuilding Together Philadelphia (RTP), an organization that helps qualifying poor homeowners with house repairs, free of charge. People apply and they receive a visit from an evaluating team to verify the information, assess the repairs that need to be done, and approve that person to receive the services. RTP was going to make some thirty visits to people in the immediate New Creation area on that same day. All their members were primarily men (just two women), and all of them were white. Almost all of them lived in the suburbs. They needed a Spanish-speaking person to visit these homes with them. That's how I ended up joining [one of their] teams. Never before did I feel so fortunate and capable. I gained their trust immediately. Furthermore, people they initially ruled

out because of misinterpretation of their circumstances and demeanors were accepted after a brief discussion and some explanations. The contrary also happened. But what I experienced was that I was accepted by both the disenfranchised Hispanic as well as the white, suburban group. I do not know how. I guess knowing both languages was a real asset. But also my understanding of the two cultures helped too. I came home so exhausted and sad about what I saw, but very excited about how I might have helped some people who would have been so misunderstood and therefore disqualified.

I continue to believe that the more we are willing to explore all the parts of our multiply constituted selves (including our own inner multiculturality—known and unknown to us) and to become curious about encountering the "others" within us—the parts of ourselves we have disavowed or otherwise split off from conscious awareness—the more open we will dare to be toward the "other" in our world. The model of pastoral care and counseling that I am advocating[54] seeks to help individuals (both women *and* men) come to know, accept, and appreciate all the distinctive parts—the many voices—that live within them. This openness to inner "others" may then allow women and men to bridge relational gaps, not simply by liberal Enlightenment values of "unity" and "solidarity" (a form of oneness), but by unfolding to embrace the other.

Might such unfolding lead to new social constructions, new recognitions, across gender, race, sexuality, and religion, to disrupt and replace existing power dynamics of dominance and submission with a new, political intersubjectivity—even among nations? This relational unfolding and refolding together—this com|plication—is the heart of an ethics for a postmodern world. We cannot have empathy for "others" whom we are too afraid to know, either within ourselves or in the social realm beyond superficial, anxiety-laden politeness or paranoid projections that inflate "others" into enemies, agents of evil, or justifiable targets of war. The more paranoid we become, the more we are likely to behave as the other's fearsome "other," continuing what has already become an endless cycle of provocation and retaliation.

In our relations, from the most intimate circles of lovers, family, and friends, to our immediate communities, to the wider world, and even to God—as Christian theism itself is unfolded and refolded

54. Cooper-White, *Many Voices*.

in new, more multiple conceptions of the divine[55]—we will find new sources of justice and creativity to sustain our efforts for justice and peace. At a time of so much simplistic rhetoric of "us and them," "good and evil"—especially with regard to race and racialized stereotypes of "other" religions and cultures—I continue to believe that it is precisely a turn toward multiplicity that might best help us to envision a generosity toward the "other" that might save us from ourselves.

While this embracing of multiplicity is informed by a postmodern feminist pastoral theology and psychology, and resonates strongly within it, it is finally worth pursuing passionately by both women *and* men. Multiplicity can offer new, more creative ways of conceiving both self/selves and other(s) as we take up the challenges of living in today's pluralistic, postmodern world—a "fluidity that is not loss but rather source-resource of new energy."[56] Our com|plication unfolds an alternative "imaginary" to the hyperrational, masculinist "progress" model of the Enlightenment in whose thrall we have dreamed too long. Multiplicity of self and others unfurls a new fold, to reveal a dream of a truly postcolonial age in which justice, care, and creative flourishing can flow freely among living beings.

55. E.g., Keller, *Face of the Deep*; Jantzen, *Becoming Divine*; and Schneider, *Beyond Monotheism*; and from a pastoral theological perspective, Cooper-White, *Many Voices*. All these approaches take seriously the postmodern feminist critique of oneness and propose alternative visions that move beyond Enlightenment categories of universality, truth, and singular rationality. See also chapters 4 and 5 above.

56. Irigaray, "The Limits of the Transference," in Irigaray, *To Speak Is Never Neutral*, 238.

SEVEN

The 'Other' Within

Multiple Selves Making a World of Difference

"How could one tolerate a foreigner if one did not know one was a stranger to oneself?"

—*Julia Kristeva*[1]

In the previous chapters, I have suggested that to embrace multiplicity has implications for ethics, and in particular, for the capacity to embrace diversity and difference. Diversity challenges us because it forces us into encounters with the Other, the not-like-me/not-like-us. It is by now a commonplace that in order to educate leaders for effective collaboration in diverse settings, a process of decentering from one's "comfort zone," and a stretching to embrace difference must take place. Further, any such education, to be effective, must take into consideration not only difference, per se, but also inequality of power—particularly in terms of entrenched social structures that silently reinforce unearned privilege. A genuine embracing of difference that can break down social inequalities and the dominating use of power requires more than a liberal "tolerance," or even a sincere but naïve form of curiosity about the "Other."

Growth in relation to diversity has been understood by counseling psychologists as a developmental process, with parallel stages

1. Kristeva, *Strangers to Ourselves*, cited in Capps, *Freud and Freudians on Religion*, 328.

applying, respectively, to persons targeted for oppression, and persons in a privileged group.[2] These stages include "1. Conformity → 2. Dissonance → 3. Resistance/immersion → 4. Introspection → and 5. "Integrative awareness/commitment." Persons of color in this schema take the journey from pressure to assimilate to the dominant culture, through questioning, anger and external resistance, to healthy pride, self-esteem, and a collaborative commitment to ending oppression. White persons move from denial and minimal race awareness to defensive awareness to shame and a desire to atone, to acceptance of responsibility for racism and an internalized commitment to ending oppression.[3]

This developmental outline can be critiqued for not fully taking into consideration the systemic and institutionalized power dynamics of racism (or other forms of oppression), or for creating too-neat parallels between white persons and persons of color. It has, however, provided a helpful framework for understanding and teaching how individuals at different stages of growth may resist, tolerate, cooperate with, or embrace diversity. It is a far more sophisticated tool for understanding individual variations in response to the challenges of diversity than assuming that once reasonable information is shared about differences, then the destructive phenomena of racism and other oppressions will be successfully resisted until they simply melt away. Nevertheless, fear, discrimination, and oppression—both internalized and externalized—persist among all of us, even those of us who have participated with a goodwill, and a relatively mature perspective, in antiracism and diversity education. What more is needed?

In this chapter I will argue that a greater appreciation of the *unconscious* dimensions of the human psyche is necessary for the formation of pastoral leaders in a diverse world. By coming to understand some of the unconscious dynamics at play within and among persons, we can build bridges of empathy that can more effectively combat

2. See the "Minority Identity Development Model," in Atkinson et al., *Counseling American Minorities*, 39–46; Cross, "The Negro-to-Black Conversion Experience"; Cross, "The Psychology of Nigrescence"; and Cross, *Shades of Black*; Sabnani et al., "White Racial Identity Development"; Helms, *Black and White Racial Identity Theory*; Pedersen et al., *Counseling across Cultures*; see also Lartey, *In Living Colour*; and Lartey, *Pastoral Theology in an Intercultural World*.

3. For more psychoanalytic reflections on whiteness, see, recently, Cataldo, "Whiteness Real and Unreal"; and Rector, "Narcissistic Dimensions of Racial Identity"; see also Thandeka, *Learning to Be White*.

racism, oppression, and exclusion of the Other. This process will not look the same for those who enjoy categorical privilege vis à vis those who do not. But the commitment to meet and understand unwelcome dimensions of our interior life is crucial on both sides of the power divide. Many of us, moreover, live in social locations that are not entirely privileged or entirely oppressed (for example, a white, middle-class woman who enjoys race and class privilege but suffers from gender oppression; or a middle-class woman of color who experiences some class privileges but suffers from both race and gender oppression; or a gay white man who assumes both gender and race privilege but suffers from the oppression of heterosexism). These examples, because they remain categorical, still do not begin to unpack all the multilayered dimensions of each individual's social location, with its unique confluence of both power and suffering. Nor does it address the multiple *meanings* given to these experiences, both in the crucible of unconscious fantasy and in the relational flux of co-constructed reality. Given such complexity, a conception of the psyche that is fluid, multiple, and relationally constituted is needed to lead us to awareness of our internal inconsistencies and complexity, which can in turn engender authentic empathy for the Other.

THE MULTIPLICITY OF THE PSYCHE

Social-work theorist Carolyn Saari has argued for "identity complexity" as an indicator of mental health.[4] This idea reaches beyond simplistic iterations of identity politics, which tend to frame both identity and culture as fixed and monolithic.[5] Genuine identity complexity reaches beyond our conscious self-identifications (including our political identities) to the inner domains of our multiply constituted self-parts and affect states—many of which are outside our awareness for much or all of the time.

As I have argued previously, each of us is internally constituted by a host of internal "objects" or mental representations, which are affect laden, and shaped in the crucible of relationships with significant external persons in our lives from infancy. These inner "parts" are not static or fixed in an oedipal or preoedipal past. Further, unlike the

4. Saari, "Identity Complexity as an Indicator of Mental Health." See also chapter 6n15, above.

5. Benhabib, "Complexity, Interdependence, Community."

roles of which we may be at least dimly aware that we may play in a family or organizational system, they are entirely unconscious until some intervention (either social or therapeutic) allows us to glimpse them by the residue of their effects on our beliefs and relationships— especially as these effects are not "rational" or "ego-syntonic" and therefore demand some explanation of ourself/selves to ourself/selves. These inner parts of our selves operate mainly at symbolic and nonverbal levels of the psyche, where they are more analogous to forces than actual persons ("objects are not people"[6]) or even to partial aspects of our conscious selves or actual external others (such as "good mother," or "bad mother," or following some therapeutic models, "inner child," "inner critic," etc.). They are dynamic and fluid, never simply replicas of actual people in our past or present life, shaped as they are by internal fantasies and impulses, as well as by social relationships with others.

It has been my contention that empathy for actual others in our relationships requires us to engage in the work of coming to know, accept, and even embrace the parts of our multiple selves that we have found most difficult to acknowledge. Whether through psychotherapy, Clinical Pastoral Education, spiritual direction, or the rough-and-tumble of social conflict and everyday relationships, we inevitably find ourselves in situations where parts of ourselves that we denied or suppressed will rise up and "act out" in ways that surprise us, shock us, even cause pain to ourselves or others. Being willing to explore the "foreign" parts of ourselves rather than to seal them over and pretend we are only exactly as we wish ourselves to be is the beginning of empathic understanding of other persons.

ROADBLOCKS TO EMPATHY: DENYING VULNERABILITY AND AGGRESSION

Two aspects of our inner selves may play an especially important role in creating a bridge to empathy: our *vulnerability* and our *aggression*. As North American Christians in particular, we may find that our societal conditioning makes it difficult for us to be fully conscious of either of these subjective states. Our North American enculturation promotes conscious awareness and adaptation to individuality, personal strength, self-sufficiency, and a "can-do" attitude that implies an almost sinful

6. Kohon, "Objects Are Not People."

quality to weakness or vulnerability. Western Christianity, for its part, names overt expressions of aggression as the sin of anger, and cloaks subjective aggressive impulses with a mantle of shame. The combination of these cultural myths results in a high level of ambivalence and anxiety about both vulnerability and aggression, since *in*vulnerability moves subjectively toward aggression, at least in the form of self-defense (just as Freud first described aggression in terms of self-preservation[7]). On the other hand, the suppression of aggression tends toward a subjective sense of vulnerability in the form of defenselessness. Patriarchy further infects these competing national and religious narratives of self-sufficiency and nonaggression with gender stereotypes about masculine strength and feminine dependency and weakness. Racism creates a double and triple bind for men and women of color, for whom aggression may be considered to be a positive attribute in some contexts but a shameful flaw or even a crime in others.

Each of us, then, will have different unconscious motives for repressing, disavowing, or dissociating our awareness of our vulnerability and our aggression, depending on our particular social location, and our personal history and intrapsychic makeup. Regardless of the specific ways in which this tension is played out in our individual psyches, these are the two affect states that we most avoid or unconsciously act out under threat.

The Other is always, by definition, an Unknown, and as such, may initially trigger an unconscious fear response. Brain science would seem to confirm that we are "hardwired" to confront the unknown with suspicion, for the sake of survival.[8] In a fraction of a second, before any "higher" rational thought can kick in within the prefrontal cortex, our "ancient brain" is busy throwing up protective barriers. If we conceptualize this in terms of a multiplicity model of mind and the unconscious, the basic affect of fear, then, taps all our prior experiences and our inner parts that carry previous experiences of fear, and the related states of both vulnerability and defensive aggression.

However, what psychoanalysis has taught us is that we can develop a greater awareness of our inner parts, so that we can better predict our autonomic responses in the face of unconsciously perceived threats and learn to soothe, manage, and override our animal reactivity. This

7. Freud, *Beyond the Pleasure Principle*, 13ff.

8. Hogue, *Remembering the Future*.

will not, paradoxically, be accomplished by pretending to transcend our bodily needs and impulses, our animal sense, because this would plunge us back again into a denial of both vulnerability and aggression—since these are part of our animal inheritance. On the contrary, by embracing our embodied selves, in all our complexity, and by befriending the very particular vulnerable and aggressive self states or "parts" that we find within ourselves, we are more likely to know and enlist those parts in meeting others who differ from ourselves and stretch us beyond our familiar comfort zones. That is, to the extent that we can tolerate feelings of vulnerability, we can modulate our anxiety into appropriate reality testing about the actual level of threat that may or may not exist. To the extent that we can be aware of our own aggression, we can mobilize its energy in the service of building up new relationships, solving associated problems or conflicts, and engaging in the necessary process of learning that can enable greater mutual understanding—rather than using it preemptively to limit or destroy the other.[9]

Awareness of our inner multiplicity serves a further purpose, however, beyond a classical ego-psychological framework of reality testing and self-control. As various schools of psychoanalytic thought have proposed across many decades, the more we remove intolerable affect-states, memories, impulses, or representations of self and others from conscious awareness (whether by repression, disavowal, or dissociative mental processes[10]), the more likely we are to project them onto or even (in the form of projective identification) *into* the other person who triggers in us an unconscious emotional reaction—a reaction driven by one or more of our internal constituent parts or "objects." Without at least some awareness of our internal landscape—or population—we will be at a loss to prevent this from happening more or less automatically in the face of an unconsciously perceived threat. Not only will we defend against knowledge of our own vulnerability and aggression, but we will project them onto the other. The other thus becomes "the Other": the *xenos*—the embodiment of strangeness. Because s/he now carries our own fear and aggression, s/he becomes the enemy, in and through whom we can "innocently" fight our own evacuated impotence, rage, and destructiveness. This is the

9. See also Greider, *Reckoning with Aggression*.
10. See chapter 3 above.

unconscious dynamic of *paranoia*. And once paranoia is set in motion in the unconscious, it is a short step from fear to hate.

What might this look like in an actual experience of diversity that triggers unconscious feelings of vulnerability and aggression?

PINKY HAS ROAD RAGE

"Pinky,"[11] a twenty-two-year-old first-year seminarian slouched in the back row of the mandated antiracism workshop, arms defensively folded. Pinky had a burly build and muscular arms that offset a cherubic round face framed by blond curls. An only child growing up in a middle-class, mostly white township in upstate New York, Pinky had been her mother's darling as a child, and the "good girl" who usually heeded her father's loving but stringent moral expectations. She was a solid *B* student and a good athlete and was raised religiously in a strict, tight-knit, Methodist church community.

The nickname "Pinky" had come from her tendency to blush violently whenever she was teased as a child. She herself had adopted the name as a way of making the slur her own, and making other kids eat their words—backed up with her fists when necessary. She had discovered the power of her own physical strength in third grade when Ricky McManus, a boy on whom she had a monstrous crush, joined in taunting her one afternoon. Fueled by fantasies of romantic rejection, she felt her humiliation convert suddenly into rage, and she efficiently decked him. She decided the day's suspension from school was worth the newfound respect she enjoyed from shocked classmates. Memories from that afternoon built her self-confidence, which in turn allowed her to safely be her parents'"good girl" most of the time—but with an emboldened demeanor.

Pinky graduated in the middle of her high school class, and attended a small liberal-arts college in the area. She was pleased when the college chaplain encouraged her to consider a call to ministry. By senior year, she had become a trusted residence-hall assistant and peer counselor. Her classmates relied on her air of confidence and compassion. To save money, Pinky decided that she would live with her parents and commute to seminary. She had high hopes for a future in pastoral care or counseling.

11. A fictional composite character.

Pinky had not been prepared, however, for the culture shock she experienced upon entering seminary. The academic demands were much tougher than anything she had known before, the approach to theology was very different from the simple affirmations of faith she was used to at her home church, and the social expectations were even more foreign. The men either shied away from her assertiveness or treated her as one of the boys. The women sometimes found her abrasive and did not seek her out to share confidences as she had experienced in college. She felt like a fish out of water, unfamiliar with the assumptions her professors made about "historical-critical exegesis" of the Bible, or "postcolonial and postmodern approaches" in church history and pastoral care. She had never heard of most of what the professors seemed to take for granted, and she wasn't sure she wanted to. Living at home provided a welcome respite at the end of each day, but she knew she was missing out on some of the casual social interactions with other students who lived in the dorm, and she felt cut off from a network of potential support. She felt anxious about what her professors and candidacy committees called "formation for ministry."

"Yeah, like being shot through a mold," she thought to herself. "Will I even recognize myself when I come out the other end?"

Pinky sat through the diversity training, longing to be outside tossing a ball or even just sitting in the library trying to get a difficult paper over and done with. At times she felt momentary twinges of insecurity, not unlike the way she had felt as a child when she was made fun of, before she had realized she could defend herself physically. But fists could not help her in this situation. Nor could her parents' assurances of how wonderful she would be as a minister. She honestly didn't know how to "be good" in this situation. She felt unequipped to cope with the strangeness of all the new information being shared in the diversity training. She didn't know how to fend off the feelings of inadequacy, guilt, and shame that threatened to wash over her. In automatic response, she assumed her old familiar stance of bravado and slumped in her seat, looking belligerent and annoyed. She used the evaluation form at the end of the day to vent feelings that the training felt like a waste of her time. Stepping gratefully out into the cold December air, she tried to shake off the day's discomfort and just get home to a hot meal and a comfortable evening on the couch.

Driving west with the last streaks of sunset in front of her, Pinky turned on some good, loud music. She found herself driving five, ten, and then twenty miles over the speed limit. Other cars seemed to clog the turnpike, trundling along at an unnecessarily law-abiding pace that started aggravating her until she began weaving among other cars, shifting lanes, and muttering under her breath. She felt like cursing, and was just about to give one especially slow driver the finger, but remembering her father's disapproval of "gutter talk," she held back at the last minute, and instead, accelerated and cut the guy off. She went hurtling down the left lane, not noticing the road slicking up in the dark. Suddenly another car shifted in front of her. Slamming on the brakes, she hit a newly forming patch of black ice and found herself spinning toward the median. The car revolved 180 degrees, and as she regained control of the steering wheel, she was startled to find herself in the left lane on the opposite side of the turnpike. Thinking fast, with traffic bearing down on her from behind, she accelerated and began to shift lanes to take the next exit and turn around. Just as her breathing began to return to normal, she saw red and blue lights flashing in her rearview mirror. She slammed her fist into the steering wheel, finally letting loose a stream of invectives, and pulled over, praying for the self-control to not scream directly at the cop who was now fast approaching the driver's side window with a blinding flashlight pointed at her face.

FROM EMPATHY TO JUSTICE

Pinky can be understood as a multiple self. Any single characterization or clinical diagnosis of Pinky's rage would be simplistic, failing to capture the complexity of her internal conflicting feelings and motivations. A complicated interplay of vulnerability and aggression are at work in this scenario, as Pinky moved through a series of affect states both familiar and unfamiliar, involving fear of difference, fear of her own complicity in racism, guilt, shame, and, in turn, defensive aggression and rage. Pinky's resistance to the training was more than (just) a truculent denial of privilege and an inability to be open to diversity—although it may well have looked like an arrogant refusal to enter into the process of learning. Pinky had already been feeling both vulnerable and angry for several months, but the "good girl" who delighted her mother and kept her father's criticisms at bay had been at the helm of her consciousness most of the time.

Many other parts of Pinky—the toddler who perhaps felt excited by her parents' hugs and kisses but thwarted by their rules and requirements; the little girl who felt shame and rage while being taunted; the third-grader who had learned to use her anger to defend herself; the girl who thrived under the occasional approving nods of her father, her teachers, and her pastor; the young woman who had made pretty good grades but was flummoxed by new academic demands for a level of critical thinking she had never been asked for before in relation to her faith; the young woman who was used to being everyone's confidante and who now felt like a social outsider; the young woman who had never thought anything about race or racism in a town that had no people of color that she could recall, and who thought of herself as a good person but now was being confronted with the possibility that she had enjoyed a race privilege she had never asked for or subjectively experienced; the frugal commuter student who realized that she had not enjoyed many things that some of her wealthier classmates seemed to take for granted—all these parts were roiling in her unconscious. They threw her into a variety of unwelcome affect states from time to time. However, she had never been given the cognitive tools, nor was she in a supportive safe context, to be able to understand her more negative feelings or to put them in perspective. So Pinky shoved back the feelings of vulnerability, shame, and incapacity that all these parts of herself threatened to bring to the surface, and without conscious intention gave in to the seductions of adrenaline that came with pounding music, dangerous speed, and caution-defying expressions of rage.

We can imagine many different scenarios in which vulnerability or aggression or a combination of the two would be implicated in a failure to meet the challenges of diversity and empathic understanding of the other. In Pinky's case, it was *aggression* that was let loose in the form of rage, like steam escaping a valve. (It should be noted that rage in itself does not lead to insight, because it is an autonomic response that boils over and in fact defends against deeper and more complex self-understanding.) But we can also imagine a scenario in which the affective balance could swing toward an unmetabolized expression of *vulnerability*: A different person, who had never learned or been allowed to use her anger at all, might have unconsciously sealed over her aggression. With her anger turned inward, she might have sunk into depression where feelings of vulnerability surface more readily but without conscious acceptance turn into rancid despair.

It would take courage for Pinky to come to know and accept the more threatening parts of herself, and (as important) it would take a relational context that would help her to feel safe enough to risk feeling the feelings that each suppressed part of herself was bearing in the secret recesses of her psyche. But Pinky is not an extreme example. We all contain parts of ourselves who know things we would rather not know, remember things we would prefer to forget, and represent aspects of personality we would rather disavow. These parts carry the emotional freight of such knowledge, memories, and identities or self states. These are the strangers that live within us every hour or every day. We want to keep them strange, yet, as Freud understood, the stranger, the uncanny, is always felt simultaneously as that which we can never know, and that which we have always known from our earliest days.[12] The "return of the repressed" is the uncanny familiar. The stranger outside ourselves who most triggers a fight-or-flight response is usually the one who taps the most familiar but hidden parts of our internal nature.

To quote Julia Kristeva:

> My discontent in living with the other—my strangeness—rests on the perturbed logic that governs this strange bundle of drive and language, of nature and symbol, constituted by the unconscious, always already shaped by the other. It is through unraveling transference—the major dynamics of otherness, of love/hatred for the other, of the foreign component of our psyche—that, on the basis of the other, I become reconciled with my own otherness-foreignness, that I play on it and live by it. Psychoanalysis is then experienced as a journey into the strangeness of the other and of oneself, toward an ethics of respect for the irreconcilable. *How could one tolerate a foreigner if one did not know one was a stranger to oneself?*[13]

By coming to know and to love the stranger(s) within, especially the most vulnerable and aggressive parts of ourselves, we can begin to engage in a kind of *internal justice making*, whereby the voices we have silenced within ourselves can come to expression. By learning what

12. Freud, "The Uncanny."

13. Kristeva, *Strangers to Ourselves*, quoted in Capps, *Freud and Freudians on Religion*, 137–38 (emphasis added).

they bear for us, and how they may have helped us to survive across a lifetime of emotional challenges, we can give them new respect and appreciation—even as we may need to parley conflicting affects and impulses toward a negotiated peace. This kind of inner peacemaking, which recognizes our unconscious complexity and multiplicity, is what makes us most able to meet the demands of external diversity. No longer continually threatened by the otherness within ourselves, we can meet and enter into genuine encounters with the others in the outer world. Such genuine openness to encounter can, in turn, lead to an engagement in the kinds of negotiations that true relationship engenders, and to a commitment to justice in which the sacrifice of certain assumptions and privileges can be understood as a larger mutual benefit to both others and ourselves.

We cannot avoid the reality of our vulnerability. As Judith Butler has written in the aftermath of September 11, 2001, we are vulnerable. Our lives are always "precarious": "This is a condition, a condition of being laid bare from the start and with which we cannot argue."[14] It is through mutual mourning and recognition of our human vulnerability and contingency, rather than through denial, that Butler sees the possibility for nonviolence and ethical relating.[15]

MULTIPLICITY IN COMMUNITY

Such appreciation of multiplicity in our inner lives has potential impact for entire communities—even nations. Freud, his daughter Anna, and others in their inner circle lived through the devastations of war upon war, culminating with the horrors of World War II and the Holocaust. They were therefore no romantics when it came to their view of human nature. In *Civilization and Its Discontents*, Freud cited numerous savage human atrocities, concluding with Plautus: "*Homo homini lupus*" ("Man is wolf to man").[16] Yet, they believed that their movement was not merely therapeutic for individuals but had political implications. The Freuds and Jung envisioned a rising tide of consciousness, which augured hope for a less brutal world.[17] In the words of Christopher Lane,

14. Butler, *Precarious Life*, 31.

15. See also Adams, "The Just Politics of Mourning."

16. Freud, *Civilization and Its Discontents*, 111.

17. Danto, *Freud's Free Clinics*; Coles, *Anna Freud and the Dream of Psychoanalysis*; Jung, *Memories, Dreams and Reflections*.

a historian of literature, culture, and psychoanalysis, "What, Freud effectively asks, could be *more* political than fantasy when it determines the fate of entire communities, nations, and even continents?"[18] To quote Kristeva again, "The ethics of psychoanalysis implies a politics: it would involve a cosmopolitanism of a new sort that, cutting across governments, economies, and markets, might work for a mankind [sic] whose solidarity is founded on the consciousness of its unconscious— desiring, destructive, fearful, empty, impossible."[19]

Freud's conception of the unconscious as a product of inner conflict and repression perhaps unconsciously reflects the war-torn and ultimately genocidal milieu of his life and times. A turn to multiplicity may bear the marks of the fragmentation and alienation of our own era. It may, in fact, be most intuitive for us first to appreciate multiplicity as it operates at the social and political level. For example, Mark Lewis Taylor advocates a postmodern shift from dependency on certain singular truth claims or dominant voices to "the nurturing of breadth in conversation:"

> Reasoning in a conversational setting attains its truths not by opting out of the heightening of difference by fixing on some fulcrum outside differences or on some foundation below them. Rather, those truths are attained by maximizing "the breadth" of the conversation, so that truths are disclosed in the conversation playing between different perspectives emerging within the widest possible fields. The conversation in which difference is really valued, then, will feature not only the vulnerability that goes with openness generally but also those experiences of difference and negativity that may be had in encounters with the most multifarious, widely arrayed 'others.' This nurturing of breadth is a feature of the conversational valuation of difference.[20]

He draws on philosopher Charles S. Peirce's image of a cable of intertwined threads, in which strength is derived from the connectedness

18. Lane, *The Psychoanalysis of Race*, 7. Both Lane and Brickman (in *Aboriginal Populations in the Mind*) advance important critiques of the oscillating romanticization and denigration of the racialized Other as "savage" or "primitive," embedded within psychoanalysis from its beginnings with the notion of "primitivity" of infantile memories and forces in the psyche. See also from a feminist perspective Khanna, *Dark Continents*.

19. Kristeva, *Strangers to Ourselves*, 333.

20. Taylor, *Remembering Esperanza*, 63.

of the whole rather than the dominance of a few: "This requires, in Charles S. Peirce's words, a trusting to "the multitude and variety of arguments rather than to the conclusiveness of any one. Its reasoning should not form a chain which is no stronger than its weakest link, but a cable whose fiber may be ever so slender, provided they are sufficiently numerous and intimately connected."[21]

This argument reprivileges those who have been on the margins, and places the individual within a larger context of interdependency. The "acknowledgement of a privilege for those excluded or absent from the conversation [,] . . . often voiceless because of death, persistent hunger, or systematic distortion of their social and political life—is the crucial way by which the fullest breadth of conversation can occur, a breadth needed for the truth of reasoning to occur and be sustained."[22]

Taylor refers to our moments of alienation, disempowerment and vulnerability at the conscious level of political relations when he writes, "exploration of *our own otherness* is also crucial to the whole breadth of conversation."[23] Without taking anything away from the call for a preferential option for the voices of the poor and disenfranchised on the conscious level of political discourse, I would argue that Taylor's recognition of our own otherness must also be applied to our internal *otherness* as well—that all political discourse is carried on waves of *unconscious* as well as *conscious* communication.

This is explicitly theological, as we understand the divine as the power of love in relationship. I have previously discussed in detail how the Christian doctrine of the Trinity provides a generous metaphor for an inherent multiplicity and relationality of God. In Kristeva's words once more, "henceforth the foreigner is neither a race or a nation. The foreigner is neither glorified as a secret *Volksgeist* nor banished as disruptive of rationalist urbanity. Uncanny, foreignness is within us: we are our own foreigners, we are divided. Even though it shows a Romanticist filiation, such as intimist restoring of the foreigner's good name undoubtedly bears the biblical tones of a foreign God or of a Foreigner apt to reveal God."[24]

21. Ibid., citing Rorty, *Philosophy and the Mirror of Nature*, 224.
22. Ibid., 64.
23. Ibid., emphasis original.
24. Kristeva, *Strangers to Ourselves*, 138.

Filipina theologian Elizabeth Dominguez draws on Genesis 1:26 to propose that "to be in the image of God is to be in community. It is not simply a man or a woman who can reflect God, but it is the community in relationship."[25] This has implications, as well, for righting imbalances of power. Quoting Chung Hyun Kyung: "Interdependence, harmony, and mutual growth are impossible when there is no balance of power. Monopolized power destroys community by destroying mutuality. Therefore, in this image of God as the community in relationship, there is no place for only one, solitary, all-powerful God who sits on the top of the hierarchical power pyramid and dominates other living beings. Where there is no mutual relationship, there is no human experience of God."[26]

The extent to which we can be aware of our inner multiplicity and take seriously the host of voices crying from the margins of our own unconscious life may well be the extent to which we are able to recognize and withdraw projections that demonize, dominate, and exclude actual other persons in the context of political life. In so doing, we participate in the eternal conversation that most brightly reveals our creation in the image and likeness of God. How else can we ever truly make a world of difference?

25. Dominguez, "A Continuing Challenge for Women's Ministry," cited in Chung, *Struggle to Be the Sun Again,* 48.

26. Chung, *Struggle to Be the Sun Again,* 48.

EIGHT

"I Do Not Do the Good I Want, but the Evil I Do Not Want Is What I Do"

Multiplicity—Good and Evil

The overall theme of this book has been to value multiplicity positively in understanding both God and persons. This begs the question, however, what about those forms of multiplicity that we know from both personal and clinical experience to be pathological, damaging, or destructive? While dissociation may be placed alongside repression as a normal, even adaptive process of self-formation, as previous chapters have discussed, we cannot ignore the ways in which damaging patterns of multiplicity as fragmentation are caused by psychological wounding—either in the form of something lacking in childhood development or in the form of active traumatic injury. What more might need to be said about unhealthy multiplicity? How might this also relate theologically to the problem of sin and evil?

Two forms of pathological multiplicity will be examined here. The first is Heinz Kohut's notion of the vertical split, which, as I will show, corresponds well to Augustine's classic doctrine of evil as negative or lack—*privatio boni* ("privation of the good"). The second is Melanie Klein's concept of internal psychic splitting. This theory, it will be argued, corresponds more closely to an alternative understanding of evil as an actual force in the cosmos that opposes the good—a dualistic understanding rejected by orthodox Christianity yet resonating with aspects of human experience, especially traumatic experience. The chapter will conclude with a reflection on theodicy and an embracing of the tragic in both psychology and theology.

THE CONCEPT OF THE VERTICAL SPLIT

In the late 1970s, Heinz Kohut, the founder of the psychoanalytic movement called self psychology, introduced the concept of the vertical split as an alternative to Freud's model of horizontal or downward splitting via repression. The concept of the vertical split was also less complex than Klein's model of unconscious splitting, and not as utterly rooted in early infancy. The vertical split was first introduced into self psychology in Kohut's article "Two Analyses of Mr. Z."[1] As described in chapter 3, the vertical split is conceived as a binary form of splitting via a psychological mechanism of "*disavowal*"[2] (rather than *repression*, as in either Freud's topographical model or his later structural model). Unlike the process of repression, in which mental contents are understood to be pushed downward out of consciousness into a deeper realm of the unconscious where they are entirely inaccessible to consciousness (except by analysis), the process of disavowal retains certain aspects of oneself as accessible to consciousness, but these are so uncomfortable to one's own sense of self that they are normally kept out of awareness.

The difference between these two forms of splitting—repression and disavowal—is illustrated in Kohut's article. (For Kohut's graphic representation, see Figure 3.5 above.) The vertical split is so named because it divides consciousness into two areas pictured on the same horizontal plane and not entirely inaccessible to each other; this contrasts to Freud's topographical model of horizontal layers, in which the deepest layer, the unconscious, is separated by a repression barrier that is normally impermeable.

The vertical split is usually identified with narcissistic pathology and is mainly manifested in behaviors, often compulsive acts that

1. Kohut, "The Two Analyses of Mr. Z."

2. The vertical split has lately been the subject of much discussion in self psychology circles, and has been described in much greater clinical detail in recent writings by Arnold Goldberg, a psychoanalyst in practice in Chicago and one of Kohut's most important editors and early interpreters. The term "disavowal" is discussed in detail in Goldberg, *Being of Two Minds*, 10ff.

the person would ordinarily find completely alien. Thus, rather than splitting the personality into conscious and unconscious domains (as in classically defined neuroses), the vertical split explains patterns of inconsistent behavior, in which different behavior patterns are governed by the two separate arenas of consciousness and corresponding inhibition or disinhibition. Individuals whose subjective experience resonates closely with this concept of the vertical split often describe this much in the same terms as those in St. Paul's self-description from Romans 7:"I do not understand my own actions . . . For I do not do the good I want, but the evil I do not want is what I do" (Romans 7:15, 19).

The vertical split has its origins, according to self psychological theory, in the lack of parental provisions as "selfobjects," reliable (or unreliable) and internalizable figures upon whom the child depends in childhood. Inadequate or inconsistent parenting over a period of crucial early years results in weak or lacking internal psychological structure, particularly on two poles:[3] the "mirroring" pole, in which the child should receive recognition, warmth, unconditional affirmation, "the gleam in the parent's eye"; and the "idealizing" pole, in which the child experiences the parental selfobjects as reliable, admirable, and idealizable—the core of values around which adult aspirations and ideals are formed. When all goes well, mirroring allows infantile grandiosity to be fed and gradually modified into a mature sense of affirmed identity, self-confidence, and appropriate pride in one's capacities and achievements; and idealizing allows infantile dependence to evolve into mature interdependence with others in relationships, and for pursuit of goals founded in a secure sense of ideals, values, and purpose. When all does not go well, however, the result is an inner experience of fragmentation, lack, and depressive emptiness, a sense that inside oneself "there is no there, there." This deep insecurity is often disguised by an external presentation of inflated self-importance, sensitivity to criticism, and narcissistic grandiosity and entitlement.[4]

With the phenomenon of the vertical split, the external presentation is the "me" with which the individual identifies: typically quite successful in some arenas, but often unable to form genuine intimate

3. Followers of Kohut, such as Ernest Wolf and others, identified additional types of selfobjects, e.g., Wolf, *Treating the Self*. Kohut himself introduced a third selfobject, the alter-ego or twinship selfobject, in Kohut, *The Restoration of the Self*.

4. For a postmodern discussion of narcissism and its origins in lack (drawing on both Freud and Lacan), see Deleuze, *Difference and Repetition*, esp. 110ff.

bonds in relationships, and baffled by the reluctance of others in one's world to recognize his or her superiority. On this side of the split, the individual often finds him- or herself attempting to ward off depression, and at times flying into inexplicable rages that are out of proportion to a perceived threat or criticism, but finally unable to soothe the self or restore a sense of proportion and harmony. When productive activity and the release of tension through rages fails to soothe, then the individual slips over onto the other side of the split and engages in compulsive behaviors in a joyless attempt at filling the inner sense of emptiness. In its most sociopathic form, these compulsive behaviors are justified by a semiconscious belief that "the world owes me" (paralleling Winnicott's "antisocial tendency").[5]

Sexual acting out, fetishes, alcohol and drug abuse, compulsive gambling, physical violence, and other behaviors destructive of self or others or both can often be understood dynamically as behavioral evidence of this vertical split born of early narcissistic deficit or injury. The predominant affect associated with those moments when the individual is aware of this "other side" of the vertical split is not guilt, as with neurotic behaviors, but profound shame: not "I *did* something bad," but "I *am* bad."

For example, a prominent and respected pastor, "Pastor George,"[6] used to engage in risky sexual behaviors when traveling on church business. Greatly admired in particular for his ability to find financial resources to fund important church projects, and for an uncanny ability to match people with needed resources, this man had a highly developed "good" side. He enjoyed a position of considerable power and prestige in the world of his denomination. His marriage, however, was one characterized by emotional distance and subtly patronizing discourse, and functioned mostly as a showcase to provide a traditional "happy marriage." When traveling, Pastor George hired prostitutes and became involved in a kind of "double life" sexually, in which he indulged masochistic fantasies, neither that he would have wanted known publicly, nor that he would he ever have revealed to his wife. Pastor George was "caught" in this behavior when he charged a number of visits to an "escort service" to his church credit card. He denied so convincingly that he had engaged in any behaviors the church

5. Winnicott, "The Antisocial Tendency."

6. A fictional composite case.

would disapprove of, that he exuded moral outrage when accused. He felt genuinely indignant, and his wife joined him in vigorously accusing the church leaders of conspiring to hurt him "out of jealousy." When the evidence came to light overwhelmingly enough that he could no longer deny it, his wife was devastated. Pastor George himself sank into a deep depression laden with intense shame, and besieged church leaders to restore his former status and reputation as quickly as possible, in a frantic effort to seal over the rupture in the wall of his disavowal and to restore his former delusion of superiority.

While self psychology certainly recognizes the impact of trauma on development, the theory overall presents itself as a *deficit model*—pathology is a result primarily of what an individual did not receive enough of in childhood, rather than an insertion of active, persecutory "objects" into the child's inner landscape. This model of personality is *structured*, not *peopled*, and pathology results from insufficient structure or structural defects, rather than from the presence of something, someone, or some*ones* "bad" inside. The subjective experience of patients from whom Kohut first derived his model was one of lack, a sense that "the center cannot hold," and frantic efforts to fill the void.

EVIL AS PRIVATION OF THE GOOD

How does this psychological deficit model correspond or correlate with Christian conceptions of good and evil? To answer this question, I want to turn very briefly to two main strands of theological tradition about good and, in particular, about the definition and nature of evil. There have been two significantly different understandings of evil: *evil as negative* (in the sense of absence or lack) and *evil as positive* (in the sense of presence of agency or ontological status)[7]; or to use feminist theologian Kathleen Sands's terminology for these two understandings: *rationalistic* and *dualistic* interpretations of evil.[8]

The negative, or rationalistic, view of evil has its origins in Augustine's concept of evil as *privatio boni*, the privation of the good. For the mature Augustine (who actually had started out from an opposite, dualistic point of view, as a Manichean), evil could not be accorded an active status in the cosmos, because that would elevate it to the level of

7. Milbank, "Evil: Negative or Positive?"; and Milbank, "Forgiveness: Negative or Positive?"

8. Sands, *Escape from Paradise,* 2.

divinity. As Augustine worked out his Christian theological doctrine, he came to insist upon the absolute original perfection and goodness of both God and creation. Evil, then, became in Augustine's theology, not a countervailing force of badness, but rather a lack or deficiency of good. For Augustine, evil had no place in God's original plan and was a human artifact. In the garden, Adam (we don't hear much about Eve in a positive light) was endowed with will, which was the perfect desire for God's perfect goodness and (borrowing from Plato) inexhaustible plenitude. The human creature was created to love God and with an innate capacity to apprehend the infinite. For Augustine, free will in its original, natural state meant the willing, or desire, for the good.

For reasons Augustine could never fully explain (although he struggled with this in *De libero arbitrio voluntatis* and elsewhere[9]), Adam perverted the will and invented what theologian Jon Milbank has termed the "fiction of choice,"[10] the illusion of self-governance in disregard for his created purpose—to love God. (Lucifer did the same thing in the angelic realm first, according to Augustine.[11]) So after the fall, human beings are prone to sin, which for Augustine meant the propensity to believe in the delusion of self-control and autonomous will.

After the fall, human beings can no longer perfectly discern what is good and perfect, although we are still able to desire the good, but now this desire is not automatic, but mediated by God's reparative gift of grace. Evil in this conceptualization is not an active force but rather a delusory self-reliance and a lack of the originally intended capacity to desire only that which truly (that is, infinitely) exists: God and all things pertaining to God's perfection—peace, love, perfect harmony. In this way, sin means that human beings are prone to confuse lesser goods with greater goods. In an instance pertinent to our case examples above, one is able to choose a desperate act of risky behavior as the good of self-soothing, but at the same time to miss the destructive consequences of such behavior to one's own and one's partner's health and security, and to tear at the fabric of community trust and accountability.

In this model for the origin of evil, there is no positive—in the sense of active—force of evil. And unlike the ancient Greeks' view, for

---

9. Augustine, *On Free Choice of the Will*; also *De Correptione et Gratia*, discussed in Wetzel, "Predestination, Pelagianism, and Foreknowledge."

10. Milbank, "Evil: Negative or Positive?"

11. Augustine, *City of God*, cited in Suchocki, *The End of Evil*, 8.

Augustine the flesh was not a particular locus for evil. Both desire for the good, and sin, could originate in the passions of the flesh, depending largely on degree. Even something that is good (for example, the desire to procreate—as we know, a large stumbling block for Augustine!—or the desire for food) can in excess become idolatrous—what Augustine termed (in one piquant translation), "the birdlime of concupiscence."[12]

Evil "exists" in this model,[13] but not in an ontological sense. It exists as an absence, as a tear in the fabric of creation; or, in the common explanation, as holes exist in Swiss cheese. Evil in the Augustinian model is emptiness, an absence, or nothingness, in which the desire for good is confused with what turns out only to be an illusion, a chimera of self-possession.

CORRESPONDENCES: THE VERTICAL SPLIT AND EVIL AS PRIVATION

There are some ready points of correspondence between this theological conception and the psychological construct of the vertical split. Both are deficit models. That is, both conceive of the origins or etiology of "bad behavior" in terms of something that is missing, not something bad that is actively present.

Me (aspects of self congruent with self-perception and public identity)	Not-me (disavowed aspects of self and behavior); lack of self-structure on poles of mirroring and idealization
Desire for the good/God's perfection (still available since the Fall, but mediated now through grace)	Failure of the will to desire the good (sin, first introduced by Adam's rebellion); evil = lack of good

Figure 8-1. The Vertical Split with an Augustinian Model of Good (Desire) and Evil (Privatio Boni)

12. Cited in Meilander, "I Renounce the Devil and All His Ways," 78.

13. Contra Evans, whose reading of Augustine, especially *De libero arbitrio*, asserts that "evil does not exist" (Evans, "Evil," 341). However, Evans herself presents a more complex discussion of evil as an historical phenomenon and hence a 'something,' resulting from the willful turning away of fallen angels and human beings in *Augustine on Evil*, e.g., 100.

In the narcissistic pathology described by the vertical split, "Me" (the aspects of my self that are congruent with my own self-perception and public identity) corresponds rather nicely with the Desire for the good/God's perfection (still available since the Fall, but mediated now through grace).[14] The "Not-me" side of the vertical split (consisting of disavowed aspects of my self and behavior), which has its origins in the lack of self-structure on the poles of mirroring and idealization, and in the lack of early parental provisions, similarly corresponds, not with an active desire to do bad things, but rather with the failure of the will to desire the good.

So, with the concept of the vertical split, "I do not do the good I want, but the evil I do not want is what I do," not because I am possessed by some active, external demon who is whispering naughty things to me from my left shoulder, or because my flesh has a mind of its own that does not "live up to" my lofty spiritual desires (the Platonic error), but because I am caught up in a desperate, shame-laden but disavowed effort to fill up the sense of emptiness inside me and soothe my painful feelings of fragmentation.

This never works, however, precisely because from this point of view evil is, in fact, that emptiness, an absence or nothingness of which Augustine writes, in which the desire for good is confused with what turns out to be only that illusion of self-possession and "the craving for undue exaltation"[15]—in other words, narcissistic inflation!

The only remedy, then, is not more compulsive acts aimed at filling one's own internal void, because this is futile. We cannot fill ourselves up. The remedy, from the point of view of self psychology, is the process Kohut calls "transmuting internalization,"[16] whereby relationships with new selfobjects facilitate the process of structuralization. By surviving (usually over and over) the experience in this new relationship of empathic ruptures, being given an interpretation that allows "me" to see more clearly the nature and origins of my split self that caused me to be vulnerable to that empathic rupture, and through this

14. It would be theoretically possible for someone to have an evil-self-concept and disavow the good, but this is not the way it is usually understood or manifested in clinical application.

15. Augustine, *City of God*, XIV.XIII, as cited in Suchocki, *The End of Evil*, 6.

16. Kohut discussed the concept of "transmuting internalization" in all three of his major works. He first introduced it in *The Analysis of the Self*, and elaborated in *The Restoration of the Self* and (posthumously) *How Does Analysis Cure?*

process experiencing the growth or repair of the inner self-structure, the split can gradually be healed. In this way, my behavior can gradually change from shame-laden, compulsive, hidden activity driven by a need for grandiose self-inflation and self-soothing, to behavior that is more integrated and genuinely relational.

In a sense, the original damage is done, but transmuting internalization functions in a way like grace—it does not replace the original goodness that was intended in creation, but it does mediate a restoration of the capacity, however imperfect, to desire the good once again. While this process of transmuting internalization may not necessarily require the services of an analyst, the aim of a self psychological analysis, as well as the potentially curative function of all loving relationships, is in the healing of the vertical split and the restoration of wholeness. This might be seen to correspond to the theological notion of the healing power of grace.

To the extent that self psychologists increasingly view this conception of psychopathology as narcissistic deficit to be more or less true for everyone, this model even corresponds with the universality of the theological construct of original sin. No one gets out of childhood with a "perfect" self structure, and so no one can escape the propensity toward self-inflation and narcissistic vulnerability of one form or another, although this may be acted out to varying degrees and may not enter into overtly destructive behaviors. In the same way, in this theological view, no one can escape the consequences of the fall, and although some individuals will behave morally more badly than others, even the saints cannot any longer perfectly will the good without the mediating and redeeming power of God's grace.

The correspondence between the vertical split then, as a psychological construct, and the theological conception of evil as *privatio boni*, works rather neatly! And that's the problem. We have just explored a rather tidy heuristic correspondence between the deficit model in self psychology and the idea of evil as privation. But is this a sufficient model to understand evil in all its guises?

EVIL AS A POSITIVE FORCE

A second prominent strand in both Christian and post-Christian theology frames evil in a very different way—not as a negation, as a privation of the good, but as a positive (in the sense of active and ontological) force in the universe, competing directly against God's goodness and seeking to undo it.[17] In the view most opposite to that of Augustine (this is the *dualistic* view), which had its fullest flower in the Manichean doctrine of the patristic era, which later re-erupted in Catharism (the object of the Albigensian Crusade in the thirteenth century).[18] Dualism has always been labeled as heresy by the church, but nevertheless is prominent in popular folk religion. Dualism sees God and the devil as virtually equal cosmic forces competing for human souls.

For the medieval pietist, this view of an active devil as Adversary[19] was reconciled with the ultimate supremacy of God by saying that in the eschaton, the devil would finally be permanently subdued, but in this interim period of travail between the first and second comings of Christ, the devil was still allowed to wreak havoc. So we have the story of Martin Luther hurling his inkwell at the devil as Luther lurked in his own study. Similarly, Ignatius of Loyola found it necessary to write *Rules for the Discernment of Spirits* (i.e., for the discernment of evil vs. good) to accompany his *Spiritual Exercises* because of his own experience of "the Evil Spirit" or Satan, who undermines the spiritual progress of maturing Christians through deception and seduction, resulting in spiritual desolation.[20] The idea of an active force of evil with sentience and agency is certainly biblical: "Be sober, be watchful. Your adversary the devil prowls around like a roaring lion, seeking someone to devour. Resist him, firm in your faith" (1 Peter 5:8–9a).

A serious and scholarly contemporary conceptualization of evil as an active force has come from post-Holocaust theologians, modern and postmodern philosophers, who contend that in the wake of the mass horrors of the twentieth century, particularly the atrocities of Nazi Germany but also Stalinist Russia and the Pol Pot genocides in

17. For the sake of concision, I am omitting discussion of another positive, or active, conception of evil: that of Irenaeus, who viewed evil as an active force but subsumed as a necessary part under God's plan as a means of perfecting an immature creation; this view is also espoused in modern times by Hick in *Evil and the God of Love*. This might also be compared with Jung's notion of God even containing evil, especially in Jung, *Answer to Job*.

18. There has been a recent resurgence of interest in the Albigensian Crusade, e.g., Costen, *The Cathars and the Albigensian Crusade*.

19. See Pagels's exhaustive historical review of the word *Satan* as a name for the devil as "adversary" or "temptation" in Pagels, *The Origin of Satan*.

20. For a lengthy discussion on Ignatius's discernment of spirits, see Toner, *A Commentary on Saint Ignatius' Rules for the Discernment of Spirits*.

Cambodia, we can no longer subscribe to a view of evil as merely privation of the good. For many modern and postmodern philosophers, the category of "free will" is not a consequence of some primordial human error but rather intrinsic to the human condition. Paul Ricoeur's idea of "fallible man" opens the way toward viewing the capacity for sin and evil as inherent in human existence.[21] Traces appear in Ricoeur of the idea that evil is not simply a "nothing" but a "something." In his concluding sentence in the book *Fallible Man*, he states: "To say that man [sic] is fallible is to say that the limitation peculiar to a being who does not coincide with himself is the primordial weakness from which evil *arises*. And yet, evil arises from this weakness only because it is *posited*. This last paradox will be at the center of the symbolics of evil."[22] Elaborating further in *The Symbolism of Evil*, he states, within his framework of the "servile will":

> Evil is not nothing; it is not a simple lack, a simple absence of order; it is the power of darkness; it is posited; in this sense it is something to be 'taken away:' I am the Lamb of God who takes away the sins of the world,' says the interior Master . . . Evil comes to a man [sic] as the 'outside' of freedom, as the other than itself in which freedom is taken captive . . . This is the schema of seduction; it signifies that evil, although it is something that is brought about, is already there, enticing . . . Evil is both something brought about now and something that is already there; to begin is to continue.[23]

Ricoeur's understanding is not strictly dualistic, however. Evil is always, for Ricoeur, subordinate to original goodness, neither symmetrical nor equal to it.[24] "However primordial badness may be, goodness is yet more primordial."[25]

21. Ricoeur, *Fallible Man*.

22. Ibid., 146 (emphasis original).

23. Ricoeur, *The Symbolism of Evil*, 155. Feminist theologian Kristine Rankka draws from this positive view of evil in her *Women and the Value of Suffering*, esp. 184–89.

24. E.g., Ricoeur, *The Symbolism of Evil*, 156. In her argument for evil as a "something," Rankka (184–85) notes the first two points Ricoeur makes about the positiveness of evil, cited above, but she omits Ricoeur's third point that evil is also subordinate to original goodness (*Symbolism of Evil*, 156).

25. Ricoeur, *Fallible Man*, 145.

John Milbank locates the modern origins of dualistic interpretations of evil in Kant.[26] In a post-Kantian sense, Milbank has asserted, the capacity to will means the capacity to will *either* good *or* evil. The senses are amoral and so tend toward self-preservation and pleasure (not unlike Freud's pleasure principle, but contrary to his idea of the death instinct). But because, for Kant and the post-Kantians, there can be no access to the infinite through the senses, we are left with the dilemma of making moral choices based in the historical moment, with no recourse to such a thing as Augustine's desire for the good to guide us.

The problem of theodicy—justifying God's "allowing" evil to exist—gets resolved in this strand of thinking in one of several ways. Either God is dead (the nihilistic solution), or God has willingly limited God's own power in favor of the gift of free will (the process-theology solution[27]) so that we might be made in God's own image, which is defined as being able to choose between good and evil for ourselves. The latter view preserves both human and divine agency, while explaining how "genuine evil" is allowed to exist.[28] It has been popularized in books like Rabbi Kushner's *When Bad Things Happen to Good People*,[29] and is a view often cited in pastoral care.

The value of this positive view of evil is in its power to describe the way many people do experience evil in the contemporary world. The vast majority of trauma survivors have not read Augustine and are unfamiliar with scholarly arguments about theodicy. They do, however, present themselves to us as legitimate experts on the experience of suffering and personal acquaintance with evil. One scholarly line of thought regarding theodicy is, in fact, that focusing on attempts to rationalize evil or justify God can serve as an intellectualizing distraction from the human reality of suffering as the proper focus for attention.[30] This may be especially true, or at least true in a distinctive

26. Milbank, "Evil: Negative or Positive?"

27. E.g., Cobb and Griffin, *Process Theology*; Griffin, *God, Power, and Evil*; Madden and Hare, *Evil and the Concept of God*.

28. See in particular Griffin's critique of Augustine in *God, Power, and Evil*, 55–71, also reprinted in Peterson, *The Problem of Evil*, 197–214.

29. Kushner, *When Bad Things Happen to Good People*.

30. Weil, *Waiting for God*, cited in Nava, "The Mystery of Evil and the Hiddenness of God," 76. See also Tilley, *The Evils of Theodicy*; Surin, *Theology and the Problem of Evil*; Gutierrez, *On Job*; Billings, "Theodicy as a 'Lived Question.'" Miroslav Volf has also rejected the category of "theodicy" on similar grounds; e.g., Volf, "Memory, Suffering, and Redemption."

way, for women's experience of evil and suffering. Nel Noddings, in her study of women and suffering, found that women experience evil as "relational and positively real."[31] She writes:

> Evil is a real presence, and moral evil is often the result of trying to do something either genuinely thought to be good or rationalized layer on layer in gross bad faith. Evil is thus intimately bound up in disputes over good . . . When we acknowledge that pain, separation, and helplessness are the basic states of consciousness associated with evil and that moral evil consists in inducing, sustaining, or failing to relieve these conditions, we can no longer ignore that we do think on and intend evil when we perform such acts. Just as disease is real and not just an illusion or absence of health, evil is real, and to control it we need to understand it and accept that the tendency toward it dwells in all of us.[32]

Noddings goes on to advocate for education as a means to understand evil, with the goal, in turn, of combating mystification and informing moral action.

Feminist theologian Kathleen Sands has faulted classical, twentieth-century feminist and postmodern theologians for not taking the existence of evil seriously enough, or for mystifying evil. She finds the distinction between a negative and a positive view of evil to be a dualism that is itself suspect.[33] Womanist theologians such as Emilie Townes, Frances Wood, and Delores Williams also point to the concreteness of the reality of the demonic as experienced in Black women's suffering. They tend to locate evil not in abstraction or in "nature," but as institutionalized in the social, political, and economic realm.[34]

Peter Homans recently commented that there are many forms of intelligence, including what he appreciatively termed "clinical intelligence."[35] In order to address this more active conceptualization of evil in relation to our psychological theories, we need to turn to our clinical intelligence and ask the question, what do *patients* experience? In my own clinical experience, individual's conceptualization of evil

---

31. Noddings, *Women and Evil*, 229. See also Rankka, *Women and the Value of Suffering*, 60ff.

32. Noddings, *Women and Evil*, 229–30.

33. Sands, *Escape from Paradise*.

34. E.g., Townes, *A Troubling in My Soul*.

35. Homans, A Response.

seems to depend on whether that person's perspective is one of being victimized or one of (however unwittingly or disavowedly) being a perpetrator. Another way of putting this might be whether the predominant characteristics of the individual's suffering fall more into the pattern of posttraumatic symptomatology or narcissistic character pathology. The vertical split provides an excellent theoretical understanding of the problems experienced due to narcissistic injury, as already described above. But what about those patients whose injury falls more into the category of active traumatization than a deficit model of parental lack?

This is where in my own clinical work and research I have found the self psychological model somewhat lacking in explanatory power. I have found object-relations theory, and particularly the contributions of the "relational" school psychoanalysis,[36] able to go further in explaining the complex intersubjective and mutual projective processes experienced in clinical work in general, but especially with trauma survivors.

EVIL VIEWED FROM OBJECT RELATIONS AND TRAUMATOLOGY

In object-relations theory, the inner world is not characterized by one binary split as in the vertical split, nor is it adequately described by going back to Freud's repression model that divided consciousness into conscious and unconscious regions. This model, originating in the work especially of theorists like Fairbairn—with his system of internal objects, the "libidinal ego,""anti-libidinal ego" or "internal saboteur," and "central ego"[37]—goes even further in populating the inner world with a vast multiplicity of mental representations. (For more detail on these concepts, see chapter 2, above.) Most of these have their origins in real external figures in the individual's life, especially in the formative first months and years of life. But following Klein,[38] inner objects are not necessarily derived from a pure, undistorted internalization of external figures taken in "whole." They are digested and metabolized by the infant's own inner mechanisms—fantasized or perceived expe-

36. For a representative collection of articles by relational theorists, see Mitchell and Aron, *Relational Psychoanalysis*. Ongoing work in this school of thought is represented in the journal *Psychoanalytic Dialogues*. This movement is discussed in more detail in chapters 3 and 4 in this volume.

37. Fairbairn, *Psychoanalytic Studies of the Personality*.

38. Klein, "Notes on Some Schizoid Mechanisms."

riences of the other that may correspond only to varying degrees with external "reality," and shaped by constitutional predispositions prior experiences, bodily sensations, fears, wishes, or the like.

The inner world, further, is filled with contradictory representations, based on the mechanism of splitting (the primitive developmental state Klein called the "paranoid schizoid position"). Based on Klein's theory, external figures or events experienced as bad are unconsciously split off from good representations of the same figures, in order to preserve those figures—especially those on whom the small child depends for survival. Both "me" and "others" are thus preserved in split-off forms. Persecutory objects may also be internalized as a survival mechanism of identifying with the oppressor. If the child is fortunate enough, there may also be alternative loving, soothing, and strengthening figures, pets, books, or even inanimate objects that carry symbolic healing power, which can be internalized as well.

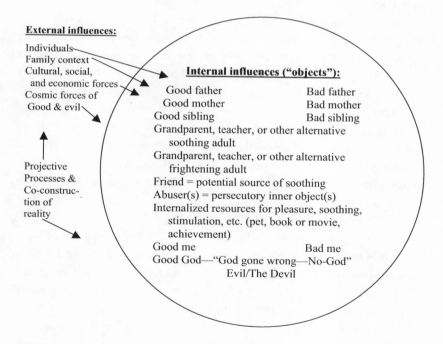

Figure 8-2. An Object-Relational Model of the Mind and Internal Splitting

In this model, behavior is not explained by the mechanism of disavowal but rather by *dissociation* and *fragmentation*. Persecutory inner objects and traumatic mental representations are not static inner images but function as live introjects that can at times govern behavior. Although most trauma victims do not experience the degree of dissocation present in Dissociative Identity Disorder (formerly known as Multiple Personality Disorder),[39] in this model of mind, all of us to varying degrees find ourselves in different affect states generated by associations between current circumstances and multiple past, state-dependent learnings and experiences.

In this model, because of the psychic necessity of splitting in an unconscious attempt to preserve the integrity of good objects, badness is projected "out there" onto other people, and also "into" them through "projective identification"[40] until new unconscious relationships are set in motion between people in an intersubjective co-construction of realities that, especially to the degree trauma has existed in the past, tend to reenact unhealed painful experiences. Whereas in healthy multiplicity the variety of inner self states is flexible and can change and grow in response to new experiences, *fragmentation* represents a traumatically fixed or static state of splitting, in which the internal parts of the self remain defensively unchanged and unchanging. Like the clenched muscles of a street fighter in defensive posture, fragmented self states, bathed in a continual flow of stress hormones, cannot move flexibly because they are in a constant state of hypervigilance against further assault. Thus, the normal multiplicity of a healthy personality is frozen into rigid patterns of dissociation in which the various parts of the self cannot relate fluidly to one another or to the outside world.

In terms of religious faith, internalized representations of God also grow from these early inner objects, as Maria Rizzuto and others have demonstrated. Theologian Jane Grovijahn, in her study of sexual abuse survivors' narratives, has identified ways in which the inner God *imago* may also be split by the traumatic experience into one or more versions of "Good God," "God gone wrong," and "No-God."[41] I would add to this the further splitting off, frequently, of an inner

39. American Psychiatric Association, *DSM-IV-TR*, 526–29.
40. Klein, "Notes on Some Schizoid Mechanisms."
41. Grovijahn, "A Theology of Survival."

representation or figure opposing God as "Evil" or "the devil." Some survivors have a rather large inner population of both avenging angels or helpers, *and* demonic figures that are fantasized or even actively experienced as something supernatural or in some other realm beyond human form.

In the object-relations model, psychopathology is a result of *trauma*, not *deficit*. Suffering is a result not of emptiness and lack but of the insertion of active, persecutory "objects" into the child's inner landscape and the splitting of good and bad aspects of others that cannot be held together and psychically survive. This model of personality *is* peopled, not structured; and pathology results, not from insufficient structure or structural defects, but from the felt *presence* of something, someone, or some*ones* "bad" inside. Patients for whom this model holds the greatest explanatory power are those who report not only emptiness, although they do frequently describe something like a "hole" deep inside, but also continual, undifferentiated psychic pain (as described so poignantly by British analyst Betty Joseph[42]).

Ask a trauma survivor about evil, and you will not likely get an abstract answer about privation of the good. Think of the rhetoric that surrounded survivors' viewing of Timothy McVeigh's execution. We heard one survivor say, "He looked at each one of us, and we felt that evil was looking directly at us." Trauma survivors, especially if their trauma was one of human design and not a natural disaster, will say that they have seen evil, can give it a name and a face. They remember malicious laughter and deliberately cruel words and actions, not only as past events, but also as an ongoing psychic reality that can even have the force of throwing them back into a dissociative reliving of past terrors. (These thoughts, which I first wrote down long before September 11, 2001, take on more poignancy and perhaps also more complexity in the wake of the terrorist attacks on New York City and Washington, DC.)

In this psychological model of trauma, it is hard to account for evil only as *privatio boni* (although one could still make a case, as Milbank does, that terrible, even catastrophic things can be done as a result of absence of the good—especially as a result of mistaking a lesser good for a greater one, a chilling explanation for how "good people" can be swept up in doing horrible things). The psychic experience of trauma

42. Joseph, "Toward the Experiencing of Psychic Pain."

survivors, however, calls forth depictions of demonic forces locked in battle with avenging angels, devils lurking on the rooftops of cathedrals, and so-called normal reality being more suspect and ephemeral than the certain knowledge of terror. Supernatural narratives from the popular culture, with avenging characters, such as *The Exorcist, Xena: Warrior Princess, Buffy the Vampire Slayer,* and more recently the Twilight vampire romances and the Harry Potter books and movies have held enduring interest for many trauma survivors, precisely because such blends of gothic and science-fiction narratives resonate with the psychic battles between good and evil that these survivors experience as their daily inner world.

For many trauma victims, internal representations of evil are not conscious and disavowed but split off in the unconscious. Evil is not located in a known though unwanted part of the self, but is located most often, at least until healing integration begins to take place, in the unconscious, and is experienced externally through projection, whether this projection falls upon an intimate partner, a publicly identified villain, or an entire nation labeled as enemy. This model also has its claims to universality. Most of us do not get out of childhood with perfect self structures, and most of us do not get out of childhood unscathed. Numerous convincing arguments show that much conflict at the level of groups and even nations is a result of our collective, mutually constructed reality based on splitting and projection of evil always somewhere outside ourselves.

CONCEPTUALIZING PATHOLOGY: MUST WE CHOOSE ONE MODEL?

As we have seen above, then, there is more than one model to understand pathological splitting. Must we choose? Is it possible to rely solely on any one of the models previously mentioned—Kohut's vertical split, Klein's concept of internal splitting and object relations, or the understanding of dissociative fragmentation in trauma theory—to understand the more destructive and pathological aspects of multiplicity of the self? It is my contention that these different understandings of pathological multiplicity address different aspects of human wounding, and therefore we need them all to comprehend the full range of ways in which healthy multiplicity can become skewed toward illness and destructive acting out (or, in theological terms, can become behavior that participates in evil and sin). With reference to "thick theory" (chapter 1 above), perhaps an openness to both constructs can provide needed complexity.

The vertical split is especially helpful to empathically understand individuals whose suffering falls most prominently under the category of *narcissistic pathology*. From the narcissistically damaged individual's point of view, evil is most often experienced as an alien part of one's self-identity and character, corresponding well with the vertical split. Early experiences are predominantly of deficit and lack, specifically lack of appropriate mirroring and provision of reliable selfobjects for idealization. The process of removing contents from ordinary awareness is a conscious process of disavowal. Evil is experienced as lack, and one's own self-defeating behavior is experienced as both unintended and unwanted, or as necessary recompense, as if one were "filling an empty hole inside" or, in its most sociopathic form, as if one lived with the sense that "the world owes me." The classical theological doctrine of evil as privation of the good fits well with this psychological model, and the pain experienced by such individuals is the pain of compulsion.

However, the concept of the vertical split is not sufficient to explain *all* conceptions of evil. In the subjective experience of traumatized persons, evil is most often described as a malevolent attribute of someone else's identity and character, based on early experiences of injury and later life experiences born of projection of inner persecutory objects outward where they are then battled or feared. For traumatized persons early experiences are not predominantly of deficit and lack but of active harm. The process of removing contents from ordinary awareness is an unconscious process of splitting and dissociation. Evil is experienced as "out there," and one's own self-defeating behaviors are understood, if at all, as righteous attacks on evil that has been projected onto or into others. The classical theological doctrine of evil as privation of the good fits less well with this psychological model and competes with views of evil as an active cosmic force battling the good. The pain experienced by these traumatized individuals is the pain of *ex*-pulsion, and the resulting experience of terror of what is out there—repeated, baffling experiences of intense attachment and rejection in relationships; internal fragmentation; and constant, undifferentiated psychic pain.

This is not a gender-neutral conclusion. While certainly both men and women experience trauma, the disproportionate number of women survivors of sexual abuse and assault in our culture may suggest that clinically the object-relational and intersubjective psychoanalytic theories, which can accommodate this experiential understanding of evil as something positive (i.e., active) within a framework of multiplicity, may be especially relevant to women's experience. The Augustinian notion of sin as pride or inordinate self-reliance (which I have correlated previously with the self psychological understanding of narcissism) has been further challenged by feminist theologians as inappropriate when applied to women and other marginalized groups within patriarchal society. In the words of Elizabeth Johnson,

> If pride be the primary block on the path to God, then indeed decentering the rapacious self is the work of grace. But the situation is quite different when this language is applied to persons already relegated to the margins of significance and excluded from the exercise of self-definition. For such persons, language of conversion as loss of self, turning from *amor sui*, functions in an ideological way to rob them of power, maintaining them in a subordinate position to the benefit of those who rule . . . Analysis of women's experience is replete with the realization that within patriarchal systems women's primordial temptation is not to pride and self-assertion but rather to the lack of it.[43]

ADDRESSING CORPORATE AND SYSTEMIC EVIL

Both the vertical split, with its correspondence to the doctrine of *privatio boni*, and the concepts of splitting and traumatic fragmentation, which retain a more dualistic understanding of good and evil as opposing forces, refer to individuals' experiences of suffering—through

43. Johnson, *She Who Is*, 64. See also an earlier exposition of this theme by Saiving, "The Human Situation: A Feminine View." Saiving proposes that patriarchal attention to sins of self-absorption is less relevant for women, and suggests as alternatives the sins of "triviality, distractibility, diffuseness; lack of an organized center or focus; dependence on others for one's own self-definition; tolerance at the expense of standards of excellence; inability to respect the boundaries of privacy; sentimentality; and mistrust of reason." Saiving's proposals have more recently been debated as inadvertently reinforcing essentialist stereotypes of women and as insufficiently critical of women's own participation in cultural evils, particularly racial and class oppression. See also Rankka, *Women and the Value of Suffering*.

experiences of lack or active injury. In fact, a focus purely on individual pathology or sin, either from a psychological or theological perspective, can unwittingly collude with the invisibility and pervasiveness of corporate and political privilege, and the ongoing perpetration of systemic evil that results in a *societal splitting* between those with access to power and those excluded from it. As trauma specialist Judith Herman has written, "Repression, dissociation, and denial are phenomena of social as well as individual consciousness."[44]

A further aspect of sin and evil, then, must finally be taken into consideration; that is, the *corporate and cultural* aspects of evil that transcend individual pathology and sin. Feminist and Womanist writers' approach to the subject of evil has tended to deemphasize classical arguments about the abstract nature of evil and individual sin and atonement, and to focus much more on what Noddings calls "cultural evil." Noddings highlights women's experience of suffering and participating in evil through complicity with the cultural conditions of poverty, racism, war, and sexism.[45] Womanist theologians especially have highlighted the systemic, institutionalized aspects of evil, as noted above.[46] Delores Williams redefines individual sin as participation in the larger social systems that devalue Black women's humanity through a process of devaluation and "invisibilization."[47]

Neither psychoanalytic model described above—self psychology or object relations—has actually paid adequate attention to the larger systemic, cultural, and social forces that are implicated in human cruelty and human suffering. But at least one reason (and perhaps the most profound reason) that evil *is* evil, is not only that it destroys individuals intrapsychically, but that it tears at the fabric of human relationship and confounds the human capacity for community. In the words of David Tracy and Hermann Häring, "Evil has no center, but is everywhere. It does not send out its raiding parties, but spreads like moods and rampant growths."[48] The image here is not one of sheer nothingness or purposeful malevolent planning, but of *metastasis.* (The rejection of the image of "raiding parties" may be more debatable after

44. Herman, *Trauma and Recovery,* 9.

45. Noddings, *Women and Evil,* 120–21.

46. Townes, *A Troubling in My Soul.*

47. Williams, "A Womanist Perspective on Sin," 146.

48. Tracy and Häring, *The Fascination of Evil,* 1.

September 11, 2001. However, in the larger sense, the image of metastasis still works: there is no precise beginning or end to contemporary terrorism, and no precise boundaries. Local, temporal acts are subsumed under larger movements and countermovements and cycles of retaliation across many centuries and continents.)

While few psychoanalytic theorists have yet adequately addressed this larger systemic and social dimension (although there are a few exceptions, from both self psychology and object relations points of view), my sense is that an appreciation of the dynamics of projection not only by individuals but by entire groups, and further application of theories of intersubjectivity, alterity, and social constructivism, may yield more important understandings of the systemic dimension of evil than the concept of the vertical split or indeed *any* theoretical conceptualization of intrapsychic pain can do by itself without the application of a wider social and cultural lens. (This seems especially poignant after September 11, in the wake of a massive cultural mobilization of Americans to split off and locate the enemy "out there," to disavow all complicity in the evils of the world, and to claim only the virtues of American ideals of freedom and democracy, without any of the pitfalls of unfettered global capitalism or militarism. The consciously held self-identity, purified of problematic elements, is then packaged in the symbol of the flag and mobilized in a rush to war.)

IMPLICATIONS FOR PASTORAL PRAXIS

Finally, what are some implications of these pathological forms of splitting, and their corresponding theodicies, for pastoral praxis? From a Christian theological perspective, we probably cannot hope for a total eradication of evil this side of the escahton. Final reconciliation of all beings is God's task and on God's timeline, not ours. Nor will we ever, I think, entirely resolve the mystery of evil from an abstract theological perspective: if we take an eschatological perspective, the very question of theodicy, in the words of Todd Billings, "remains open and anomalous rather than answered and (hence) forgotten."[49] I

49. "Evil is not explained; it is protested against by acting as if a reign of peace were prior to this world of violence. As Gutierrez says in *On Job*, 'Only if we take seriously the suffering of the innocent and live the mystery of the cross amid that suffering, but in the light of Easter, can we prevent our theology from being "windy arguments" (Job 16:3)' (sic 103). The question of theodicy, and the life of the Christian,

agree with the growing number of contemporary theologians who assert that an overpreoccupation with abstract questions of theodicy can undermine our very efforts to get about the business of addressing the results of evil and the suffering of the world.

My own theological leaning, and it is a leaning only, is finally toward the Augustinian view—not because I am convinced by any argumentation in the doctrine itself, but because it makes the most sense from a *psychoanalytic* framework: All splitting, including a dualistic construct of good and evil, belongs to Klein's paranoid schizoid worldview. Evil cannot finally be split off from human affairs, not our own, not anyone's. The "depressive position" (Klein's term for the developmental state in which integration can occur) acknowledges the tragic and poignant reality that all seeming opposites, including good and evil (mother, breast, father, me), are finally held together. Finally, when splitting is healed and projections are withdrawn and reincorporated in the conscious life, to whatever extent that is fleetingly possible, evil may be understood as a tear in the very fabric of the good itself, and not apart from it. Especially in the form of the confusion of lesser for greater goods,[50] this integrated view of evil is a convincing and tragic explanation for the complexity of human life.

This view of the complexity of the moral life incorporates what feminist theologian Wendy Farley has identified as the classical tragic components to human suffering: finitude, conflict, and fragility.[51] This is not to abandon responsibility; on the contrary, to quote another feminist theologian, Kristine Rankka: "What a tragic view of reality and suffering might do, for example, is move one from self-blame or from the projection of responsibility to change things outside oneself to a more mature realization of one's own appropriate responsibility within a context of limitation and finitude."[52]

---

is lived between the suffering of the cross and the increasingly penetrating light of Easter. As such, the question of theodicy remains open and anomalous rather than answered and (hence) forgotten" (Billings, "Theodicy as a 'Lived Question,'" 9).

50. Edward Farley offers a parallel, convincing discussion of the human hunger to eliminate vulnerability, insecurity, and contingency by relying on "mundane goods" (such as religions, sciences, nations, social movements, etc.), and in turn collapsing the "eternal horizon" (borrowing Ricoeur's terminology) into these goods, which is idolatry. Farley, *Good and Evil*, 130–35.

51. Farley, *Tragic Vision and Divine Compassion*, 27–31; see also Rankka, esp. 174–81.

52. Rankka, *Women and the Value of Suffering*, 196.

The depressive position relinquishes, albeit with sadness, the possibility of perfection, and acknowledges the seeming inextricability of evil from the very fabric of the good, and the ever-present reality of suffering, at least on this side of the eschaton.

However, our work is not, finally, abstract argumentation about the nature of good and evil, but compassionate solidarity with the suffering, and concrete acts of healing. As Jürgen Moltmann wrote in *The Trinity and the Kingdom*, "the question of theodicy is *not a speculative question*; it is a critical one ... [the question] is the open wound of life in this world."[53] However we decide abstractly to frame the existence of evil, healing is possible, and improvement in individuals' capacity to relate lovingly and work productively (*lieben und arbeiten*)[54] is not unrealistic—if we do not confuse the mutual and intersubjective work of healing with the one-sided *perfecting* of others in our care. If we work as pastoral caregivers and therapists to facilitate the healing of splitting (whether of the narcissistic splitting of emptiness, compulsive behavior and disavowal, or of the posttraumatic splitting of projection, terror, and fragmentation), our work has the potential for participating in the mending of creation (*tikkun ʿolam* in Jewish mystical tradition). By so doing, we can participate positively in the good: if not in the perfect, then at least in the "good enough." And for this human lifetime, that, perhaps, will be enough.

---

53. Moltmann, *The Trinity and the Kingdom*, 49 (emphasis added), also cited in Billings, "Theodicy as a 'Lived Question,'" 1.

54. Well-known phrase attributed to Freud as the summary of health. The original phrase, in Freud, *Civilization and Its Discontents* reads, "the compulsion to work ... and the power of love" (101).

NINE

Braided Selves

Theological and Psychological Reflections
on "Core Selves," Multiplicity, and the Sense
of Cohesion

The couple was resplendent in their Civil War–period dress as they
swept forward in the line to receive Communion at my family's church
in Gettysburg, Pennsylvania—he in his Union General's dark blue
with shining brass buttons, sword hanging at his side, and she in a
pink dimity dress with high lace collar and billowing hoop skirt. It was
Fourth of July weekend, and the town was full of Battle enthusiasts
who had traveled, some from great distances, to reenact the high-
water mark of the Civil War in exacting detail, high on history, chasing
a "period rush."[1] The husband and wife knelt at the Communion rail,
careful to arrange sword and skirt with proper etiquette. The pastor
placed the Communion bread into their gloved hands: "The body of
Christ, given for you."

But who were "you"? I wondered later, as my husband and I
sipped our twentieth-century lattés at the Ragged Edge, a café staffed
by local college personnel. Were "you" well-informed tourists, attending worship in our historic church because it had served as a hospital

---

1. Horwitz, *Confederates in the Attic,* esp. 275–81; Weeks, *Gettysburg,* esp. 209–14.
Weeks quotes one reenactor (214) who asserted, "We *are* the characters we're playing"
(quoting Allred, "Catharsis, Revision, and Re-enactment," 7).

during the days following the Battle, planks laid out across pews to receive the bodies of the wounded? Were "you" religiously committed Christians, lifelong Lutherans, perhaps, who sought your regular weekly sustenance of faith in Word and Sacrament? Or were you here as your Civil War personas, not only reenacting the Battle, but enjoying a period rush here, too, as the General and his wife attending church in seemly fashion?

What was the "efficacy" of such a sacrament, the priest in me also wondered? *Who* was communed? To what "communion" of the baptized did they belong, and in which century? And who were they in relationship to God? Was there some essential or "core self" whom God would always recognize as a singular, distinctive person, uniquely and eternally written into the Book of Life, regardless of the era of their dress or their subjective experience of the moment?

IS THERE A CORE SELF?

Now, over a decade later, I recognize that these questions themselves are based on a suspect foundation—namely, that there is (or should be) some essential, real, or "core" self by which each person is uniquely, irreducibly, and perhaps even eternally defined. Even after I had been steeped in psychoanalytic and postmodern literature about multiple subjects and subjectivities, and writing constructive theological work on the multiplicity of both persons and God, the question "Who were these people, *really*?" was irrepressible. We are children of the Enlightenment, and our personal anthropologies have been saturated with the notion that there is, finally, a true, core self at the heart of each person, and that this core self is the defining factor in human personality. Beneath all the various roles a person may play in his or her life in love and in work, and even in (re)enactment, a person is finally one, singular entity—or, in more philosophical or theological language, one *soul*. This belief in the singularity of a person is no doubt heightened in the dominant culture of the United States, where the founding eighteenth-century myth of independence and the Romantic era's "pioneering spirit" and "rugged individual" combine to emphasize the self-sufficiency of each human being as free citizen.

The foundation, however, is crumbling—or, perhaps, more accurately, has been *found out* to be no foundation at all but rather a kind of façade. Our rugged individual is at best a well-functioning persona, and at worst a Potemkin house, presenting a seemingly solid front to the world while concealing everything, anything, chaos, creativity, despair, multitudes. To twist Gertrude Stein's famous line, there *is* a "there" there[2]—but it is not *one* "there," not one self. The façade has been pocked and chipped away over the past century by postmodern philosophy, neuroscience, psychoanalysis, postcolonial theory, feminist and queer theory, and even quantum physics, until we are able to see through cracks and fissures and larger voids into a subjectivity that is more expansive, more variegated, yet more fragile and interdependent than we were ever able to imagine.

In the previous chapters, I have engaged the question of multiple selves/multiple subjects in relation to the construction of both a theological anthropology and a theology of multiplicity, drawing on the Christian doctrine of the Trinity. Following relational psychoanalytic theory, I have advocated for an expanded view of the human subject—at both conscious and unconscious levels—as a web or network of self states. These states are not monolithic but in themselves encompass whole worldviews, ranges of affect, systems of meaning making, and tendencies to particular types of bodily activity. In this theory, we are not understood as a unitive, integral Self, but as a conglomerate of self states, affect states, and entire personalities formed in identification with objects or part-objects we have internalized from our experiences of other persons since birth. These self states and internal personalities, further, do not function as autonomous, structured "beings," but continue to grow and change in unconscious dynamic interaction, both among themselves internally, and in connection with other persons beyond the "self."

Freud's metapsychology, when examined in light of unity vs. multiplicity, supports a view of person and mind. From some of Freud's earliest work, notably *The Interpretation of Dreams*,[3] his theorizing about the unconscious and later elaboration in the form of three "institutions" of the mind—ego, id, and super-ego[4]—established a way of thinking about our mental life as a fundamental disunity. The ego, in both Freud's and Jung's theories, thinks it knows more than it does.

---

2. Stein's original statement, in reference to her childhood home in Oakland, California, was, "There is no there there," in *Everybody's Autobiography*.

3. Freud, *The Interpretation of Dreams*.

4. Freud, *Three Essays*.

It was Freud's genius to assert in the face of the materialist-oriented scientific world of fin-de-siècle Vienna that we are not masters of our own houses, but that our actions are more often than not controlled by internal forces and dynamics beyond our conscious knowledge or control. Freud further paved the way for recognizing that we internal-ize others (objects) as part of the process of mental formation,[5] and that this process itself is swayed by internal forces of fantasy and desire, as well as the actual good and bad experiences coming from the en-vironment.[6] This attention to internal objects led to the development of "object-relations theory" in the generation after Freud (including Melanie Klein, W. R. D. Fairbairn, and D. W. Winnicott). These theorists emphasized attachment to external persons ("objects") as the primary motivational force in human development. In this theory, the psyche is gradually constructed from the infant's unconscious internalization of multiple, affect-laden "objects" (an amalgam of actual people as experienced by the child; parts of people, such as the mother's breast; and the child's own fantasized versions of those people and parts).[7] Object-relations theory has been expanded further by contemporary relational-psychoanalytic theory, with its concept of the normativity of multiple selves, to guide both theoretical conceptualization and clinical practice.[8]

This concept of multiplicity of persons has been brought into dialogue with pastoral psychology and theology to propose a concept of God as equally and transcendentally multiple, fluid, mutable, and relational—intimately responsive to the complexity of human life and

5. Freud, *Mourning and Melancholia.*

6. This shift from an emphasis on actual external trauma toward attention to the inner, unconscious dynamics of the psyche, has sometimes been critiqued as an "abandonment of the seduction theory" (e.g., Masson, *The Assault on Truth*) and a betrayal of sexual abuse survivors in Freud's practice. While there is certainly some truth to this, e.g., the disastrous case of "Dora" (in Freud, "Fragment of an Analysis of a Case of Hysteria"), a review of Freud's entire opus demonstrates that he never completely abandoned his concern for the impact of actual trauma. However, his rec-ognition of the inner forces of desire in the form of the drives of sex and aggression led to a significant shift from a more materialist view of the human personality to one that recognizes the complexity and motivational impact of intrapsychic as well as interpersonal dynamics. For a detailed contemporary discussion of the longstanding theoretical controversy between trauma vs. fantasy as the cause of psychopathology, see Mitchell and Black, *Freud and Beyond*, 207–14.

7. For more detail, see chapter 2 above.

8. See chapters 3–4 above.

all created nature.[9] Drawing from various contemporary theologians, I have embraced a conception of the divine in terms of inherent community, relationality, and mutual desire. This expansive, multiple divinity is the "Manyone [many/one],"[10] the *Elohim* whose multiplicity is still discernible in the book of Genesis as the "chaotic plenary source from which all being does not so much emerge, upward, as it 'unfolds,'"[11] eternally expanding in relationship as "primordial communion."[12] As a Christian theologian, I have been led from this specifically to consider the Trinity as "a spacious room—even matrix/womb" a deconcretized, kenotic space for metaphorical play and imagination. I have proposed a pastoral Trinitarian metaphor of the divine as Creative Profusion, Incarnational Desire, and Living Inspiration.[13]

This conceptualization of both human persons and God as multiple still begs the question, however, might there still be a *core* self—a central, defining self—amid the myriad of self-parts, self states, and subjectivities contained within a larger multiple self?

CORE SELF: SOME HISTORY BEHIND THE IDEA

The notion of a core, nuclear, true, or essential self is ubiquitous in psychotherapy, including pastoral counseling. Each of these terms—*core, true,* and *essential*—has its own (often unacknowledged) intellectual lineage. The idea of a "core self" has the most recent genesis, in the specialized treatment of childhood sexual-abuse survivors, especially those diagnosed with Dissociative Identity Disorder (formerly called Multiple Personality Disorder) as a result of severe and repeated trauma. As trauma treatment was developed and refined in the 1980s, a "core self" frequently emerged among the many personality states commonly identified by dissociative patients and their therapists.[14] The subjective experience of rediscovering this core self had a thera-

9. See esp. chapters 3–5, above.

10. Keller, *Face of the Deep.* For more detailed discussion of this point, including Hebrew Bible exegetical references, see Chapter 4 above, and Cooper-White, *Many Voices,* 74–75.

11. Deleuze, *Difference and Repetition;* also discussed in Keller, *Face of the Deep,* 168, and in chapter 4 above.

12. Johnson, *She Who Is,* 227.

13. See chapter 5 above; elaborated in Cooper-White, *Many Voices,* 81–94.

14. E.g., Fink, "The Core Self." For a much more popularized version, see the website http://www.coreintegrity.org/.

peutic effect of anchoring the patient back to a sense of an original reality and identity.

Heinz Kohut and the Core or Nuclear Self

In the psychoanalytic literature, Heinz Kohut occasionally used the term "core self" interchangeably with his concept of a "nuclear self," to refer to "the central sector of the personality."[15] As he broke with classical Freudian theory, Kohut asserted a "psychology of the self" based less on internal drives and conflict, and more on the impact of environment and parental provisions in development. For Kohut, the "core" or "nuclear self" represented an internal psychic structure undergirding "our sense of being an independent center of initiative and perception, integrated with our most central ambitions and ideals and with our experience that our body and mind form a unit in space and a continuum in time."[16] For Kohut, this nuclear self provided a sense of self-cohesion to existence.

The term "core self" was used similarly around the same time in empirical studies directly observing infant behavior to refer to babies' developing sense of self-regulation.[17] The language of "core self" has increasingly migrated from these various contexts, and is now frequently used by clinicians to refer more generally to the center or most "true and authentic" source of personality and identity. It should be noted, however, that in neither Kohut's writings nor the infant-observation literature is the core self postulated as a constitutional, inherent essence. The responsiveness of the parents and other caretakers has a profound effect on the child's sense of agency and identity.

For Kohut, moreover, the nuclear self was not a single unit but a "bipolar" schema. He posited that the child's sense of structural cohesion derived from two structural pillars or "poles," built up gradually from the parents' provision of two crucial relational (or "selfobject") functions: mirroring (the parents' empathic responsiveness to the child's grandiosity through recognition and age-appropriate applause) and idealizing (the parents' empathic responsiveness to the child's

15. Kohut, *The Restoration of the Self*, 177–78. The use of the term "nuclear self" echoes the earlier ego psychologist Edward Glover, who conceived of a "primitive," and "preconflictual" infant ego formation in *The Birth of the Ego*, 32, 34ff., 73.

16. Kohut, *The Restoration of the Self*, 177.

17. Stern, *The Interpersonal World of the Infant*.

idealization of the parents' reliability and strength). Thus, the development of the self was understood as complex, with "many shades and varieties or types," formed through a "variety of environmental factors . . . which, singly or in combination with each other, account for the specific characteristics of the nuclear self and for its firmness, weakness, or vulnerability."[18]

Winnicott and the True Self

True self is a term associated with the British object-relations psychoanalyst D. W. Winnicott. In "Ego Distortion in Terms of True and False Self,"[19] Winnicott described a type of patient who operates in the world out of a compliant, somewhat anesthetized "false self." Such a person, Winnicott posited, internalized parental prohibitions and expectations so deeply that his or her spontaneity was crushed in early childhood, and the "true self," which contained the child's spontaneity and aliveness, was effectively suppressed.[20] The goal of therapy with such patients was to help them reconnect with this buried true self, in order to restore their full range of affect, creativity, and zest for life.

The problem with this term is not so much in its original usage, but that like "core self," it has leaked into common clinical parlance apart from its context in Winnicott's writings.[21] Winnicott did not intend to create a binary metaphysic in which the self is composed solely of a "true" and a "false" self. Winnicott clearly worked within a Kleinian "object-relations" model of multiple internalized and fantasized objects in dynamic relation. He identified the early play of subjectivities in the psychic "transitional space" between infant and mother as the basis for all creativity, even culture and religion.

Subjectivity, then, according to Winnicott, is neither monolithic (supposing only the "true self" to be "real") nor binary (with reified

18. Ibid., 187.

19. Winnicott, "Ego Distortion in Terms of True and False Self."

20. To complicate terminology further, Bollas uses the term "core of the self" to describe the same dynamic process between the growing infant and parental expectations, in which the original "core" or "unique idiom of psychic organization" gives way to becoming "our parents' child, instructed by the implicit logic of their unconscious relational intelligence in the family's way of being: we become a complex theory for being a self that the toddler does not think about but acquires operationally." In *Being a Character*, 51.

21. See also Mitchell, "Contemporary Perspectives on Self," 133.

"true" and "false" selves in Manichean opposition). The "false self" and "true self" in Winnicott's conception of the person do not have any reified ontological status, but rather represent two different self *states* or experiences of the larger interior world of object relations— the one more deadened, its vitality having been sacrificed to external prohibitions and compromises; and the other a state of aliveness and imaginative potential. To the extent that the "false self" state becomes habitual in certain persons, it is a particular diagnosis, which Winnicott thought required a therapeutic regression to an earlier, less tamped-down part of the personality, possibly from infancy. But contact with and even restoration of the patient to this "true self" state, if that were entirely possible, would not eliminate the multiplicity of internal objects and associated affects and projective processes at work within the complexity of the psyche.

The third term, *essential self*, belongs to a strand of thought within philosophy that there is one, true, fundamental nature behind or within everything, and this true nature or "essence" is what ultimately defines it—that without which a thing could not be itself. While some psychoanalysts have traced this concept, particularly as it appears as a guiding belief about the nature of persons ("essentialism") to the influence of the Enlightenment,[22] it has its origins in the Greek philosopher Plato. Plato posited that for every phenomenon in our earthly experience there is an Ideal, a perfect Form from which each thing derives its essential substance. We can only perceive these Forms indirectly through the senses. Earthly existence is like a cave, in which we can perceive objects outside only by their shadows.[23] The Ideal or Form of a person is the Soul, which has an eternal life independent of the body, and which flies after death back to Heaven, the pure realm of the Ideals. The concept of essences or Ideals, and the various mutating forms they may take in earthly reality, has a long and tortuous history in philosophy, which need not be elaborated here. In Christianity, it became a point of contention in discussions both of the nature of the Trinity (how God could be one "substance"—*ousia*—yet three "persons"—*hypostases*) and, later, of transubstantiation in the Eucharist (in Aquinas's appropriation of Aristotle's distinction between "essences" and "accidents").

22. E.g., Kirshner, "The Concept of the Self in Psychoanalytic Theory"; Stein, "Geometry of the 'True Self' (Winnicott)."

23. Plato, *The Republic*, 270–75.

Both instances retained the primacy of essence and the One. In the eighteenth century, Descartes's search for one irreducible foundation for the reality of the self led to the fusion of rationality ("*Cogito, ergo sum*") with essential selfhood, creating the autonomous, modern subject. In nineteenth-century psychology, the idea of essences is perhaps most readily apparent in Jung's theory of universal archetypes, which Jung posited as universal dynamic forces in the collective unconscious, discernible through myths and legends of many cultures across all human history.[24]

Feminist, postmodern, postcolonial, and queer theorists have mounted a multifaceted critique of essentialism as perpetuating a mind-body split that reinforces the subjugation of women, sexual minorities, and persons of color. Essentialism, as defined by the white, male, Western "self," represented an ongoing valorization of imperialist notions of the white Western self as rational and autonomous, and marked the non-Western "Other" as both exotic and inferior. Such critiques however, often remain in academic contexts and do not trickle into popular culture. In Western culture to this day, the belief in some Ideal or defining essence continues to influence popular conceptions of mind, self, and soul, including smorgasbord-style popular spiritual movements and implicit models of integration and what it means to be a self in counseling and psychotherapy.

Even the use of the word *self* "itself" to denote a concrete ontological entity, " is a reification, a misuse of the reflexive pronoun."[25] Jane Flax, cited earlier in this book, has also argued for the language of *subjectivity* and *subjects* rather than "self" and "selves":

> Language to discuss multiple subjectivity requires terms with less bounded or solid connotations than 'self.' Subjectivity is a complex verb rather than a noun. It is a dynamic, constantly rewoven web of processes. The constitution of each subject is a continual and idiosyncratic process. The meanings of these processes for the subject and her or his experiences of them are shifting and often reconstituted. The term *subjectivity* also captures the multiple positions of subjects as agent and object, as neither purely determined nor determining."[26]

24. For an excellent discussion of the archetypes, both historically and in contemporary critical usage, see Samuels, *Jung and the Post-Jungians*, 19–43.

25. Mitchell, "Contemporary Perspectives on Self," 24; also citing Ryle, *The Concept of Mind* and Ludwig Wittgenstein.

26. Flax, "Taking Multiplicity Seriously," 578.

The terms *core self, True Self, essential self, soul,* and even *self* itself, then, have often been used interchangeably[27] to mean the real person as who s/he "really is"—both as the subjective sense of having an authentic identity, and as a character or set of character traits (including native virtues and besetting sins) that can be defined externally as "personality" or way of being a person in the world. In psychotherapy, heavily influenced by twentieth-century humanism and existentialism, "finding oneself" is held explicitly or implicitly as a kind of ideal state to be reached through a therapeutic process of integration[28] or "self-actualization,"[29] as layers of unconscious repression, family socialization, and acculturation are brought into conscious awareness and then chosen or discarded in favor of a more self-determined state of being.

Angels and Demons

As an ideal, this bears a slippery relation to morality in the form of "character," with the implication that a healing of "character pathology" (the earlier, twentieth-century ego-psychology term for the DSM[30] Axis II "personality disorders") should result in a higher capacity for moral judgment. As Philip Rieff so trenchantly pointed out, psychology does not operate with the pure scientific neutrality Freud so vigorously (and defensively) asserted.[31] Just as the term *character* has been equated with virtue both in twentieth-century social and educational movements[32]

27. E.g., Shengold uses the term "soul" without any explicit spiritual or theological meaning in *Soul Murder*.

28. For a detailed critique of integration as the goal of psychotherapy, see chapter 4 above.

29. Maslow, *Motivation and Personality*; and Maslow, *Toward a Psychology of Being*.

30. The most recent version is the *Diagnostic and Statistical Manual of Mental Disorders (DSM-IV-TR)*. *DSM-5* is currently under development. For more information, see American Psychiatric Association, "DSM-5 Development." Online: http://www.dsm5.org. For further discussion of the *DSM* and the value of diagnosis, see chapter 1 above.

31. Rieff, *Freud: The Mind of the Moralist*.

32. The relationship between character and civic virtues in American life was classically described as "habits of the heart" by Tocqueville, *Democracy in America*, 336. This term was adopted by sociologist Robert Bellah to argue against individualism as self-absorption, in favor of a return to civic participation in Bellah, *Habits of the Heart*. Taking an opposite position valorizing individualism, Bennett advocates for the cultivation of individual virtues in Bennett, *The Book of Virtues*, designed to call Americans to the renewal of attention to personal character. The authoritarian and individualistic themes underlying Bennett's argument are evident in Bennett's

and in academic philosophy ("virtue ethics"[33]), so in psychology its diagnostic meaning retains the color of social mores. Character can be characterized as weak or strong, bad or good, and clinical labels such as *borderline, dependent, depressive,* or *narcissistic*—especially when patients are perceived as difficult—can function judgmentally as reinscriptions of familiar "deadly sins" (anger, sloth, acedia, pride) or classic humors (choleric, phlegmatic, melancholic, sanguine).

This slippage of a true, core, or essential self toward the idea of an ideal or "higher self" has a long heritage going back to the dualistic notion of a self or soul, torn between the angel and the demon on the right and left shoulder, battling for control. This moral dualism, interestingly, has also been addressed in contemporary psychological terms as a battle between a more sober, mature self oriented toward long-term aims vs. a more impulsive self interested in immediate pleasure. The developmental capacity to delay gratification has been framed in recent decades in terms of individuals and communities' capability of "self-binding"[34]—that is, finding strategies by which the impulsive short-term self can be "bound" or constrained, in favor of long-term goals and/or the greater good. Psychologist Paul Bloom, whose most recent work has addressed "how pleasure works,"[35] acknowledges that

introduction to a letter of F. Scott Fitzgerald to his daughter: "In this letter we see the molding of character: a father gently but explicitly telling his daughter what her duties are" (Bennett, *The Book of Virtues*, 225), and in Bennett's introduction to the Funeral Oration of Pericles: "The speech reminds the participants of democracy two and a half millennia later that the character of the state is determined by the virtues of individual citizens" (ibid., 244). For a popular application of virtues education, see the Virtues Project at www.virtuesproject.com/.

33. The relationship between virtue and character can be traced to Aristotle; for a detailed discussion, see Sherman, *The Fabric of Character*. Well-known contemporary authors include Foot, *Virtues and Vices*; and *Natural Goodness*; MacIntyre, *After Virtue*; see also Flanagan and Rorty, *Identity, Character, and Morality*. For a review of the literature, including critiques, see also "Virtue Ethics," *Stanford Encyclopedia of Philosophy*, http://plato.stanford.edu/entries/ethics-virtue/#2/. Princeton philosopher Harman interrogates the connection between character and virtue in Harman, "Virtue Ethics without Character Traits," drawing from Thomson, who by distinguishing between "good" and "right" also paves the way for separating character from right actions, in Thomson, "The Right and the Good"; and Merritt, "Virtue Ethics and the Social Psychology of Character."

34. Term coined by economist Schelling, "Ergonomics, or the Art of Self-Management" and elaborated by psychologist Elster in Elster, *Ulysses and the Sirens*; Elster, *Ulysses Unbound;* and Elster, "Don't Burn Your Bridge before You Come to It."

35. Bloom, *How Pleasure Works*.

the short-term self, like the devil on the shoulder, has many wiles, and self-binding is no easy task: "It's not that the flesh is weak; sometimes the flesh is pretty damn smart."[36] Bloom summarizes this discussion: "even if each of us [as individuals] is a community, all the members shouldn't get equal say. Some members are best thought of as small-minded children—and we don't give 6-year-olds the right to vote. Just as in society, the adults within us have the right—indeed, the obligation—to rein in the children."[37]

The language of "true self" creeps into this argument as well, when Bloom, citing Jon Elster,[38] describes this "adult" self as "a truer self, because it tries to bind the short-term, drunk self. The long-term, sober self is the adult." Bloom, however, contests those who would always rule in favor of the "long-term, sober self—i.e., the more purely rational self.[39] Bloom wants to leave room for spontaneity and imagination—a multiplicity of selves that values "imaginary worlds."[40] He writes: "The main problem with all of this is that the long-term self is not always right. Sometimes the short-term self should not be bound."[41] Citing the cruel excesses of rationality that defended slavery and the Holocaust, Bloom concludes that a balance is needed. Bloom concludes: "I wouldn't want to live next door to someone whose behavior was dominated by his short-term selves, and I wouldn't want to be such a person, either. But there is also something wrong with people who go too far in the other direction. We benefit, intellectually and personally, from the interplay between different selves, from the balance between long-term contemplation and short-term impulse. We should be wary about tipping the scales too far. The community of selves shouldn't be a democracy, but it shouldn't be a dictatorship either."[42]

PROBLEMATIZING THE "CORE SELF"

This idea(l), then, of a central, true, core, essential, or even "higher" self, together with its moral overtones, permeates our Western understand-

36. Bloom, "First Person Plural," 97.
37. Ibid.
38. E.g., Elster, *Ulysses Unbound*.
39. Ibid.
40. Bloom, *How Pleasure Works*, esp. 197–202.
41. Bloom, "First Person Plural," 98.
42. Ibid.

ing of what it means to be a human being. But, like all idea(l)s, the "core self" is a social construction, and as such, can be interrogated as to its cultural, political, and social purposes. As a part of the dominant culture's understanding of the human person, whom does the construct of a "core" or essential self or character benefit? Whom does it marginalize, exclude, or even violate? As a paradigm[43] or *Weltanschauung*, what are the questions it invites, and what are the questions that cannot be imagined within its limits?

The problematic aspect of a "core" or essential self is not so much what it contains, but what it excludes, i.e., the inherent relationality and interdependence of persons. The notion of a core self reinforces individualism and the belief that somewhere, "deep down"[44] inside a person, there is finally an insoluble unity. As long as there is a core, no matter how much multiplicity, variation, inconsistency, and even chaos there may be in the outer layers of the personality, there is finally a place deep within the person that is an unconflicted, unalloyed, defining One. This may be of comfort particularly to those who have experienced only violation, rupture, and traumatic fragmentation. Paradoxically, the more fragmented I am (as opposed to a healthy, fluid dissociability), the more I am likely to feel trapped in whatever state I am currently in as my only self (however painful or frightening that state may be), because I cannot flow readily among my many self states and cannot imagine ever feeling any different.[45] Relational analysts have distinguished between multiplicity (as normative fluidity, mutability, and diversity of the self) and fragmentation (a pathological sense of being in pieces without any reliable cohesiveness or going-on-being),[46] or at least conceptualize them as opposite ends of a spectrum.[47] All of us probably need some subjective sense of a floor to stand on, or an anchor in the storm.

---

43. Kuhn, *The Structure of Scientific Revolutions*.

44. For a critique of vertical "depth" in Freud's classic conception of the unconscious, see chapter 3, above. For further elaboration on the multidimensionality of the mind, especially with reference to Deleuze's image of the rhizome, see chapter 4, above; and Cooper-White, *Many Voices*, 51–63.

45. Bromberg, "Standing in the Spaces," 516–17.

46. Ibid.; and Flax, "Multiples."

47. Davies, "Multiple Perspectives on Multiplicity." For more on clinical implications, see also Davies, "Getting Cold Feet . . ."

Lisa Cataldo, a relational analyst, has argued brilliantly for retaining *both* multiplicity *and* a sense of self-cohesion, as mutually dependent, illusory constructs, operating in a kind of dialectical tension:

> Without a sense of cohesive, continuous self, we have nowhere to stand. Or rather we might ask, "who is standing in the spaces?" Bromberg does not say, but I cannot help but think of Winnicott's image of the child who has not had good enough holding in infancy; this is the child (and later, adult) who experiences him or herself as "falling forever," a terrifying way to exist . . . As much as I have experienced and affirmed my own multiplicity, I keep coming back to the question, "if we are only standing in the spaces, what keeps us from falling forever?"
>
> I think we need to expand Bromberg's idea that the creative space is in the spaces between selves. The creative space is not between selves only, but in the space between a sense of self as multiple and a sense of self as unified and continuous. They are mutually dependent illusions. It is moving between these illusions that gives us a sense of "real"—the more we are able to be both multiple and singular, the more we are able to play in the real world of our experience. And the more we are able to play with multiplicity and unity as possible images of God.[48]

However, as long as the "floor" or the "anchor" is conceived as existing only within ourselves, we remain isolated—literally (if impossibly) *self-contained*. Winnicott critiqued the notion of isolated selves in his well-known statement, "There is no such thing as an infant . . . whenever one finds an infant, one finds maternal care."[49] Neither the floor nor the anchor in Winnicott's conception exist initially within the self, but in the arms and on the breast of the nursing mother.[50] When the mother is "good enough," and the infant feels reliably held and responded to, it gradually internalizes the holding function into itself. This is a developmental achievement[51] always occurring (with more or

---

48. Cataldo, "Multiple Selves, Multiple Gods?"

49. Winnicott, "The Theory of the Parent-Infant Relationship."

50. Winnicott speaks of mothers specifically. This has been critiqued as devaluing the nurturing role of fathers and other caregivers, and today we would be more likely to use the gender-neutral term *parent*. I use his language here not to suggest that fathers and other caregivers cannot provide a holding function, but to retain his emphasis, drawn from Klein, on the "nursing pair" and his emphasis on the biological connection between the infant and the breast.

51. Bromberg, "'Speak! That I May See You.'" See also Ogden, *The Primitive Edge of Experience*, 9.

less success) in and through relationship—even if such relationality is unrecognized or denied. Intersubjectivity theorists frame this dialectic of singularity vs. plurality in terms of a background-foreground relationship, in which the subjective experience of being one or many depends on the relational intersubjective context in which one "stands" at any given moment.[52]

Furthermore, the One, the isolate, the individual and individualistic "I," has negative social and political ramifications. A solitary construct of what it means to be human participates in an exaggerated heroic narrative, which cannot be disentangled from the myths of conquest that undergird both imperialism and colonialism. Dominance maintained through violence is recast as heroism, and the "I" asserts its individuality while standing on the invisible-ized bodies of the conquered. Such individuality is a self-serving illusion, won|one at the unacknowledged price of others' lives. There is no such actual oneness, only the *illusion* of oneness, maintained by excluding and even forbidding knowledge about and relationship with the subjugated other. Devotion to oneness benefits the "One" who masquerades as the universal, whereas multiplicity makes space for the marginalized, those constructed as "Other" in the binary dualism of One vs. Many.

Insistence upon such isolated oneness is reinscribed in theologies that emphasize a single, monolithic, imperial God. To quote theologian Laurel Schneider again:

> Oneness, as a basic claim about God, simply does not make sense. The world in its tenacious natality, mutability, and flesh has always exceeded and undermined oneness and totality, whether in Akhenaten's Egypt, Josiah's Israel, Constantine's Rome, or Luther's Germany. It repeatedly puts the lie to the One God's attempts at closure and control. For multiplicity, it turns out, is not just the flesh behind the mask of the One, it is the mask and masquerade of totality as well, popping the seams of the One's oneness in every instance. Multiplicity, which is not a synonym for "many," is a preliminary gesture, an experiment in naming a logic that is supple, adaptive, and rhizomatic rather than fixed, or merely predictive. Multiplicity turns out the story of the One, in the paradoxical sense of rejecting the One's totality and in the sense of producing it. This can be no either/or reduction. When the flow of multiplicity disrupts the pretensions of the One, we

52. E.g., Orange et al., *Working Intersubjectively*, 88.

discover that God, so often a synonym for the One, is more
and less than one, after all.[53]

The genius of Trinitarian theology, and the Cappadocians' beautiful
imagery of *perichōrēsis*, is that it holds divine oneness and multiplicity
in a never-ending creative tension. The image of the three "persons,"
Anselm's three Unimaginables (*nescio quids*),[54] holds relationality as a
primary attribute of divinity, and at the same time invites humanity
into the divine relation by incorporating the embodied human Jesus
as one of the (at least) Three-in-One.

"CORE SELF" AS PART, NOT CENTER

If we reject the binary division between "core self" and "multiple self" as
definitive of what it means to be a person, does this mean that the sense
of a "core self" is illusory, and multiplicity is what is real? As Cataldo
has noted,[55] *both* concepts are illusory, in the Winnicottian sense that
reality can only be known through the mediation of illusion, play, and
imagination, in the transitional spaces among and between internal
objects and external relationships. Or, we might say, both concepts are
equally "real" or "true," in the way that all constructs function to create
the reality they purport to define. If singularity and multiplicity are
ontological assertions, however, they must remain mutually exclusive.
Only if both constitute separate self states or subjectivities can they be
mutually compatible. As constructs representing different experiences
of one's own solidity or complexity, they can be represented as "existing" not in binary opposition, but on a continuum of experience.[56]

To return to the question, then, whether there might still be a
"core self" amid the myriad of self-parts, self states, and subjectivities contained within a larger multiple self—I would answer yes, but
only if understood as an *aspect* of all one's subjectivities, and not as an
actual, definitive, or central locus of identity, agency, and purpose. I
think there is no question that some people (I would not say all) experience their mental and emotional well-being as "grounded" in a

53. Schneider, *Beyond Monotheism,* ix–x. For a related quotation, see also chapter
4 above.

54. Anselm, of Canterbury, *Monologion* 78:142, cited in Johnson, *She Who Is,* 203.

55. Cataldo, "Multiple Selves, Multiple Gods?" 49.

56. Davies, "Multiple Perspectives on Multiplicity."

unified, coherent sense of "I," or organizing fantasy or "self-concept,"[57] which has an enduring set of character traits, desires, agentic capacity, and even an overarching sense of purpose or "calling." I would also agree that an unremitting sense of fragmentation and absence of going-on-being, or a sense of "falling forever" without any ground to stand on (or mother's arms to catch you) can be a terrifying and anguished mode of existence. However, I do not believe that the felt *sense* of having a "core self" or "ground of being" (and I use this term deliberately for both its psychological and theological connotations) is the same thing as there *actually being one*.

This leads me, therefore, to see multiplicity as the overarching paradigm,[58] within which the concept of the One is admissible, but only as one illusory part. It is a subjective feeling of being grounded in an essential truth, yet it is not necessarily as "true" as it feels, because it excludes the knowledge of itself as a contingent part of a larger whole. Its confidence depends on a denial of multiplicity. There is still no singular "truth" or "essence" defining the whole.

Nor does the "core self" have an identifiable, fixed location within the self. If it is one of many illusory self-experiences rather than a reified existential entity, then as a particular self-experience it can be situated spatially in several different ways, depending on the metaphor being used (endpoint on a continuum, center of a sphere, the very bottom of things). If we reject the notion that the "self" is bounded in either two or three dimensions, except as our physical bodies move through time and space, then it might be possible to conceive of the self/selves/subject in more expansive terms. In chapters 4 and 6 above, I engaged two metaphors from Gilles Deleuze: the *rhizome*,[59] to contest models of the unconscious that drill down into a singular deep origin or root; and the *fold*,[60] to offer a more organic, mutable, and unpredictable model of mind. There are origins but no single point of origin, depths and shadows but no single locatable, penetrable "depth." There is a shape—in the way an iris corm or a fall of silk drapery has

57. Grossman, "The Self as Fantasy."

58. This is opposite from the conclusion drawn by infant observation researcher Lachmann, whose "singular self process model" posits integration as the overarching principle, within which diversity and complexity can be tolerated (Lachman, "How Many Selves Make a Person?").

59. See chapter 4 above and Cooper-White, *Many Voices*, 57–61.

60. See chapter 6 above.

a shape—but it is fluid and ever changing—formed, contingent, and permeable to forces beyond itself.

Moving beyond dualisms or fixed geometrical structures for metaphors of self and mind, the "core" is meaningless as a structural reality.[61] The subjective perception that "I" am being "true to myself," "keeping it all together," "grounded," or "centered," can arise along various nodal points of my experience from moment to moment, or in a more enduring way, even as the "ground" shifts and crumbles imperceptibly "under my feet"—making way for my hungry, expanding, foraging roots. But that "I"—including my sense of "core self"—will change and grow, even as relationships and circumstances impinge and mold me intersubjectively, at both conscious and unconscious levels.

This too, has ethical resonances. Mutability of the self makes way for new relations. A willingness to surrender a particular subjective experience of "core self" in favor of other selves, or even a revised sense of what is "core," is necessary for true mutuality to occur in relations with others. To quote Korean feminist scholar Wonhee Anne Joh:

> I find the notion of the "annihilation of the self" a meaningful part of my spirituality of resistance and transformation—individual and social—when I understand it as a call to practice emptying out of self so that I might better let a multiplicity of selves into my being in the world. Such emptying out and letting in gives birth to a "co-arising" of many selves in relation with, to, and for one another. The annihilation of self then is a call to practice a kind of way of being in the world whose arch is bent toward the other. To use Gayatri Spivak's term, such a way of being in the world, bent and directed toward the other, is a kind of love that seeks to slowly make possible a non-coercive rearrangement of desire. To be sure, [Mary Potter] Engel's call for "deheroization" as a form of letting go of one's self and "taking the hand of another in love" is precisely such a practice that allows for the possibility of "non-coercive rearrangement of desire"—our interior life of desire, as well as our desire for social transformation.[62]

This is certainly not to reinscribe notions of self-denial and self-annihilation that have been used by dominating powers (whether church

61. I disagree here with Bromberg's distinction between "dissociative process" and "dissociative structure." Any notion of "psychic *structure*" must remain metaphorical to avoid being reinscribed as an ontological attribute of intrapsychic experience.

62. Joh, "Authoring a Multiplicity of Selves and No-Self," 171.

or state). Joh, too, rejects a spirituality of "no-self" when it is imposed on women as a means of suppressing resistance to oppression. The "self" that is annihilated in Joh's claim here is akin to the heroic concept of a "core self" that is solitary, self-sufficient, and relatively immutable due to its impermeability.

As I argued in the previous chapter, the concept of multiple selves/subjects is a powerful bridge to empathy, especially toward others we perceive to be different. A genuine openness to difference, one that can move beyond social inequalities and the dominating power, "requires more than a liberal 'tolerance,' or even a sincere but naïve form of curiosity about the 'Other.'"[63] To experience genuine empathy for other persons outside ourselves calls us to engage and even befriend the parts of our multiple selves that we have most denied or wished to disavow. Being willing to explore our alien self-parts, and to recognize that the very fact of alienness is built into the fabric of our own character, is the beginning of empathic understanding of other persons, with all of their own complexity and alienness. In the words of Julia Kristeva, "How could one tolerate a foreigner if one did not know one was a stranger to oneself?"[64]

Such openness requires courage, because it invites a level of annihilation of any certainty we may have clung to for our sense of identity, security, even "reality." To quote religion scholar Jill Petersen Adams:

> In recognizing our shared vulnerability, I must allow myself to be "undone" by the Other. Butler poetically writes: "For if I am confounded by you, then you are already of me, and I am nowhere without you. You are what I gain through" the disorientation and loss that comes from trying to speak to an Other. "This is how the human comes into being, again and again, as *that which we have yet to know*." Ideally, both ethically and politically, the realization that the other is *always* that which we have yet to know, is *forever* unknowable, stays our hand at the moment of potential violence.[65]

Being thus "undone" in order to be capable of reaching out toward the Other requires a sense of having a self to undo in the first place (and,

63. See chapter 7 above.

64. Kristeva, *Strangers to Ourselves*, cited in Capps, *Freud and Freudians on Religion*, 328.

65. Adams, "The Just Politics of Mourning," 49 (emphasis added).

presumably, to do again). But this *sense* of having a self, whether experienced as being one-self at the core, or as being a cohesive amalgam of multiple selves does not need to be conceived as primary, central, or foundational—except in the most metaphorical sense. Paradoxically, the capacity to feel secure enough to tolerate and use one's own multiplicity is related to the infantile experience of being held, and this always requires the actual experience of holding by a "good enough," reliable enough (m)Other outside one-self.

BRAIDED SELVES: ACHIEVING THE ILLUSION OF COHESION

So what does hold each of us together as healthy "multiples"? If we are not, as we once imagined, bound by the gravity of an inner core, what keeps us from flying to pieces? What keeps our healthy multiplicity from dissolving into unhealthy splitting, or even fragmentation as defined in the previous chapter? And what allows us to perceive ourselves (at least most days) to be the same person from day to day and year to year? What constitutes our going-on-being?

The Feeling of Being Oneself: Weaving the Braid

To return to the metaphor of the fold, I suggested in chapter 6 above, that there is a thread, or threads, holding together the fabric of our mental lives, at least as we experience our selves from moment to moment. Rather than identifying this thread as a singular conscious identity formation, I proposed a metaphor for the multiple self as *braid*, whose strength derives precisely from the interweaving of its disparate conscious and unconscious threads.[66] I identified the experience of inhabiting one body, a mature sense of spirituality, and a commitment to embodied ethical practices as three threads constituting the braided self, with relationality as an overarching theme.

I would like to identify relationality further here as actually functioning as a fourth thread *within* the braid in order to focus attention on its distinctive attributes in contributing to the sense of identity and continuity of self experience. I would now identify four strands that "hold" a sense of self together without erasing or undoing our multiplicity: 1) our bodies, 2) our relationships, 3) our spirituality; and

66. See chapter 5 above.

4) our embodied ethical practices.[67] This fourfold braid is conceptualized not as a single straight line, but as a three-dimensional weaving
or net-work. This web or net of threads, taken together, constitutes a
"whole"—but a whole whose very coherence and binding power is
made up of our multiple subjective experiences and states of being-
in-relation. As a net can flexibly hold a multiplicity as heavy as a catch
of fish or as light as two butterflies, this braid can flex and move with
everything that changes within and without and yet is strong enough
to provide a subjective sense of form that constitutes a subjectivity,
a contingent and provisional "I" that coheres even as it moves and
shape-shifts across time and space.

As in all theories of what constitutes a healthy self, there are certainly value judgments embedded in this conceptualization—quite
explicitly so. I draw from a Judeo-Christian ethic of love and justice,
from the particularity of my own context as a Christian theologian. The
concept of the multiplicity of selves, then, as a pastoral theological anthropology, valorizes increasing knowledge and harmonious relations
among the parts of a person as well as the "arch bent toward the other,"
that "non-coercive rearrangement of desire" with others in relation.[68]

Life in the Body

The most obvious unifying factor in our experience of ourselves is that
we live in one body. We are contained by the primal boundary of our
skin, and as infants it is primarily through the skin that we first experience the boundary between ourselves and the rest of the world.[69]
While there is some convincing evidence that our bodies react quite
differently in relation to our many different self states,[70] even persons
suffering with Dissociative Identity Disorder do not have multiple
bodies. Our various affective states and selves must share a physical

---

67. Ibid.

68. Joh, "Authoring a Multiplicity of Selves and No-Self," 171.

69. Bick, "The Experience of Skin in Early Object Relations"; and Bick, "Further
Considerations on the Function of the Skin in Early Object Relations"; see also
Ogden's concept of the "autistic-contiguous position," in which tactile contact es-
tablishes the first boundary between the sense of self and (m)other; see Ogden, *The
Primitive Edge of Experience*, 31.

70. Bass, "Sweet Are the Uses of Adversity"; Stolorow and Atwood, "The Mind and
the Body"; Davies and Frawley, *Treating the Adult Survivor*, 68–72; van der Kolk, "The
Body Keeps the Score."

being—blood, bones, organs, nerves, flesh, hair, and all. Our bodily experiences become a part of the shared history of our many selves. The arrowhead-shaped scar on my elbow, the wrinkles and freckles kissed and seared into my skin by the sun, the fracture line on my kneecap—these are permanent reminders of the fifty-three years "I" in all my subjective states have dwelled in this particular, irreproducible "temple" that is my body.

Although my body may respond very differently to different conscious and unconscious states of being, especially emotional states, and may do the bidding of different self-parts as I move through my days (curled up, stretched out, taut with anger, soft with compassion, laboring dutifully, running bravely toward, shrinking back, lounging heedlessly, arcing sensually), I am able in some sense to know myself through all these variations as one person because I am located in this living, pulsing, breathing animal-being of skin and bones.

Life in Relationship

Being held by others in infancy in a state of utter dependency, as Winnicott understood, is the beginning of a lifelong sense of security or insecurity.[71] We also come cognitively to know who we are because our relationships locate us both temporally and spatially and, in particular, give us a name. The power of naming is well recognized, as in the book of Genesis. Naming is a form of stewardship in this Judeo-Christian creation story. As human beings, we are called to care for one another as stewards, because we also have the power to name and define one another. The power of naming can be used or abused. On one hand, when we are limited and confined by myths that maintain dominance and subordination, naming becomes a strategy for subjugation of the "Other." On the other hand, naming is a powerful force for encouragement and nurture by "good enough" parents, siblings, friends, and intimate partners. None of us can escape the mirrors that others hold up to us, mirrors that can tell us truths about our diverse selves, tell us lies, and show us pictures of what we might or might not be in the future.

Our sense of identity and ongoingness of being oneself depends, for good or for ill, on this naming and mirroring by others. Relational analyst Donnel Stern has chosen the term *witness* to highlight the

71. Analogous to Erikson's first developmental stage, "basic trust vs. basic mistrust," in Erikson, *Childhood and Society*, 247.

importance of mutual *recognition*, as "partners in thought," in the formation of selves from infancy onward. This term might even be understood as having theological resonance: the New Testament Greek word translated "witness" is *martys*. Leaning on this biblical connotation, we are able to emphasize the spiritual significance—and even the costliness (as martyrs/witnesses to the multiple truths of one another's subjectivities)—of relationality with one another as formative of our personhood.[72]

Spirituality

I have specified spirituality as an element that shapes our sense of identity because it evokes those qualities of experience, often previously assigned to an essential or "core" self, that appear to shape our sense of purpose or "calling," and represent our most cherished values and ideals. These aspects of subjectivity are akin to what James Fowler identified as "faith": "our way of finding coherence in and giving meaning to the multiple forces and relationships that make up our lives . . . a person's way of seeing him- or herself in relation to others against a background of shared meaning and purpose."[73] While I have argued against the notion that such shaping values reside inherently in some essential, central part of our being, our "soul" or "character," I do not dispute the presence of such values and ideals as a part of the self-experience—and, in keeping with multiplicity of the self in general, these values and ideals are both multiple and intersubjectively constructed in relationships. They are both conscious and unconscious, and so may be diverse, even conflicting. There may be a "majority view" that directs our lives more or less coherently, but we all contain worlds within us, some of which are repressed or habitually disavowed. The more we can bring these differing values into consciousness and honest dialogue, the better we may be able to understand what function the various "faiths" perform in our inner life. The better we are able to mediate among them toward a more harmonious, collaborative feeling of purpose and meaning (akin to Carl Rogers's idea of "congruence"[74]), the more reliable we may also

72. Stern, *Partners in Thought*, esp. 110ff.; see also Stern, *Unformulated Experience*, for an elaboration of this theological reflection, see Cooper-White, "Suffering."

73. Fowler, *Stages of Faith*, 4.

74. Rogers, *On Becoming a Person*.

be able to be in our relations with others. But the meaning making in which we engage is not a simple process of consciously deciding to be a certain kind of person, or plumbing the depths to discover our one "true" character or soul. Healthy multiplicity is a lifelong negotiation, not a model of finality, certainty, or perfection.

Within Christian traditions of spirituality, again, there are resources to enhance this sense of inner collaboration, rather than collapsing back into a vision of undifferentiated oneness. Bonhoeffer's well-known poem "Who Am I?" resolves an anguishing sense of contradictions and multiple subjectivities by resting in the faith statement that "Whoever I am, Thou knowest, O God, I am Thine!"[75] Just as our God-imagoes reflect our infantile state of utter dependency and cannot be separated entirely from our earliest experiences of our seemingly omniscient and omnipotent parents, the function of maternal holding that we internalize for our sense of personal security in the world is also reflected in this description of divine holding. We are held by God, as surely or even more surely than by any earthly parent. In Julian's words, "when we fall, quickly [God] raises us up with his loving embrace and his gracious touch. And when we are strengthened by his sweet working, then we willingly choose him by grace, that we shall be his servants and his lovers, constantly and forever."[76]

Embodied Ethical Practices

Finally we also experience a sense of identity as it grows and is formed over time by our actual behaviors and actions in the world. Our bodies not only experience passively, but act. Our agency and our sense of agency are intertwined with our actual history, involving our bodies, our relationships, and our spirituality—our sense of values, meaning and purpose—and the ways in which we have acted in the world. To quote Elaine Graham, theological "truth" itself, because of "the contingency and situatedness of human existence and knowledge, and the provisionality of our apprehension of the divine," would be understood as realized within and through human practices and material transformation."[77]

75. Bonhoeffer, "Who Am I?"

76. Julian, of Norwich, *Showings*, 300.

77. Graham, *Making the Difference*, 227, also citing Benhabib, *Situating the Self*; and Browning, *A Fundamental Practical Theology*, 2–10. For a further elaboration of

Our actions are not identical with our *memories* of actions or events. Memory is multiple, mutable, and always subject to interpretation and reinterpretation. It is neither fixed nor factual.[78] It also cannot be reduced only to narrative,[79] although what is narrated about and to us deeply influences and shapes our sense of identity and our actions. Our concrete practices amid other living beings, while subject to selective and fluid interpretation by others, leave a mark in our communities and on the earth. We have impact both for good and for ill, and the tracings we leave behind are maps by which others may come to know something about us, quite apart from our own subjective sense of identity and purpose. As these maps are read back to us by others, we may confirm old directions or discern new pathways. The history we have written on the world, to be read intersubjectively by ourselves and others, gives us a further sense of going-on-being, but always with the possibility of change and new creation.

I have argued throughout this volume and elsewhere for a construction of theological anthropology as prior to the positing of a doctrine of God, because all conceptions of God are necessarily incomplete, partial, and filtered through the lenses of a human perspective. All concepts are projections of our internalized personal, familial, and cultural inheritances, and in spite of its transcendent subject matter, theology does not escape the trap of conceptualization (the hermeneutical circle). In Christian theology, the biblical assertion that we are made in the "image and likeness of God" provides a hinge, however, that both offers and demands a symmetry in our conceptions of God and humankind. Multiplicity, then, as a metaphor for theological anthropology, must have descriptive power in relation to our experiences of both ourselves and the divine. Even as the Trinity provides one such specific imagery for the multiplicity and intrinsic relationality of God, so the image of a threefold braid provides a Trinitarian metaphor for multiple selves in a state of well-being. We are "like God" in our capacity for multiplicity, fluidity, creativity, and loving relationality, just as we experience God through our multiply-constituted subjectivity as

---

Graham's "theology of practice," see Graham, *Transforming Practice.*

78. For more detail, see Cooper-White, *Shared Wisdom*, 50–52.

79. For a careful review of narrative social psychology in relation to theological anthropology, see Turner, "First Person Plural"; cf., Bauman, *The Individualized Society*; and Gergen, *The Saturated Self.*

being "like us"—unimaginably, transcendently yet immanently, multiple, fluid, creative, and lovingly related.

Such doctrinal musings, however, do not necessarily lead us to anything new unless they also are lived into through our practices. Finally, a theology and theological anthropology of multiplicity must be situated as ortho*praxis*, not merely orthodoxy. If our sense of cohesion is drawn from life lived in the body and its relationships, both with God (spirituality) and other human beings (practices of love and justice), then we cannot *not* find ourselves in the realm of ethics. In Schneider's words:

> If God is love, God cannot be One . . . Love is a synonym, therefore, for incarnation just as both are a synonym for divine multiplicity. To follow a God who becomes flesh is to make room for more than One. It is a posture of openness to the world as it comes to us, of loving the discordant, plenipotential worlds more than the desire to overcome, to colonize, or even to "save" them.
>
> Love, the only ethics imaginable in a theology of divine multiplicity, is a promise, not a threat. It is the presence/s of the divine, available for encounter if we leave the scripts aside, if we are prepared to have our hearts broken by beauty, awe, and the redemption of responsibility.[80]

Most especially, we will inhabit our lives through the choices and relations of every ordinary day—through what Ada María Isasi-Díaz calls *lo cotidiano* (the daily).[81] As we engage our own alienness, with courage and compassion, we are better able to open the door of compassion toward the "alien" beyond ourselves. As multiple subjects, we are able to engage difference with a greater degree of flexibility, creativity, and empathy for their competing desires and truth claims.

We are *all* "reenactors," daily reinhabiting the subjectivities that act in and through the flux of the world, never quite the same way twice,[82] but guided by braided threads of body, relationship, spirituality, and ethical practices of recommitment and responsiveness to

---

80. Schneider, *Beyond Monotheism*, 207.

81. Isasi-Díaz, *Mujerista Theology*, 63–73.

82. Cf., Deleuze, *Difference and Repetition*. Milbank uses the term "nonidentical repetition" in Milbank, *The Word Made Strange*, 55–83, to refer both to the plenitude of God's creative gift, and also the pattern of Jesus's life as it may be repeated uniquely in each new context and person (Milbank, "Postmodern Critical Augustinianism," 276).

new demands for love and justice. Like the ancient Greek philosopher Terence, we are able to say, "Nothing human is alien to me,"[83] thereby daily (re-)exercising an embodied intuition for the "Other" that extends more deeply into the margins of our own contexts. We are more able to envision new horizons of meaning, because our vision is expanded beyond encapsulated identities that can only reinscribe singular positions and commitments. Such expanded vision is necessary to move beyond our reified oppositions, which perpetuate patterns of dominance, conflict, hatred, and anomie.

EPILOGUE

So what of the Civil War reenactors described at the beginning of this chapter? Who were they? I would argue that they were in some sense *all* of the persons they presented as they walked forward to receive the sacrament that summer Sunday—including the identities given to them by others at birth, their selves-in-relation as they engaged in community, their subjective selves in a state of worship, their nineteenth-century "impressions"[84] whom they inhabited for intense periods of time as reenactors. The entire conscious and unconscious multiplicity of their embodied selves can only be known fully and finally by God. We only came to "know" them by their particular acts among us that one day, but they are continually being known in their various communities and contexts, and continually formed in their multiple selfhood, by the quality of the sum total of their embodied ethical engagements with others in the world. They are "their own persons," but also much more—in all their complexity, conscious and unconscious, they are *ours*. We are all reenactors, braided selves moving through our particular times and places, leaving and reworking our distinctive tracings on the earth. Beyond this, our knowledge dissolves again into mystery and faith: that in all our fathomless complexity we are known and loved by God—more valuable than two sparrows, always attended when falling, every self counted.[85]

83. Terence, *Heautontimorumenos*, I.i.25.

84. Term used by reenactors for the person or type of person on whom they pattern their reenactment persona. Horwitz, *Confederates in the Attic*, 127; Weeks, *Gettysburg*, 214.

85. A play on Matthew 10:29–30.

Bibliography

Adams, Jill Petersen. "The Just Politics of Mourning and Judith Butler's *Precarious Life.*" Paper presented to the Psychology, Culture and Religion Group, American Academy of Religion Annual Meeting, November 2008. Online: http://pcr.revdak.com/2008/adams.judith_butler.html/.

Ainsworth, Mary D. S., et al. *Patterns of Attachment: A Psychological Study of the Strange Situation.* Hillsdale, NJ: Erlbaum, 1978.

Ali, Carroll A. Watkins. *Survival and Liberation: Pastoral Theology in African American Context.* St. Louis: Chalice, 1999.

Allred, Randal. "Catharsis, Revision, and Re-enactment: Negotiating the Meaning of the American Civil War." *Journal of American Culture* 19.4 (1996) 1–13.

Altman, Neil. *The Analyst in the Inner City: Race, Class, and Culture through a Psychoanalytic Lens.* Relational Perspectives Book Series 3. Hillsdale, NJ: Analytic, 1995.

———. *The Analyst in the Inner City: Race, Class, and Culture through a Psychoanalytic Lens.* 2nd ed. Relational Perspectives Book Series 40. New York: Routledge, 2010.

American Psychiatric Association. *Diagnostic and Statistical Manual of Mental Disorders DSM-IV-TR.* 4th rev. ed. with text revision. Washington, DC: American Psychiatric Publishing, 2000.

———. "DSM-5 Development." Online: http://www.dsm5.org/.

Anderson, Benedict R. O'G. *Imagined Communities: Reflections on the Origin and Spread of Nationalism.* London: Verso, 1983.

Anderson, Herbert, and Edward Foley. *Mighty Stories, Dangerous Rituals: Weaving Together the Human and the Divine.* 1st paperback ed. San Francisco: Jossey-Bass, 2001.

Anderson, Herbert, and Susan Johnson. *Regarding Children: A New Respect for Children and Families.* Family Living in Pastoral Perspective. Louisville: Westminster John Knox, 1994.

Anselm of Canterbury. *Monologion.* In *Basic Writings,* translated by S. N. Deane, 81–190. LaSalle, IL: Open Court, 2001.

Arlow, Jacob A., and Charles Brenner. *Psychoanalytic Concepts and the Structural Theory.* Journal of the American Psychoanalytic Association. Monograph Series 3. New York: International Universities Press, 1964.

Armistead, M. Kathryn. *God-Images: In the Healing Process.* Minneapolis: Fortress, 1995.

Aron, Lewis. *A Meeting of Minds: Mutuality in Psychoanalysis*. Relational Perspectives Book Series 4. Hillsdale, NJ: Analytic Press, 1996.

Arthur, John. "This Is the Feast of Victory for Our God." In *The Hymnal 1982* (#417, 418). New York: Church Hymnal Corporation, 1985.

Atkinson, Donald R., et al., editors. *Counseling American Minorities*. 6th ed. Boston: McGraw-Hill, 2004.

Augustine, Saint. *On Free Choice of the Will (De Libero Arbitrio)*. Translated by Thomas Williams. Indianapolis: Hackett, 1993.

Asquith, Glenn H., editor. *Visions from a Little Known Country: A Boisen Reader*. Decatur, GA: Journal of Pastoral Care Publications, 1992.

Avis, Paul. *God and the Creative Imagination: Metaphor, Symbol and Myth in Religion and Theology*. London: Routledge, 1999.

Baker-Fletcher, Karen. "The Strength of My Life." In *Embracing the Spirit: Womanist Perspectives on Hope, Salvation, and Transformation*, edited by Emilie M. Townes, 122–39. Maryknoll, NY: Orbis, 1997.

Barth, Karl. *The Humanity of God*. Translated by John Newton Thomas and Thomas Wieser. Richmond: John Knox, 1960.

———. *The Epistle to the Romans*. Translated by Edwyn C. Hoskins. 6th ed. London: Oxford University Press, 1968.

———. *Church Dogmatics*. Edited by G. W. Bromiley and T. F. Torrance. 5 vols. London: T. & T. Clark, 2009.

Basch, Michael. *Understanding Psychotherapy: The Science Behind the Art*. New York: Basic Books, 1988.

Bass, Graham. "Sweet Are the Uses of Adversity: Psychic Integration through Body-Centered Work." In *Bodies in Treatment: The Unspoken Dimension*, edited by Frances Sommer Anderson, 151–68. Relational Perspectives Book Series. Hillsdale, NJ: Analytic, 2007.

Baudrillard, Jean. *Simulation and Simulacra*. Translated by Sheila Faria Glaser. Ann Arbor: University of Michigan Press, 1995.

Bauman, Zygmunt. *The Individualized Society*. Cambridge, UK: Polity, 2001.

Bechtel, William, and Adele Abrahamsen. *Connectionism and the Mind: An Introduction to Parallel Processing in Networks*. Cambridge, MA: Blackwell, 1991.

———. "The Contribution of Mother-Infant Mutual Influence to the Origins of Self- and Object Representations." In *Relational Perspectives in Psychoanalysis*, edited by Neil J. Skolnick and Susan C. Warshaw, 83–117. Hillsdale, NJ: Analytic, 1992.

Beebe, Beatrice, and Frank M. Lachmann. "The Contribution of Mother-Infant Mutual Influence to the Origins of Self- and Object Representations." In *Relational Perspectives in Psychoanalysis*, edited by Neil J. Skolnick and Susan C. Warshaw, 83–117. Hillsdale, NJ: Analytic, 1992.

Belenky, Mary, et al. *Women's Ways of Knowing: The Development of Self, Voice, and Mind*. 10th anniversary ed. New York: Basic Books, 1997.

Bellah, Robert. *Habits of the Heart: Individualism and Commitment in American Life*. 3rd ed. Berkeley: University of California Press, 2007.

Benhabib, Seyla. *Situating the Self*. Cambridge, UK: Polity, 1992.

———. "Complexity, Interdependence, Community." In *Women, Culture, and Development: A Study of Human Capabilities*, edited by Martha C. Nussbaum and Jonathan Glover, 235–55. WIDER Studies in Development Economics. Oxford: Clarendon, 2005.

Bennett, William J. *The Book of Virtues*. New York: Simon & Schuster, 1996.

Berger, Peter. L., and Thomas Luckmann. *The Social Construction of Reality*. New York: Doubleday, 1966.

Bhabha, Homi K. "The Third Space." Interview by Jonathan Rutherford. In *Identity: Community, Culture, Difference*, edited by Jonathan Rutherford, 207–21. London: Lawrence & Wishart, 1990.

———. *The Location of Culture*. London: Routledge, 1994.

Bick, Esther. "The Experience of the Skin in Early Object Relations." *International Journal of Psycho-Analysis* 49 (1968) 484–86.

———. "Further Considerations on the Function of the Skin in Early Object Relations: Findings from Infant Observation Integrated into Child and Adult Analysis." *British Journal of Psychotherapy* 2 (1986) 292–99.

Billings, Todd. "Theodicy as a 'Lived Question': Moving beyond a Theoretical Approach to Theodicy." *Journal for Christian Theological Research* 5:2 (2000) 1–9.

Bion, Wilfred. R. *Experiences in Groups*. London: Tavistock, 1959.

———. *Transformations: Change from Learning to Growth*. London: Heinemann, 1965.

———. *Attention and Interpretation: A Scientific Approach to Insight in Psycho-Analysis and Groups*. London: Tavistock, 1970.

Black, Max. *Models and Metaphors: Studies in Language and Philosophy*. Ithaca, NY: Cornell University Press, 1962.

Bloom, Paul. "First Person Plural." *The Atlantic*, November 2008, 90–98.

———. *How Pleasure Works: The New Science of Why We Like What We Like*. New York: Norton, 2010.

Boesky, Dale. "Structural Theory." In *Psychoanalysis: The Major Concepts*, edited by Burness E. Moore and Bernard D. Fine, 494–507. New Haven: Yale University Press, 1995.

Boff, Leonardo. *Trinity and Society*. Translated by Paul Burns. Theology and Liberation Series. Maryknoll, NY: Orbis, 1998.

———. *Holy Trinity, Perfect Community*. Translated by Phillip Berryman. Maryknoll, NY: Orbis, 2000.

Boisen, Anton. *The Exploration of the Inner World: A Study of Mental Disorder and Religious Experience*. 1936. Pennsylvania Paperbacks. Philadelphia: University of Pennyslvania Press, 1971.

Bollas, Christopher. *The Shadow of the Object: Psychoanalysis of the Unthought Known*. New York: Columbia University Press, 1987.

———. *Being a Character: Psychoanalysis and Self Experience*. 1992. New York: Routledge, 2003.

Bonhoeffer, Dietrich. "Who Am I?" *Christianity and Crisis*, March 4, 1946. Online: http://www.religion-online.org/showarticle.asp?title=385.

Bonting, Sjoerd. *Creation and Double Chaos: Science and Theology in Discussion*. Minneapolis: Fortress, 2005.

Bowen, Murray. *Family Therapy in Clinical Practice*. New York: Aronson, 1978.

Bowlby, John. "An Information Processing Approach to Defense." In *Loss: Sadness and Depression*, 44–74. Attachment and Loss 3. The International Psycho-Analytic Library 109. New York: Basic Books, 1980.

———. *Attachment*. 2nd ed. Attachment and Loss 1. New York: Basic Books, 2000.

Braun, Bennett G. *The Treatment of Multiple Personality Disorder*. Washington, DC: American Psychiatric Press, 1986.

Brickman, Celia. *Aboriginal Populations in the Mind: Race and Primitivity in Psycho-analysis*. New York: Columbia University Press, 2003.

Bromberg, Philip M. "'Speak! That I May See You': Some Reflections on Dissociation, Reality, and Psychoanalytic Listening." *Psychoanalytic Dialogues* 4 (1994) 517–47.

———. "Standing in the Spaces: The Multiplicity of Self and the Psychoanalytic Relationship." *Contemporary Psychoanalysis* 32 (1996) 509–35.

———. *Standing in the Spaces: Essays on Clinical Process, Trauma, and Dissociation.* Hillsdale, NJ: Analytic, 1998.

Brown, Eric. "Plato's Ethics and Politics in *The Republic*." In *Stanford Encyclopedia of Philosophy*, 2009. Online: http://plato.stanford.edu/entries/plato-ethics-politics/.

Brown, Lyn Mikel, and Carol Gilligan. *Meeting at the Crossroads: Women's Psychology and Girls' Development.* Cambridge, MA: Harvard University Press, 1992.

Browning, Don S. *A Fundamental Practical Theology: Descriptive and Strategic Proposals.* Minneapolis: Fortress, 1991.

Browning, Don S., and Terry D. Cooper. *Religious Thought and the Modern Psychologies.* 2nd ed. Minneapolis: Fortress, 2004.

Buber, Martin. *I and Thou.* Translated by Walter Kaufman. Hudson River Editions. New York: Scribner, 1970.

Butler, Judith. *Gender Trouble: Feminism and the Subversion of Identity.* New York: Routledge, 1990.

———. *Bodies That Matter: On the Discursive Limits of "Sex."* New York: Routledge, 1993.

———. *Precarious Life: The Powers of Mourning and Violence.* London: Verso. 2004.

C. G. Jung Institute of San Francisco. *Jung Journal: Culture and Psyche* (Formerly *San Francisco Jung Institute Library Journal*.) Online: http://www.sfjung.org/jung_journal.asp/.

Capps, Donald. *Freud and Freudians on Religion: A Reader.* New Haven: Yale University Press, 2001.

Carotenuto, Aldo. *A Secret Symmetry: Sabina Spielrein Between Jung and Freud.* Translated by Arno Pomerans et al. New York: Pantheon, 1982.

Carter, Betty, et al. *The Expanded Family Life Cycle: Individual, Family and Social Perspective,* 4th ed. Upper Saddle River, NJ: Prentice Hall, 2010.

Casement, Patrick. *On Learning from the Patient.* New York: Guilford, 1985.

Cataldo, Lisa. "Multiple Selves, Multiple Gods? Functional Polytheism and the Postmodern Religious Patient." *Pastoral Psychology* 57:1–2 (2008) 45–58.

———. "Whiteness Real and Unreal: Destruction, Survival and Racial Melancholia." Paper presented to the Psychology, Culture and Religion Group, American Academy of Religion Annual Meeting, Chicago, IL, November 3, 2008.

Charcot, Jean-Martin. *Clinical Lectures on Diseases of the Nervous System.* Translated by Thomas D. Savill. New Sydenham Publications 128. London: New Sydenham Society, 1889.

Chung, Hyun Kyun. *Struggle to Be the Sun Again: Introducing Asian Women's Theology.* Maryknoll: Orbis, 1990.

Cixous, Hélène. *The Hélène Cixous Reader.* Edited by Susan Sellers. New York: Routledge, 1994.

Cixous, Hélène, and Catherine Clément. *The Newly Born Woman.* Translated by Betsy Wing. Minneapolis: University of Minnesota Press, 1986.

Clayton, Philip, and Arthur Peacocke, editors. *In Whom We Live and Move and Have our Being: Panentheistic Reflections on God's Presence in a Scientific World.* Grand Rapids: Eerdmans, 2004.

Clebsch, William, and Charles Jaekle. *Pastoral Care in Historical Perspective, An Essay with Exhibits*. Englewood Cliffs, NJ: Prentice-Hall, 1964.

Clément, Catherine. Interview with Gilles Deleuze. *L'Arc 49* (1980) 99–102.

Clinton, Dan. "Deleuze and Guattari, 'Rhizome,' Annotation." *Theories of Media* (2003). Online: http://csmt.uchicago.edu/annotations/deleuzerhizome.htm.

Cobb, John B., Jr. *Christ in a Pluralistic Age*. Philadelphia: Westminster, 1975.

———. "Relativization of the Trinity." In *Trinity in Process: A Relational Theology of God*, edited by Joseph Bracken and Majorie Suchocki, 1–22. New York: Continuum, 1997.

Cobb, John B., Jr., and David Ray Griffin. *Process Theology: An Introductory Exposition*. Philadelphia: Westminster, 1976.

Cohen, Ted. "Metaphor and the Cultivation of Intimacy." In *On Metaphor*, edited by Sheldon Sacks, 1–10. Chicago: University of Chicago Press, 1978.

Coles, Robert. *Anna Freud: The Dream of Psychoanalysis*. Radcliffe Biography Series. Reading, MA: Addison-Wesley, 1993.

Cone, James. *A Black Theology of Liberation*. 40th anniversary edition. Maryknoll, NY: Orbis, 2010

Conterio, Karen, and Wendy Lado, with Jennifer Kingson Bloom. *Bodily Harm: The Breakthrough Healing Program for Self-injurers*. New York: Hyperion, 1998.

Cooper-White, Pamela. "Two Vampires of 1828." *Opera Quarterly* 5 (1987) 22–57.

———. "Opening the Eyes: Understanding the Impact of Trauma on Development." In *In Her Own Time: Women and Developmental Issues in Pastoral Care*, edited by Jeanne Stevenson-Moessner, 87–101. Minneapolis: Fortress, 2000.

———. "The Use of the Self in Psychotherapy: A Comparative Study of Pastoral Counselors and Clinical Social Workers." *American Journal of Pastoral Counseling*. 4:4 (2001) 5–35.

———. "Higher Powers and Infernal Regions: Models of Mind in Freud's Interpretation of Dreams and Contemporary Psychoanalysis, and their Implications for Pastoral Care," *Pastoral Psychology* 50 (2002) 319–43.

———. *Shared Wisdom: Use of the Self in Pastoral Care and Counseling*. Minneapolis: Fortress, 2004.

———. *Many Voices: Pastoral Psychotherapy in Relational and Theological Perspective*. Minneapolis: Fortress, 2007.

———. "Introduction to Special Issue on Multiplicity." *Pastoral Psychology* 57:1–2 (2008) 1–16.

———. "A Critical Tradition: Psychoanalysis and Its Implications for Pastoral Care." In *Pastoral Psychology and Psychology of Religion in Dialogue: Implications for Pastoral Care/Pastoralpsychologie und Religionspsychologie im Dialog: Impulse für die Seelsorge*, edited by Kathleen Greider et al. Stuttgart: Kohlhammer, forthcoming, 2011.

———. "Suffering." In *The Blackwell Handbook of Practical Theology*, edited by Bonnie Miller-McLemore. Oxford, UK: Blackwell, forthcoming, 2011.

Corbett, Ken. "More Life: Centrality and Marginality in Human Development." *Psychoanalytic Dialogues* 11 (2001) 313–35.

Costen, Michael. *The Cathars and the Albigensian Crusade*. Manchester, UK: Manchester University Press, 1997.

Cross, William E., Jr. "The Negro-to-Black Conversion Experience: Toward a Psychology of Black Liberation." *Black World* 20 (1971) 13–27.

———. *Shades of Black: Diversity in African-American Identity*. Philadelphia: Temple University Press, 1991.

————. "The Psychology of Nigrescence: Revising the Cross Model." In *Handbook of Multicultural Counseling*, edited by Joseph G. Ponterotto et al., 93–122. Thousand Oaks, CA: Sage, 1995.

Cunningham, David S. *These Three Are One: The Practice of Trinitarian Theology*. Challenges in Contemporary Theology. Malden, MA: Blackwell, 1998.

Daloz, Laurent A. P., et al. *Common Fire: Lives of Commitment in a Complex World*. Boston: Beacon, 1996.

Danto, Elizabeth Ann. *Freud's Free Clinics: Psychoanalysis & Social Justice, 1918–1938*. New York: Columbia University Press, 2005.

Davies, Jody Messler, and Mary Gail Frawley. *Treating the Adult Survivor of Childhood Sexual Abuse: A Psychoanalytic Perspective*. New York: Basic Books, 1994.

————. "Dissociation, Repression, and Reality Testing in the Countertransference: The Controversy over Memory and False Memory in the Psychoanalytic Treatment of Adult Survivors of Childhood Sexual Abuse." *Psychoanalytic Dialogues* 6 (1996) 189–218.

————. "Linking the 'Pre-analytic' and the Postclassical: Integration, Dissociation, and the Multiplicity of Unconscious Process." *Contemporary Psychoanalysis*, 32 (1996) 553–76.

————. "Multiple Perspectives on Multiplicity." *Psychoanalytic Dialogues* 8 (1998) 195–206.

————. "Getting Cold Feet, Defining 'Safe-Enough' Borders: Dissociation, Multiplicity, and Integration in the Analyst's Experience." *Psychoanalytic Quarterly* 68 (1999) 184–208.

"Decalcomania." In *The American Heritage Dictionary of the English Language*. 4th ed. Boston: Houghton Mifflin, 2000. Online: http://dictionary.reference.com/browse/decalcomania.

Deleuze, Gilles. *Difference and Repetition*. 1968. Translated by Paul Patton. New York: Columbia University Press, 1994.

————. *The Fold: Leibniz and the Baroque*. 1988. Translated by Tom Conley. Minneapolis: University of Minnesota Press 1993.

Deleuze, Gilles, and Felix Guattari. *What Is Philosophy?* 1991. Translated by Hugh Tomlinson and Graham Burchell. European Perspectives. New York: Columbia University Press, 1994.

————. *A Thousand Plateaus: Capitalism and Schizophrenia*. 1980. Translated by Brian Massumi. Minneapolis: University of Minnesota Press, 1987.

DeMarinis, Valerie. *Critical Caring: A Feminist Model for Pastoral Psychology*. Louisville: Westminster John Knox, 1993.

————. "The Body's Sacred Containing: An Emerging Dialogue between Feminist Studies and Ritual Studies for Pastoral Psychotherapy." *Journal of Supervision and Training for Ministry* 18 (1998–1999) 86–93.

Derrida, Jacques. *Of Grammatology*. 1967. Translated by Gayatri Chakravorty Spivak. Baltimore: Johns Hopkins University Press, 1976.

————. *Writing and Difference*. Translated, with an introduction and additional notes, by Alan Bass. Chicago: University of Chicago Press, 1978.

Descartes, René. *"Discourse on Method"; and "Meditations on First Philosophy."* Translated by Donald A. Cress. 4th ed. Indianapolis: Hackett, 1998.

Dillard, Annie. *Pilgrim at Tinker Creek*. New York: Harper's Magazine Press, 1974.

Doehring, Carrie. "Minding the Gap When Cognitive Neuroscience Is a Cognate Discipline in Pastoral Theology: Lessons from Neurotheology. *Journal of Pastoral Theology* 20, no. 2 (2010) 93–108.

Dominguez, Elizabeth. "A Continuing Challenge for Women's Ministry." In *God's Image* 2 (1983) 7–8.

Doy, Gen. *Drapery: Classicism and Barbarism in Visual Culture.* London: Tauris, 2002.

DuBois, W. E. B. *The Souls of Black Folk.* Modern Library Edition. New York: Random House, 2003.

Dykstra, Craig. "Imagination and the Pastoral Life." *The Christian Century,* March 8, 2008, 26–31. Online: http://www.religion-online.org/showarticle.asp?title=3523.

———. "Pastoral and Ecclesial Imagination." In *For Life Abundant: Practical Theology, Theological Education, and Christian Ministry,* edited by Dorothy C. Bass and Craig Dykstra, 41–61. Grand Rapids: Eerdmans, 2008.

Eco, Umberto. *The Aesthetics of Chaosmos: The Middle Ages of James Joyce.* Translated by Ellen Esrock. Cambridge: Harvard University Press, 1989. Excerpted online: http://www.noteaccess.com/APPROACHES/Chaosmos.htm/.

Eiesland, Nancy. *The Disabled God: Toward a Liberatory Theology of Disability.* Nashville: Abingdon, 1994.

Elder, Glen H., Jr., et al., editors. *Children in Time and Place: Developmental and Historical Insights.* Cambridge Studies in Social and Emotional Development. Cambridge, UK: Cambridge University Press, 1994.

———. *Children of the Great Depression: Social Change in Life Experience.* 25th anniversary edition. Boulder, CO: Westview, 1999.

Eliot, T. S. *The Four Quartets.* A Harvest/HBJ Book. New York: Harcourt Brace Jovanovich, 1971.

Elster, Jon. *Ulysses and the Sirens: Studies in Rationality and Irrationality.* Rev. ed. Cambridge Paperback Series. Cambridge, UK: Cambridge University Press, 1984.

———. *Ulysses Unbound: Studies in Rationality, Precommitment, and Constraints.* Cambridge, UK: Cambridge University Press, 2000.

———. "Don't Burn Your Bridge before You Come to It: Ambiguities and Complexities of Commitment." *Texas Law Review* 91 (2003) 1751–88.

Emde, Robert. "The Affective Self: Continuities and Transformation from Infancy." In *Frontiers of Infant Psychiatry,* vol. 2, edited by Justin D. Call et al., 38–54. New York: Basic Books, 1984.

———. "The Prerepresentational Self and its Affective Core." *Psychoanalytic Study of the Child* 38 (1983) 165–92.

Erikson, Erik H. *Childhood and Society.* 2nd ed. New York: Norton, 1963.

———. *Identity and the Life Cycle.* New York: Norton, 1980.

Evans, G. R. "Evil." In *Augustine through the Ages: An Encyclopedia,* edited by Allan G. Fitzgerald et al., 340–44. Grand Rapids: Eerdmans, 1999.

———. *Augustine on Evil.* Cambridge, UK: Cambridge University Press, 1982.

Fairbairn, W. R. D. *Psychoanalytic Studies of the Personality.* Boston: Routledge, 1952.

———. *An Object Relations Theory of the Personality.* New York: Basic Books, 1954.

Farber, Sharon Klayman. *When the Body Is the Target: Self-Harm, Pain, and Traumatic Attachments.* Northvale, NJ: Aronson, 2002.

Farley, Edward. *Good and Evil: Interpreting a Human Condition.* Minneapolis: Fortress, 1990.

———. "Practical Theology." In *Dictionary of Pastoral Care and Counseling,* edited by Rodney J. Hunter et al., 934–36. Nashville: Abingdon, 2005.

Farley, Wendy. *Tragic Vision and Divine Compassion: A Contemporary Theodicy.* Louisville: Westminster John Knox, 1990.

Ferenczi, Sándor. "The Confusion of Tongues between Adults and Children: The Language of Tenderness and Passion." In *Final Contributions to the Problems and Methods of Psychoanalysis*, by Sándor Ferenczi, 156–67. Edited by Michael Balint. Translated by Eric Mosbacher. Brunner/Mazel Classics in Psychoanalysis 6. London: Karnac, 1980.

Fewell, Danna N., and David M Gunn. *Gender, Power, and Promise: The Subject of the Bible's First Story*. Nashville: Abingdon, 1993.

Fink, David L. "The Core Self: A Developmental Perspective on the Dissociative Disorders." *Dissociation* 1:2 (1988) 43–47.

Flanagan, Owen, and Amélie Oksenberg Rorty, editors. *Identity, Character, and Morality*. Cambridge, MA: MIT Press, 1990.

Flax, Jane. "Multiples: On the Contemporary Politics of Subjectivity." In *Disputed Subjects: Essays on Psychoanalysis, Politics and Philosophy*, by Jane Flax, 92–110. New York: Routledge, 1993.

————. "The Play of Justice." In *Disputed Subjects: Essays on Psychoanalysis, Politics and Philosophy*, by Jane Flax, 111–28. New York: Routledge, 1993.

————. *Disputed Subjects: Essays on Psychoanalysis, Politics and Philosophy*. New York: Routledge, 1993.

————. "Taking Multiplicity Seriously," *Contemporary Psychoanalysis* 32 (1996) 577–93.

Foot, Philippa. *Virtues and Vices, and Other Essays in Moral Philosophy*. Oxford: Blackwell, 1978.

————. *Natural Goodness*. Oxford: Clarendon, 2001.

Foucault, Michel. "Intellectuals and Power: A Conversation between Michel Foucault and Gilles Deleuze." In *Language, Counter-memory, Practice: Selected Essays and Interviews by Michel Foucault*, edited by Donald F. Bouchard, 205–17. Translated by Donald F. Bouchard and Sherry Simon. Ithaca, NY: Cornell University Press, 1977.

————. *The History of Sexuality: An Introduction*. Translated by Robert Hurley. New York: Pantheon, 1978.

————. "Power and Strategies." In Michel Foucault, *Power/Knowledge: Selected Interviews and Other Writings, 1972–1977*, edited by Colin Gordon, 134–45. New York: Pantheon, 1980.

————. *Power/Knowledge: Selected Interviews and Other Writings, 1972–1977*. Edited by Colin Gordon. New York: Pantheon, 1980.

————. *Madness and Civilization: A History of Insanity in the Age of Reason*. Translated by Richard Howard. New York: Vintage, 1988.

————. *The Birth of the Clinic: An Archaeology of Medical Perception*. Translated by A. M. Sheridan Smith. New York: Vintage, 1994.

Fowler, James. *Stages of Faith: The Psychology of Human Development*, 2nd ed. San Francisco: HarperSanFrancisco, 1995.

Freud, Anna. *The Psycho-Analysis of Children*. Rev. ed. London: Hogarth, 1932.

————. "The Concept of Developmental Lines." *Psychoanalytic Study of the Child* 18 (1963) 245–65.

————. "The Concept of Developmental Lines: Their Diagnostic Significance." *Psychoanalytic Study of the Child* 36 (1981) 129–36.

Freud, Sigmund. *The Standard Edition of the Complete Psychological Works of Sigmund Freud*. Edited and translated by James Strachey. 24 vols. London: Hogarth, 1961. (Hereafter cited as *SE*.)

————. *Project for a Scientific Psychology* (1895/1950). *SE* 1:281–391.

————."Further Remarks on the Neuro-Psychoses of Defense"(1896). *SE* 3:163–88.

————. *The Interpretation of Dreams* (1900). *SE* 4–5 (entire).

————. *Fragment of an Analysis of a Case of Hysteria* ["Dora"] (1905). *SE* 7:1–122.

————. *Three Essays on the Theory of Sexuality* (1905). *SE* 7:125–245.

————."The Dynamics of the Transference"(1912). *SE* 12:97–108.

————. "Recommendations to Physicians Practicing Psycho-analysis." (1912). *SE* 12:111–20.

————. *Mourning and Melancholia* (1917). *SE* 14:243–48.

————. *Introductory Lectures on Psychoanalysis* (1916–1917). *SE* 15–16 (entire).

————. "From the History of an Infantile Neurosis" ['Wolf Man'] (1918). *SE* 17:1–124.

————."The Uncanny"(1919). *SE* 17:217–56.

————. *Beyond the Pleasure Principle* (1920). *SE* 18:1–64.

————. *The Ego and the Id* (1923). *SE* 19:1–66.

————. *Inhibitions, Symptoms and Anxiety* (1926). *SE* 20:75–176.

————. *The Question of Lay Analysis* (1926). *SE* 20:179–258.

————. *Civilization and Its Discontents* (1930). *SE* 21:57–146.

————. *An Outline of Psychoanalysis* (1938). *SE* 23:139–208.

Friedman, Edwin H. *Generation to Generation: Family Process in Church and Synagogue.* The Guilford Family Therapy Series. New York: Guilford, 1985.

Gast, John. *American Progress or Westward the Course of Destiny* (1873). Digital file from b&w film copy neg. ID # cph 3a04647. http://www.loc.gov/pictures/resource/cph.3a04647/. Library of Congress Prints and Photographs Division Washington, DC 20540 USA.

Gay, Peter. *Freud: A Life for Our Time.* New York: Norton, 2006.

Geertz, Clifford."From the Native's Point of View: On the Nature of Anthropological Understanding." In *Local Knowledge: Further Essays in Interpretive Anthropology,* 55–72. New York: Basic Books, 1983.

————. "Thick Description: Toward an Interpretative Theory of Culture." In *The Interpretation of Cultures,* edited by Clifford Geertz, 3–32. New York: Basic Books, 1973.

Gergen, Kenneth J. *The Saturated Self: Dilemmas of Identity in Contemporary Life.* New York: Basic Books, 1991.

Gerkin, Charles. *The Living Human Document: Re-visioning Pastoral Counseling in a Hermeneutical Mode.* Nashville: Abingdon, 1984.

Gibbs, Raymond W., Jr. "Metaphor and Thought: The State of the Art." In *The Cambridge Handbook of Metaphor and Thought,* edited by Raymond W. Gibbs, Jr., 3–13. New York: Cambridge University Press, 2008.

Gilligan, Carol. *In a Different Voice: Psychological Theory and Women's Development.* Cambridge, MA: Harvard University Press, 1982.

Ginsburg, Herbert P., and Sylvia Opper. *Piaget's Theory of Intellectual Development,* 3rd ed. Englewood Cliffs, NJ: Prentice Hall, 1988.

Glover, Edward. *The Birth of the Ego: A Nuclear Hypothesis.* New York: International Universities Press, 1968.

Goldberg, Arnold. *Being of Two Minds: The Vertical Split in Psychoanalysis and Psychotherapy.* Hillsdale, NJ: Analytic, 1999.

Goleman, Daniel P. *Emotional Intelligence.* New York: Bantam, 1997.

Graham, Elaine. *Making the Difference: Gender, Personhood, and Theology.* London: Mowbray, 1995.

———. *Transforming Practice: Pastoral Theology in an Age of Uncertainty*. 1996. Eugene, OR: Wipf & Stock, 2002.

Green, André. "The Dead Mother." In *On Private Madness*, 142–73. Maresfield Library. London: Karnac, 1997.

Greenberg, Amy S. *Manifest Manhood and the Antebellum American Empire*. Cambridge, UK: Cambridge University Press, 2005.

Greenberg, Jay R. *Oedipus and Beyond: A Clinical Theory*. Cambridge, MA: Harvard University Press, 1991.

Greenberg, Jay R., and Stephen A. Mitchell. "Object Relations and Psychoanalytic Models." In *Object Relations in Psychoanalytic Theory*, 9–20. Cambridge, MA: Harvard University Press, 1983.

Greenspan, Stanley I. *The Growth of the Mind: And the Endangered Origins of Intelligence*. Reading, MA: Addison-Wesley, 1997.

Gregory of Nyssa. *Life of Saint Macrina*. Translated by Kevin Corrigan. Toronto: Peregrina, 1996. Original document: Migne, *Patrologia graeca*, 46:960–1000. Online: http://www.fordham.edu/halsall/basis/macrina.html#bib/.

Greider, Kathleen G. *Reckoning with Aggression: Theology, Violence, and Vitality*. Louisville: Westminster John Knox, 1997.

Griffin, David Ray. *God, Power, and Evil: A Process Theodicy*. Philadelphia: Westminster, 1976.

Grossman, William I. "The Self as Fantasy: Fantasy as Theory." *Journal of the American Psychoanalytic Association* 30 (1982) 919–38.

Grosz, Elizabeth. "Irigaray and the Divine." In *Transfigurations: Theology and the French Feminists*, edited by C. W. Maggie Kim et al., 199–214. 1993. Eugene, OR: Wipf & Stock, 2002.

Grovijahn, Jane. "A Theology of Survival." PhD diss., Graduate Theological Union, Berkeley, CA, 1997.

Guntrip, Harry J. "Deeper Perception of the Schizoid Problem." In *Personal Relations Therapy: The Collected Papers of H. J. S. Guntrip*, edited by Jeremy Hazell, 127–56. Library of Object Relations. Northvale, NJ: Aronson, 1994.

———. *Schizoid Phenomena, Object-Relations and the Self*. New York: International Universities Press, 1969.

Gutierrez, Gustavo. *On Job: God-Talk and the Suffering of the Innocent*. Translated by Matthew J. O'Connell. Maryknoll, NY: Orbis, 1987.

Habermas, Jürgen. *Legitimation Crisis*. Translated by Thomas McCarthy. Boston: Beacon, 1975.

Hammond, Guyton. "An Examination of Tillich's Method of Correlation." *Journal of the American Academy of Religion* 32 (1964) 248–51.

Hanh, Thich Nhat. *Peace Is Every Step: The Path of Mindfulness in Everyday Life*. New York: Bantam, 1992.

Haresh B. Sabnani, et al. "White Racial Identity Development and Cross-cultural Counselor Training: A Stage Model." *The Counseling Psychologist* 19 (1991) 76–102.

Harman, Gilbert. "Virtue Ethics without Character Traits." Online: http://www.princeton.edu/~harman/Papers/Thomson.html/.

Harris, Adrienne. "False Memory? False Memory Syndrome? The So-called False Memory Syndrome?" *Psychoanalytic Dialogues* 6 (1996) 155–87.

Hartmann, Heinz. *Ego Psychology and the Problem of Adaptation*. Translated by David Rapaport. Journal of the American Psychoanalytic Association. Monograph Series 1. New York: International Universities Press, 1958.

Helms, Janet E., editor. *Black and White Racial Identity: Theory, Research, and Practice.* Contributions in Afro-American and African Studies 129. New York: Greenwood, 1990.

Hemingway, Ernest. *A Farewell to Arms.* New York: Scribner, 1929.

Herman, Judith Lewis. *Trauma and Recovery.* Revised ed. New York: Basic Books, 1997.

Hick, John. *Evil and the God of Love.* Rev. ed. San Francisco: Harper & Row, 1978.

Hoffman, Irwin Z. "Discussion: Toward a Social-Constructivist View." *Psychoanalytic Dialogues* 1 (1991) 74–105.

Hofstadter, Douglas. *Gödel, Escher, Bach: An Eternal Golden Braid.* 20th anniversary ed. New York: Basic Books, 1999.

Hogue, David A. *Remembering the Future, Imagining the Past: Story, Ritual, and the Human Brain.* Cleveland: Pilgrim, 2003.

Holifield, E. Brooks. *A History of Pastoral Care in America: From Salvation to Self-Realization.* Nashville: Abingdon, 1983.

———. "Anton Boisen." In *Dictionary of Pastoral Care and Counseling,* edited by Rodney J. Hunter and Nancy J. Ramsay, 104–5. Rev. ed. Nashville: Abingdon, 2005.

Homans, Peter. Response to Person, Culture and Religion Panel on the 100th Anniversary of Freud's *Interpretation of Dreams,* American Academy of Religion annual meeting, Boston, MA, November, 1999.

Hopkins, Gerard Manley. *The Poems of Gerard Manley Hopkins.* Edited by W. H. Gardner and N. H. Mackenzie. 4th ed. London: Oxford University Press, 1967.

Horwitz, Tony. *Confederates in the Attic: Dispatches from the Unfinished Civil War.* New York: Vintage, 1998.

Hunter, Rodney J., and Nancy J. Ramsay, editors. *Dictionary of Pastoral Care and Counseling.* Rev. ed. Nashville: Abingdon, 2005.

Husserl, Edmund. *Cartesian Meditations: An Introduction to Phenomenology.* Translated by Dorion Cairns. The Hague: Nijhoff, 1977.

Irigaray, Luce. *This Sex Which Is Not One.* Translated by Catherine Porter. Ithaca, NY: Cornell University Press, 1985.

———. *Speculum of the Other Woman.* Translated by Gillian Gill. Ithaca, NY: Cornell University Press, 1985.

———. "Divine Women." Translated by Stephen Muecke. Local Consumption Occasional Paper 8. Sydney, Australia: n.p., 1986.

———. *An Ethics of Sexual Difference.* Translated by Carolyn Burke and Gillian Gill. Ithaca, NY: Cornell University Press, 1993.

———. "Equal to Whom?" In *Differences: A Journal of Feminist Cultural Studies* 1:2 (1989) 59–76; reprinted in *The Postmodern God: A Theological Reader,* edited by Graham Ward, 198–214. Blackwell Readings in Modern Theology. Malden, MA: Blackwell, 1997.

———. *To Speak Is Never Neutral.* Translated by Gail Schwab. New York: Routledge, 2002.

Isasi-Díaz, Ada María. *Mujerista Theology: A Theology for the Twenty-First Century.* Maryknoll, 1996.

Janet, Pierre. *The Major Symptoms of Hysteria.* New York: MacMillan, 1907.

Jantzen, Grace M. *Becoming Divine: Towards a Feminist Philosophy of Religion.* Bloomington: Indiana University Press, 1999.

————. "Luce Iragaray: Introduction." In *The Postmodern God: A Theological Reader*, edited by Graham Ward, 191–97. Blackwell Readings in Modern Theology. Malden, MA: Blackwell, 1997.

Joh, Wonhee Anne. "Authoring a Multiplicity of Selves and No-Self" (Roundtable Discussion: Mysticism and Feminist Spirituality), *Journal of Feminist Studies in Religion* 24 (2008) 169–72.

Johnson, Elizabeth. *She Who Is: The Mystery of God in Feminist Theological Discourse*. 10th anniversary edition. New York: Crossroad, 2002.

Jones, Ernest. *The Life and Work of Sigmund Freud*. 3 vols. New York: Basic Books, 1953–1957.

Jones, Susan. "This God Who Is Not One: Irigaray and Barth on the Divine." In *Transfigurations: Theology and the French Feminists*, edited by Maggie C. W. Kim et al., 109–41. Minneapolis: Fortress, 1993.

Jordan, Judith V., editor. *Women's Growth in Diversity: More Writings from the Stone Center*. New York: Guilford, 1997.

Joseph, Betty. "Toward the Experiencing of Psychic Pain." In *Psychic Equilibrium and Psychic Change*, 88–97. New Library of Psychoanalysis 9. London: Tavistock/Routledge, 1989.

Julian, of Norwich. *Showings*. Classics of Western Spirituality. New York: Paulist, 1978.

Jung, C. G. *The Collected Works of C. G. Jung (CW)*. Vol. 5, *Symbols of Transformation*. Edited and translated by Gerhard Adler and R. F. C. Hull. 2nd ed. Bollingen Series 20. Princeton, NJ: Princeton University Press, 1976.

————. *Psychological Types* (1921). *CW* 6.

————. *Answer to Job* (1952). *CW* 11:355–470.

————. *The Archetypes and the Collective Unconscious* (1954). *CW* 9, Part I.

————. *Memories, Dreams and Reflections*. Edited by Aniela Jaffé. Translated by Richard and Clara Winston. Rev. ed. New York: Vintage, 1989.

Kaufman, Gordon. *In the Beginning—Creativity*. Minneapolis: Fortress, 2004.

Kegan, Robert. *The Evolving Self: Problem and Process in Human Development*. Cambridge, MA: Harvard University Press, 1982.

————. *In Over Our Heads: The Mental Demands of Modern Life*. Cambridge, MA: Harvard University Press, 1994.

Keller, Catherine. *Face of the Deep: A Theology of Becoming*. London: Routledge, 2003.

Kerr, John. *A Most Dangerous Method: The Story of Jung, Freud, and Sabina Spielrein*. New York: Vintage, 1993.

Kestenbaum, Ellyn. *Culture on Ice: Figure Skating & Cultural Meaning*. Middletown, CT: Wesleyan University Press, 2003.

Khanna, Ranjana. *Dark Continents: Psychoanalysis and Colonialism*. Post-contemporary Interventions. Durham, NC: Duke University Press, 2003.

Kim, C. W. Maggie, et al., editors. *Transfigurations: Theology and the French Feminists*. Minneapolis: Fortress, 1993.

Kirshner, Lewis. "The Concept of the Self in Psychoanalytic Theory and Its Philosophical Foundations." *Journal of the American Psychoanalytic Association* 39 (1991) 157–82.

Klein, Melanie. *Envy and Gratitude: A Study of Unconscious Sources*. London: Tavistock, 1957.

————. *Love, Guilt, and Reparation, and Other Works 1921-1945*. Edited by Roger Money-Kyrle. The Writings of Melanie Klein 1. New York: Free Press, 1975.

———. "Notes on Some Schizoid Mechanisms." In *Envy and Gratitude and Other Works, 1946–1963*, edited by Robert Money-Kyrle, 1–24. The Writings of Melanie Klein 3. New York: Free Press, 1975.

———. *Envy and Gratitude and Other Works, 1946–1963*. Edited by Roger Money-Kyrle. The Writings of Melanie Klein 3. New York: Free Press, 1975.

Kluckholn, Clyde, and Henry A. Murray, editors. *Personality in Nature, Society and Culture*. 2nd ed. New York: Knopf, 1953.

Kohlberg, Lawrence. *Collected Papers on Moral Development and Moral Education*. Cambridge, MA: Moral Education & Research Foundation, Harvard University, 1975

———. "Continuities and Discontinuities in Childhood and Adult Moral Development Revisited." In *Collected Papers on Moral Development and Moral Education*. Cambridge, MA: Moral Education Research & Foundation, Harvard University, 1975.

Kohon, Gregorio. "Objects Are Not People." *Free Associations* 2 (1985) 19–30.

Kohut, Heinz. "Introspection, Empathy, and Psychoanalysis: An Examination of the Relationship between Mode of Observation and Theory." *Journal of the American Psychoanalytic Association* 7 (1959) 459–83.

———. *The Analysis of the Self: A Systematic Approach to the Psychoanalytic Treatment of Narcissistic Personality Disorders*. The Psychoanalytic Study of the Child. Monograph 4. New York: International Universities Press, 1971.

———. *The Restoration of the Self*. New York: International Universities Press, 1977.

———. "The Two Analyses of Mr. Z." *International Journal of Psycho-Analysis* 60 (1979) 3–27.

———. *How Does Analysis Cure?* Edited by Arnold Goldberg and Paul Stepansky. Chicago: University of Chicago Press, 1984.

Kristeva, Julia. *Revolution in Poetic Language*. Translated by Margaret Waller. New York: Columbia University Press, 1984.

———. *The Kristeva Reader*. Edited by Toril Moi. New York: Columbia University Press, 1986.

———. *Strangers to Ourselves*. Translated by Leon Roudiez. European Perspectives. New York: Columbia University Press, 1991.

Kuhn, Thomas S. *The Structure of Scientific Revolutions*. 3rd ed. Chicago: University of Chicago Press, 1996.

Kushner, Harold. *When Bad Things Happen to Good People*. New York: Schocken, 1981.

Kutchins, Herb, and Stuart A. Kirk. *Making Us Crazy: DSM; The Psychiatric Bible and the Creation of Mental Disorders*. New York: Free Press, 1997.

Lacan, Jacques. *Écrits: A Selection*. Translated by Alan Sheridan. New York: Norton, 1977.

———. "The Mirror Stage as Formative of the Function of the *I* Function as Revealed in Psychoanalytic Experience." In *Écrits: The First Complete Edition in English*, translated by Bruce Fink in collaboration with Héloïse Fink and Russell Grigg, 75–81. New York: Norton, 2005.

———. *Écrits: The First Complete Edition in English*. Translated by Bruce Fink in collaboration with Héloïse Fink, and Russell Grigg. New York: Norton, 2005.

Lachmann, Frank M. "How Many Selves Make a Person?" *Contemporary Psychoanalysis* 32 (1996) 595–614.

LaCugna, Catherine Mowry. *God for Us: The Trinity and Christian Life*. San Francisco: HarperSanFrancisco, 1991.

Lakoff, George, and Mark Johnson. *Metaphors We Live By*. Chicago: University of Chicago Press, 1980.

Lane, Christopher, editor. *The Psychoanalysis of Race*. New York: Columbia University Press, 1998.

Lartey, Emmanuel Y. *In Living Colour: An Intercultural Approach to Pastoral Care and Counseling*. 2nd ed. London: Jessica Kingsley, 2003.

———. *Pastoral Theology in an Intercultural World* Peterborough: Epworth, 2007.

Lear, Jonathan. *Freud*. Routledge Philosophers. New York: Routledge, 2005.

Lemert, Charles C., and Garth Gillan. *Michel Foucault: Social Theory as Transgression*. New York: Columbia University Press, 1982.

Lemke, Jay. "Postmodernism and Critical Theory," 1998. Link [7] in *Important Theories for Research Topics on This Website*. Online: http://academic.brooklyn.cuny.edu/education/jlemke/theories.htm.

Levinas, Emmanuel. *Totality and Infinity: An Essay on Exteriority*. Translated by Alphonso Lingis. Duquesne Studies. Philosophical Series 24. Pittsburgh: Duquesne University Press, 1969.

Lewis, Helen B. "Shame and Guilt in Human Nature." In *Object and Self, A Developmental Approach: Essays in Honor of Edith Jacobson*, edited by Saul Tuttman et al., 235–65. New York: International Universities Press, 1981.

Little, Margaret. "My Experience of Analysis with Fairbairn and Winnicott (How Complete a Result Does Psychoanalytic Therapy Achieve?")" *International Review of Psycho-Analysis* 2 (1975) 145–56.

Loder, James E. *The Logic of the Spirit: Human Development in Theological Perspective*. San Francisco: Jossey-Bass, 1998.

Loewald, Hans W. "Instinct Theory, Object Relations, and Psychic Structure Formation." In *Papers on Psychoanalysis*, 207–18. New Haven: Yale University Press, 1980.

Loftus, Elizabeth, and Katherine Ketcham. *The Myth of Repressed Memory: False Memories and Allegations of Sexual Abuse*. New York: St. Martin's, 1994.

Loomer, Bernard. "Tillich's Theology of Correlation." *Journal of Religion* 36 (1956) 150–56.

———. *The Size of God: The Theology of Bernard Loomer in Context*. Edited by William Dean and Larry Axel. Macon, GA: Mercer University Press, 1987.

———. "Two Conceptions of Power." *Process Studies* 6 (1976) 5–32.

Lukoff, David, et al. "Toward a More Culturally Sensitive DSM-IV: Psychoreligious and Psychospiritual Problems." *Journal of Nervous and Mental Disease* 180 (1992) 673–82.

Lyotard, Jean-Francois. *The Postmodern Condition: A Report on Knowledge*. Translated by Geoff Bennington and Brian Massumi. Theory and History of Literature 10. Minneapolis: University of Minnesota Press, 1984.

MacIntyre, Alasdair. *After Virtue: A Study in Moral Theory*. 3rd ed. Notre Dame, IN: University of Notre Dame Press, 2007.

Macquarrie, John. *Principles of Christian Theology*. 2nd ed. New York: Scribner, 1977.

Madden, Edward, and Peter Hare. *Evil and the Concept of God*. American Lecture Series 706. A Monograph in the Bannerstone Division of American Lectures in Philosophy. Springfield, IL: Thomas, 1968.

Maslow, Abraham H. *Motivation and Personality*. 3rd ed. New York: HarperCollins, 1987.

Maslow, Abraham H., and Richard Lowry. *Toward a Psychology of Being*. 3rd ed. New York: Wiley, 1998.

Masson, J. Moussaieff. *The Assault on Truth: Freud's Suppression of the Seduction Theory*. New York: Pocket Books, 1998.

McFague, Sallie. *Metaphorical Theology: Models of God in Religious Language*. Philadelphia: Fortress, 1982.

———. *Models of God: Theology for an Ecological, Nuclear Age*. Philadelphia: Fortress, 1987.

McGoldrick, Monica, et al. *Genograms: Assessment and Intervention*. 3rd ed. New York: Norton, 2008.

McLean, George F. "Philosophical Notions of the Person." In *Psychology, Phenomenology, and Chinese Philosophy: Chinese Philosophical Studies VI*, edited by Vincent Shen et al., 41–69. Cultural Heritage and Contemporary Change. Sereis 3, Asia 6. Washington, DC: Council for Research in Values and Philosophy, 1994.

McWilliams, Nancy. *Psychoanalytic Case Formulation*. New York: Guilford, 1999.

———. *Psychoanalytic Psychotherapy: A Practitioner's Guide*. New York: Guilford, 2004.

Meilander, Gilbert. "I Renounce the Devil and All His Ways." In *Sin, Death, and the Devil*, edited by Carl E. Braaten and Robert W. Jenson, 76–93. Grand Rapids: Eerdmans, 2000.

Meissner, W. W. *Life and Faith: Psychological Perspectives on Religious Experience*. Washington, DC: Georgetown University Press, 1987.

Merritt, Maria. "Virtue Ethics and the Social Psychology of Character." PhD diss., University of California, Berkeley, 1999.

"Metaphor." In *Random House Dictionary, Inc. 2010*. Online: http://dictionary. reference.com/browse/metaphor/.

"Metaphor—Definition." *WordIQ.com*. Online: http://www.wordiq.com/definition/ Metaphor/.

Meyers, Diana Tietjens. *Subjection & Subjectivity: Psychoanalytic Feminism & Moral Philosophy*. Thinking Gender. New York: Routledge, 1994.

Milbank, John. "Postmodern Critical Augustinianism: A Short *Summa* in Forty-Two Responses to Unasked Questions." In *The Postmodern God: A Theological Reader*, edited by Graham Ward, 265–78. Blackwell Readings in Modern Theology. Malden, MA: Blackwell, 1997.

———. *The Word Made Strange: Theology, Language, Culture*. Oxford: Blackwell, 1997.

———. "Evil: Negative or Positive?" and "Forgiveness: Negative or Positive?" Paddock Lectures, General Theological Seminary, New York, NY, October 2000.

———. *Theology and Social Theory: Beyond Secular Reason*. 2nd ed. Oxford: Blackwell, 2006.

Miller-McLemore, Bonnie. "The Living Human Web: Pastoral Theology at the Turn of the Century." In *Through the Eyes of Women: Insights for Pastoral Care*, edited by Jeanne Stevenson-Moessner, 9–26. Minneapolis: Fortress, 1996.

———. "Cognitive Neuroscience and the Question of Theological Method." *Journal of Pastoral Theology* 20 (2010) 64–92.

Minsky, Marvin. *The Society of Mind*. New York: Simon & Schuster, 1986.

Mitchell, Stephen A. *Relational Concepts in Psychoanalysis: An Integration*. Cambridge, MA: Harvard University Press, 1988.

———. "Contemporary Perspectives on Self." *Psychoanalytic Dialogues* 1 (1991) 121–48.

———. "Multiple Selves, Singular Self." In *Hope and Dread in Psychoanalysis*, 95–122. New York: Basic Books, 1995.

————. *Hope and Dread in Psychoanalysis.* New York: Basic Books, 1995.

————. *Relationality: From Attachment to Subjectivity.* Relational Perspectives Book Series 20. Hillsdale, NJ: Analytic, 2003.

Mitchell, Stephen A., and Lewis Aron, editors. *Relational Psychoanalysis.* Vol. 1, *The Emergence of a Tradition.* Relational Perspectives Book Series 14. Hillsdale, NJ: Analytic, 1999.

Mitchell, Stephen A., and Margaret J. Black. *Freud and Beyond: A History of Modern Psychoanalytic Thought.* New York: Basic Books, 1995.

Moi, Toril. *Sexual/Textual Politics: Feminist Literary Theory.* London: Routledge, 1988.

Mollenkott, Virginia Ramey. *Godding: Human Responsibility and the Bible.* New York: Crossroad, 1987.

Moltmann, Jürgen. *The Trinity and the Kingdom.* Translated by Margaret Kohl. Minneapolis: Fortress, 1993.

————. *Theology of Hope: On the Ground and the Implications of a Christian Eschatology.* Minneapolis: Fortress, 1993.

————. "Eschatology." In *Dictionary of Pastoral Care and Counseling,* edited by Rodney J. Hunter and Nancy Ramsay, 360–62. Rev. ed. Nashville: Abingdon, 2005.

Moltmann-Wendel, Elisabeth. *I Am My Body: A Theology of Embodiment.* Translated by John Bowden. New York: Continuum, 1995.

Montaigne, Michel de. *Essays of Michael, Lord of Montaigne.* Translated by John Florio. 3 vols. Boston: Houghton Mifflin, 1902–1904.

Morton, Nelle. *The Journey Is Home.* Boston: Beacon, 1985.

Moskowitz, Michael, et al., editors. *The Neurobiological and Developmental Basis for Psychotherapeutic Intervention.* The Library of Clinical Psychoanalysis. Northvale, NJ: Aronson, 1997.

Nava, Alexander. "The Mystery of Evil and the Hiddenness of God: Some Thoughts on Simone Weil." In *The Fascination of Evil,* edited by Hermann Häring and David Tracy, 74–84. London: SCM, 1998.

Nicholas of Cusa, Cardinal. *Selected Spiritual Writings.* Translated and introduced by H. Lawrence Bond. New York: Paulist, 1997.

Noddings, Nel. *Women and Evil.* Berkeley: University of California Press, 1989.

Nouwen, Henri J. M. *Behold the Beauty of the Lord: Praying with Icons.* Notre Dame, IN: Ave Maria, 1987.

Obholzer, Anton, et al., editors. *The Unconscious at Work: Individual and Organizational Stress in the Human Services,* by the members of the Tavistock Clinic "Consulting to Institutions" Workshop. London: Routledge, 1994.

Ogden, Thomas H. *The Primitive Edge of Experience.* Northvale, NJ: Aronson, 1989.

Orange, Donna M. et al. *Working Intersubjectively: Contextualism in Psychoanalytic Practice.* Psychoanalytic Inquiry Book Series 17. Hillsdale, NJ: Analytic, 1994.

Pagels, Elaine. *The Origin of Satan: How Christians Demonized Jews, Pagans, and Heretics.* New York: Vintage, 1996.

Pearson, Alison. *I Don't Know How She Does It: The Life of Kate Reddy, Working Mother.* New York: Knopf, 2002.

Pedersen, Paul B. et al., editors. *Counseling across Cultures.* 5th ed. Thousand Oaks, CA: Sage, 2002.

Perry, Bruce D. et al. "Childhood Trauma, the Neurobiology of Adaptation and Use-Dependent Development of the Brain: How States Become Traits." *Infant Mental Health Journal* 16 (1995) 271–91.

Peterson, Michael L., editor. *The Problem of Evil: Selected Readings.* Library of Religious Philosophy 8. Notre Dame: University of Notre Dame Press, 1992.

Piaget, Jean. *The Construction of Reality in the Child.* Translated by Margaret Cook. New York: Basic Books, 1954.

Plato. *The Republic.* Translated with an introduction and notes by Robin Waterfield. Oxford World's Classics. Oxford: Oxford University Press, 2008.

Polkinghorne, John. Trinity Institute Lectures "Ordered Freedom: An Anglican Paradox." Presented at Trinity Episcopal Church, New York City, 1997.

———. *Quarks, Chaos & Christianity: Questions to Science and Religion.* New York: Crossroad, 1997.

Pruyser, Paul W. *The Minister as Diagnostician: Personal Problems in Pastoral Perspective.* Philadelphia: Westminster, 1976.

Ramsay, Nancy J. *Pastoral Diagnosis: A Resource for Ministries of Care and Counseling.* Minneapolis: Fortress, 1998.

———, editor. *Pastoral Care and Counseling: Redefining the Paradigms.* Nashville: Abingdon, 2004. Also reprinted in Hunter and Ramsay, editors. *Dictionary of Pastoral Care and Counseling.* Rev. ed. 1349–1452.

Rankka, Kristine M. *Women and the Value of Suffering: An Aw(e)ful Rowing toward God.* Collegeville, MN: Liturgical, 1998.

Rector, Lallene. "Narcissistic Dimensions of Racial Identity: The Role of Selfobject Experiences in the Development and Maintenance of 'Whiteness.'" Paper presented to the Psychology, Culture. and Religion Group at the American Academy of Religion annual meeting, Chicago, IL, November 3, 2008.

Reik, Theodor. *Listening with the Third Ear: The Inner Experience of a Psychoanalyst.* New York: Farrar, Straus, 1948.

"Rhizome." In *The American Heritage Dictionary of the English Language.* 4th ed. Boston: Houghton Mifflin, 2000. Online: http://dictionary.reference.com/browse/rhizome.

Richards, I. A. *The Philosophy of Rhetoric.* The Mary Flexner Lectures on the Humanities, 1936. London: Oxford University Press, 1965.

Ricoeur, Paul. *The Symbolism of Evil.* Translated by Emerson Buchanan. Religious Perspectives 17. New York: Harper & Row, 1967.

———. "Biblical Hermeneutics." *Semeia* 4 (1975) 29–148.

———. *Interpretation Theory: Discourse and the Surplus of Meaning.* Fort Worth: Texas Christian University Press, 1976.

———. "The Metaphorical Process." In *On Metaphor,* edited by Sheldon Sacks, 141–58. Chicago: University of Chicago Press, 1978.

———. *The Rule of Metaphor: Multi-disciplinary Studies of the Creation of Meaning in Language,* translated by Robert Czerny with Kathleen McLaughlin and John Costello. London: Routledge & Kegan Paul, 1978.

———. *Essays on Biblical Interpretation.* Edited with an introduction by Lewis S. Mudge. Philadelphia: Fortress, 1980.

———. *Fallible Man.* Revised translation by Charles A. Kelbley. *The Philosophy of the Will.* New York: Fordham University Press, 1986.

Rieff, Phillip. *Freud, The Mind of the Moralist.* 3rd ed. Chicago: University of Chicago Press, 1979.

Rivera-Pagán, Luis N. "Doing Pastoral Theology in a Post-Colonial Context: Some Observations from the Caribbean." *Journal of Pastoral Theology,* 17:2 (2007) 1–27.

Rizzuto, Ana-Maria. *The Birth of the Living God: A Psychoanalytic Study.* Chicago: University of Chicago Press, 1979.

Rogers, Carl R. *On Becoming a Person: A Therapist's View of Pyschotherapy*. Boston: Houghton Mifflin, 1961.

Roland, Alan. *In Search of Self in India and Japan: Toward a Cross-Cultural Psychology*. Princeton, NJ: Princeton University Press, 1989.

Rorty, Richard. *Philosophy and the Mirror of Nature*. Princeton: Princeton University Press, 1979.

Rowling, J. K. *Harry Potter and the Prisoner of Azkaban*. New York: Scholastic, 1999.

Ryder, R. "The Cohort as a Concept in the Study of Social Change." *American Sociological Review* 30 (1965) 843–61.

Ryle, Gilbert. *The Concept of Mind*. Chicago: University of Chicago Press, 2002.

Saari, Carolyn. "Identity Complexity as an Indicator of Mental Health." *Clinical Social Work Journal* 21 (1993) 11–23.

Sabnani, Haresh et al. "White Racial Identity Development and Cross-Cultural Counseling Training." *The Counseling Psychologist* 19 (1991) 76–102.

Saiving, Valerie. "The Human Situation: A Feminine View." *Journal of Religion* 40 (1960) 100–112. Also reprinted in *Womanspirit Rising: A Feminist Reader in Religion*, edited by Carol P. Christ and Judith Plaskow, 25–42. Harper Forum Books. San Francisco: Harper & Row, 1979.

Salovey, Peter, and David J. Sluyter, editors. *Emotional Development and Emotional Intelligence: Educational Implications*. New York: Basic Books, 1997.

Samuels, Andrew. *Jung and the Post-Jungians*. London: Routledge & Kegan Paul, 1985.

Sands, Kathleen M. *Escape from Paradise: Evil and Tragedy in Feminist Theology*. Minneapolis: Fortress, 1994.

Schelling, Thomas. "Ergonomics, or the Art of Self-Management." *American Economic Review: Papers and Proceedings* 68 (1978) 290–94.

Schlauch, Chris R. "Re-Visioning Pastoral Diagnosis." In *Clinical Handbook of Pastoral Counseling*, edited by Robert J. Wicks et al., 2:51–101. 3 vols. New York: Paulist, 1993.

Schneider, Laurel C. *Beyond Monotheism: A Theology of Multiplicity*. London and New York: Routledge, 2008.

Schore, Allan. *Affect Regulation and the Origin of the Self: The Neurobiology of Emotional Development*. Hillsdale, NJ: Erlbaum, 1999.

———. *Affect Dysregulation & Disorders of the Self*. 2 vols. Norton Series on Interpersonal Neurobiology. New York: Norton, 2003.

———. *Affect Regulation & the Repair of the Self*. Norton Series on Interpersonal Neurobiology. New York: Norton, 2003.

Segal, Hanna. "Notes on Symbol Formation." In *The Work of Hanna Segal: A Kleinian Approach to Clinical Practice*, 49–65. Northvale, NJ: Aronson, 1981.

Seligman, Linda. *Selecting Effective Treatments: A Comprehensive, Systematic Guide to Treating Mental Disorders*. 3rd ed. San Francisco: Jossey-Bass, 2007.

Serres, Michel. *Genesis*. Translated by Genevieve James and James Nielson. Studies in Literature and Science. Ann Arbor: University of Michigan Press, 1995.

Serres, Michel, and Bruno Latour. *Conversations on Science, Culture, and Time*. Translated by Roxanne Lapidus. Studies in Literature and Science. Ann Arbor: University of Michigan Press, 1995.

Shange, Ntozake. *for colored girls who have considered suicide/when the rainbow is enuf: a choreopoem*. New York: Macmillan, 1977.

Shengold, Leonard. *"Father, Don't You See I'm Burning?": Reflections on Sex, Narcissism, Symbolism, and Murder—from Everything to Nothing*. New Haven: Yale University Press, 1991.

————. *Soul Murder: The Effects of Childhood Abuse and Deprivation.* New York: Fawcett Columbine, 1991.

Sherman, Nancy. *The Fabric of Character: Aristotle's Theory of Virtue.* Oxford: Clarendon, 1991.

Siegel, Daniel J. *The Developing Mind: Toward a Neurobiology of Interpersonal Experience.* New York: Guilford, 1999.

Slavin, Malcolm Owen. "Is One Self Enough?: Multiplicity in Self-Organization and the Capacity to Negotiate Relational Conflict." *Contemporary Psychoanalysis* 32 (1996) 595–614.

Spitz, René. "Hospitalism: An Inquiry into the Genesis of Psychiatric Conditions in Early Childhood." *Psychoanalytic Study of the Child* 1 (1945) 53–74.

Spivak, Gayatri Chakravorty. "Can the Subaltern Speak?: Speculations on Widow Sacrifice." *Wedge* 7:8 (1985) 120–30.

————. *A Critique of Postcolonial Reason: Toward a History of the Vanishing Present.* Cambridge, MA: Harvard University Press, 1999.

————. *The Spivak Reader: Selected Works of Gayatri Chakravorty Spivak.* Edited by Donna Landry and Gerald MacLean. New York: Routledge, 1996.

Stein, Gertrude. *Everybody's Autobiography.* New York: Random House, 1937.

Stein, Herbert. "Geometry of the 'True Self' (Winnicott): On a Psychoanalytic Leibniz Study by F. Eckstein in 1931," *Zeitschrift für klinische Psychologie* 33 (1985) 367–76.

Stern, Daniel N. *The Interpersonal World of the Infant: A View from Psychoanalysis and Developmental Psychology.* New York: Basic Books, 1985.

Stern, Donnel B. "Commentary on Papers by Davies and Harris." *Psychoanalytic Dialogues* 6 (1996) 261–66.

————. *Unformulated Experience: From Dissociation to Imagination in Psychoanalysis.* Relational Perspectives Book Series 8. Hillsdale, NJ: Analytic, 1997.

————. *Partners in Thought: Working with Unformulated Experience.* Psychoanalysis in a New Key 12. New York: Routledge: Taylor & Francis Group, 2009.

Stern, Steven. "The Self as a Relational Structure: A Dialogue with Multiple-self Theory." *Psychoanalytic Dialogues* 12 (2002) 693–714.

Stolorow, Robert D., and George Atwood. "The Mind and the Body." *Psychoanalytic Dialogues* 1 (1991) 181–95.

Stolorow, Robert D., and George Atwood. *Contexts of Being: The Intersubjective Foundations of Psychological Life.* Psychoanalytic Inquiry Book Series 12 Hillsdale, NJ: Analytic, 1992.

Stolorow, Robert D., et al., editors. *Psychoanalytic Treatment: An Intersubjective Approach.* Psychoanalytic Inquiry Book Series 8. Hillsdale, NJ: Analytic, 1987.

Stolorow, Robert D., et al., editors. *The Intersubjective Perspective.* Northvale, NJ: Aronson, 1994.

Suchocki, Marjorie Hewitt. *God, Christ, Church: A Practical Guide to Process Theology.* New York: Crossroad, 1982.

————. *The End of Evil: Process Eschatology in Historical Context.* SUNY Series in Philosophy. Albany: State University of New York Press, 1988.

Surin, Kenneth. *Theology and the Problem of Evil.* Signposts in Theology. Oxford: Blackwell, 1986.

Taylor, Jill McLean, et al. *Between Voice and Silence: Women and Girls, Race and Relationship.* Cambridge, MA: Harvard University Press, 1995.

Taylor, Mark Lewis. *Remembering Esperanza: A Cultural-Political Theology for North America,* annotated edition. Minneapolis: Fortress, 2005.

Terence, *Heautontimorumenos (The Self-Tormenter)*. In *Terence: The Complete Comedies; Modern Verse Translations*, by Palmer Bovie et al., 71–144. Edited, with a foreword by Palmer Bovie. New Brunswick, NJ: Rutgers University Press, 1974.

Thandeka, *Learning to Be White: Money, Race, and God in America*. New York: Continuum, 2000.

Thomson, Judith Jarvis. "The Right and the Good." *Journal of Philosophy* 94 (1997) 273–98.

Thornton, Sharon G. *Broken Yet Beloved: A Pastoral Theology of the Cross*. St. Louis: Chalice, 2002.

Tilley, Terrence. *The Evils of Theodicy*. Washington, DC: Georgetown University Press, 1991.

Tillich, Paul. *Systematic Theology*. Vol. 1, *Reason and Revelation*. Chicago: University of Chicago Press, 1951.

———. *Systematic Theology*, Vol. 3, *Life and the Spirit. History and the Kingdom of God*. Chicago: University of Chicago Press, 1976.

Tomkins, Silvan S. *Affect, Imagery, Consciousness*. Vol. 1, *The Positive Affects*. New York: Springer, 1962.

———. *Affect, Imagery, Consciousness*. Vol. 2, *The Negative Affects*. New York: Springer, 1963.

Toner, Jules. *A Commentary on Saint Ignatius' Rules for the Discernment of Spirits*. Series III. Original Studies, Composed in English. St. Louis: Institute of Jesuit Sources, 1982.

Tocqueville, Alexis de. *"Democracy in America"; and "Two Essays on America."* Translated by Gerald E. Bevan with an introduction and notes by Isaac Kramnick. Penguin Classics. London: Penguin, 2003.

Townes, Emilie, editor. *A Troubling in My Soul: Womanist Perspectives on Evil and Suffering*. Bishop Henry McNeal Turner Studies in North American Black Religion 8. Maryknoll, NY: Orbis, 1993.

———, editor. *Embracing the Spirit: Womanist Perspectives on Hope, Salvation and Transformation*. Bishop Henry McNeal Turner/Sojourner Truth series in Black Religion 13. Maryknoll: Orbis, 1997.

Tracy, David. *Blessed Rage for Order: The New Pluralism in Theology*. Chicago: University of Chicago Press, 1996.

Turkle, Sherry. *The Second Self: Computers and the Human Spirit*. 20th anniversary edition. Cambridge, MA: MIT Press, 2005.

Turner, Léon. "First Person Plural: Self-unity and Self-multiplicity in Theology's Dialogue with Psychology." *Zygon* 42 (2007) 7–24.

Turner, Victor. *Dramas, Fields, and Metaphors: Symbolic Action in Human Society*. Symbol, Myth, and Ritual Series. Ithaca: Cornell University Press, 1974.

Vaillant, George. *Adaptation to Life*. Cambridge, MA: Harvard University Press, 1995.

Van der Kolk, Bessel A. "The Body Keeps the Score: Memory and the Evolving Psychobiology of Posttraumatic Stress." *Harvard Review of Psychiatry* 1 (1994) 253–65.

Van der Kolk, Bessel A., and Rita Fisler. "Dissociation and the Fragmentary Nature of Traumatic Memories: Overview and Exploratory Study." *Journal of Traumatic Stress* 8 (1995) 505–26.

Van der Kolk, Bessel A., et al. *Traumatic Stress: The Effects of Overwhelming Experience on Mind, Body, and Society*. New York: Guilford, 1996.

"Virtue Ethics." In *Stanford Encyclopedia of Philosophy*. Online: http://plato.stanford. edu/entries/ethics-virtue/#2/.

Volf, Miroslav. "Memory, Suffering, and Redemption." Lecture sponsored by the Philadelphia Theological Institute, Philadelphia, PA, delivered October 21, 2001.

Ward, Graham, editor. *The Postmodern God: A Theological Reader*. Blackwell Readings in Modern Theology. Malden, MA: Blackwell, 1997.

Weeks, Jim. *Gettysburg: Memory, Market, and an American Shrine*. Princeton, NJ: Princeton University Press, 2003.

Weil, Simone. *Waiting for God*. Translated by Emma Cruafurd. New York: Putnam, 1951.

Weiner, Edmund C., and John A. Simpson, editors. *The Compact Edition of the Oxford English Dictionary*. 2 vols. Oxford: Oxford University Press, 1971.

Wells, Samuel. *Improvisation: The Drama of Christian Ethics*. Grand Rapids: Brazos, 2004.

Wetzel, James. "Predestination, Pelagianism, and Foreknowledge." In *The Cambridge Companion to Augustine*, edited by Eleonore Stump and Norman Kreztmann, 54–56. Cambridge, UK: Cambridge University Press, 2001.

Whitehead, Alfred North. *Process and Reality: An Essay in Cosmology*. Gifford Lectures, 1927–1928. New York: Free Press, 1978.

Whitman, Walt. *Walt Whitman's "Song of Myself": A Sourcebook and Critical Edition*. Edited by Ezra Greenspan. Routledge Guides to Literature. New York: Routledge, 2005.

Williams, Delores. "A Womanist Perspective on Sin." In *A Troubling in My Soul: Womanist Perspectives on Evil and Suffering*, edited by Emilie Townes, 130–49. Bishop Henry McNeal Turner Studies in North American Black Religion 8. Marynknoll, NY: Orbis, 1993.

———. *Sisters in the Wilderness: The Challenge of Womanist God-Talk*. Maryknoll, NY: Orbis, 1993.

Wilson-Kastner, Patricia. *Faith, Feminism and the Christ*. Philadelphia: Fortress, 1983.

Wimberly, Edward P. *African American Pastoral Care*. Rev. ed. Nashville: Abingdon, 2008.

Winnicott, D. W. "The Antisocial Tendency." In *Through Paediatrics to Psycho-Analysis: Collected Papers*, 305–15. New York: Brunner/Mazel, 1992.

———. "Further Thoughts on Babies as Persons." In *The Child, the Family, and the Outside World*, 85–92. A Pelican Book. Harmondsworth, UK: Penguin, 1964.

———. "Ego Distortion in Terms of True Self and False Self." In *The Maturational Processes and the Facilitating Environment*, 140–52. International Psycho-Analytical Library 64. London: Hogarth, 1965.

———. "The Theory of the Parent-Infant Relationship." In *The Maturational Processes and the Facilitating Environment*, 37–55. International Psycho-Analytical Library 64. London: Hogarth, 1965.

———. *The Maturational Processes and the Facilitating Environment*. International Psycho-Analytical Library 64. London: Hogarth, 1965.

———. "Transitional Objects and Transitional Phenomena." In *Playing and Reality*, 1–25. New York: Basic Books, 1971.

———. "The Use of an Object and Relating Through Identifications." In *Playing and Reality*, 86–94. New York: Routledge, 1971.

———. *Playing and Reality*. New York: Basic Books, 1971.

Wittgenstein, Ludwig. *Philosophical Investigations.* Translated by G. E. M. Anscombe. Oxford: Blackwell, 1953.

Wolf, Ernest S. *Treating the Self.* New York: Guilford, 1988.

Yalom, Irvin D. *Love's Executioner and Other Tales of Psychotherapy.* New York: Basic Books, 1989.

Young, Frances. *The Art of Performance: Towards a Theology of Holy Scripture.* London: Darton, Longman and Todd, 1990.

Zornberg, Avivah Gottlieb. *The Beginning of Desire: Reflections on Genesis.* New York: Image, 1996.

Zuckerman, Phil. *Society without God: What the Least Religious Nations Can Tell Us about Contentment.* New York: New York University Press, 2008.